MANAGERS AND WORKERS

MANAGERS AND WORKERS

Origins of the Twentieth-Century Factory System in the United States, 1880–1920

Second Edition

DANIEL NELSON

THE UNIVERSITY OF WISCONSIN PRESS

The University of Wisconsin Press
114 North Murray Street
Madison, Wisconsin 53715

3 Henrietta Street
London WC2E 8LU, England

Library of Congress Cataloging-in-Publication Data
Nelson, Daniel, 1941–
    Managers and workers: origins of the twentieth-century factory
system in the United States, 1880–1920 / Daniel Nelson. —Rev. ed.
    262 pp.   cm.
    Includes bibliographical references and index.
    ISBN 0-299-14880-7. —ISBN 0-299-14884-X (pbk.)
    1. Factory system—United States—History.   2. Personnel
management—United States—History.   3. Industrial sociology—
United States—History.   I. Title.
HD2356.U5N44   1995
658.3'009073—dc20   95-6356

Contents

Tables

Preface

The principle of a factory is that each laborer, working separately, is controlled by some associating principle which directs his producing powers to effect a common result, which is the object of all collectively to attain. [Carroll Wright, "The Factory System of the United States," *Tenth Census of the United States,* 1880, vol. 2, *Manufactures,* (Washington, 1883), p. 553]

In most accounts of the evolution of the modern economy, the growth of the factory system plays a major role, often as a symbol of the industrial revolution.[1] This approach made sense in the nineteenth century and perhaps even early in the twentieth century when the memory of the handicraft shop was still fresh. But it made less sense in the early 1970s, when *Managers and Workers* was written, and it makes even less sense today, as the second or twentieth-century factory system is superceded by a third factory system featuring smaller, more mechanized, and more intensely controlled manufacturing operations and a wider spectrum of social relationships. In retrospect the nineteenth-century factory system appears not as a decisive phase in the history of manufacturing but as the first of several steps toward the present. *Managers and Workers* focuses on the transitional years, when the classic factory system and above all the "associating principal" gave way to new forms of organization and management, evident in the largest and most technologically advanced manufacturing plants by the 1920s.

The dominant themes of this process—the substitution of formal, centralized controls for ad hoc, decentralized controls and the increasing influence of the management over the factory and its labor force—were the bases of the twentieth-century factory system. There were three basic elements in the transformation: a technological dynamic, as technical innovation produced, often inadvertently, fundamental changes in the factory environment and in the human relationships that derived from it; a managerial dynamic, as administrators attempted to impose order and system on the manufacturing organization; and a personnel dynamic, as managers began deliberate efforts to organize and control the factory labor force. In practice the three were inseparable and often indistinguishable, and they affected every plant differently. Yet by 1920 the trend was clear.

Although there were exceptions, these changes appeared first and had their greatest impact in large manufacturing plants.[2] The new factory system made sense only in certain settings. It was closely associated with mass production technologies, which alone might have accounted for the prominence of large plants. But other forces also had an impact. In textile mills, for example, managers introduced many innovations, though in other ways they remained within the traditionalist camp. The large size of the labor force and the high proportion of female employees in the typical textile plant, rather than the character of production, accounted for this selective creativity. In other settings it is difficult to draw a hard and fast line, though most small plants were unaffected. There was nothing inevitable about the changes outlined here, and there is no suggestion of moral superiority. The new factory system was not inherently better or worse than the classic factory system; the devil, as they say, was in the details.

Several terms used throughout the text have specific technical meanings. I have adopted Bruce Laurie and Mark Schmitz's distinctions between factories and other types of manufacturing plants. Thus, a *factory* used water, steam, or electric power to operate machinery; a *manufactory* employed six or more workers but did not use power machinery; and an *artisan* shop had no power machinery and fewer than six employees.[3] I have also adopted Alfred D. Chandler's definition of *mass production* as a manufacturing technology that was capital-, energy-, materials-, and management-intensive, as opposed to technologies that were labor-intensive.[4]

I have deliberately narrowed the scope of the study in several ways. I have, for example, avoided a detailed treatment of technological change except where it had a direct impact on management and the manager-worker relationship; of corporate policy making; of wage trends and the general labor movement; and of other topics that would be essential for a comprehensive study of American manufacturing. This selectivity has made it possible to focus on the most significant arena of change, the relationship between the factory manager and the factory employee.

Managers and Workers was originally published in 1975, on the eve of a veritable explosion of important, often brilliant studies of American industry. Very few of those works directly addressed the subject of this book, but many of them are indispensable to an understanding of the rise of production and personnel management. In revising the manuscript, I have kept as much of the original text as possible and simply added citations to the most significant of the newer works. Where the new material provided a better or clearer interpretation of an incident or development, I have rewritten the original text. Although the footnotes are not a comprehensive guide to the scholarly literature of the last twenty years, they should provide a useful guide to the most notable recent books on the American factory at an all-important stage in its evolution.

I have also added a new chapter (chapter 7) on the organizational responses of factory workers to managerial innovation. This chapter has a somewhat different purpose. It is not primarily to bring the text up to date, for surprisingly little recent labor history has explicitly addressed the factory employee's role as a worker. Rather, it is to explain how factory workers reacted to the technological and organizational changes that were transforming the manufacturing workplace. The best way to do that, as chapter 7 emphasizes, is to focus on their efforts to create unions and to ensure that the upheavals occurring around them benefited them as well as their employers.

I am indebted to Allen Fitchen and his colleagues at the University of Wisconsin Press, who encouraged and supported this endeavor on the twentieth anniversary of the original publication. David Goldberg read chapter 7 and made many useful suggestions. I alone am responsible for any remaining flaws.

The original book was dedicated to Lorraine, with gratitude and affection. Thankfully, that feature of the text needed no revision.

DANIEL NELSON
December 1994

MANAGERS AND WORKERS

1 The Setting

It is almost as difficult to persuade those who have the responsibility of conducting large industrial undertakings that a complete and intelligent office organization will save money, time and worry, as it was a few years ago to convince them that the use of modern machine tools was indispensable to good workmanship with cheap production. [J. Slater Lewis, *The Commercial Organization of Factories* (London, 1896), p. xxvii]

My own experience as a workman with the monotony and lack of outlook of the machine shop of the middle 'nineties has given me a very real sense of the meaningful and fundamental break Taylor made with the past. [Harlow Person, *Scientific Management in American Industry* (New York, 1929) p. xviii]

In 1800 the typical American manufacturer was a master artisan or mill proprietor, the typical employee a handicraft worker, and the typical plant a room or series of rooms in the artisan's home or in a small building adjacent to a stream that supplied the power for more complicated manufacturing operations. In 1880 the manufacturer was likely to be a factory owner or manager, the employee a machine operator, and the plant a multistory brick or stone structure powered by water or steam.[1] Economic growth and technological innovation had created the factory system.

The advent of the factory was a development of dramatic, often striking importance for participants, competitors, and consumers of industrial goods. Virtually all mid-century Americans were aware of Lowell, its massive mills and its armies of unconventional operatives.[2] But Lowell was only part of the story, a highly unrepresentative part at that. A half century later, Carroll Wright, the U.S. commissioner of labor, attempted with some success to put the entire process in perspective. His investigation is summarized in table 1. Wright examined a group of products that were manufactured by hand methods early in the century and by machine methods in the 1890s. He then asked, How were those products made before and after the advent of power machinery? The products are listed in Table 1 by savings in hours, the best measure of the impact of factory production. The table explains why cotton cloth quickly superseded homespun, why factory-made clocks soon adorned all but the most

Table 1. Hand and machine manufacture

Industry	Number of operations		Number of workers		Hours to complete	
	Hand	Machine	Hand	Machine	Hand	Machine
Cotton goods	13	38	3	184	5025	66
Clocks	400	985	14	NA	218,758	6879
Rifle barrels	44	106	2	86	9800	374
Paper envelopes	4	19	4	29	435	32
Carriages (components)	5	12	3	14	648	42
Carpets	13	26	16	134	1538	155
Boots, shoes	72	123	1	174	1334	155
Bolts	4	19	2	10	74	12
Carriages (assembly)	38	63	6	110	172	39
Files	16	28	19	28	377	89
Men's clothing	15	21	3	76	1464	481
Canned foods	15	20	54	189	258	122
Clay jars	7	15	8	18	26	14

Source: Thirteenth Annual Report of the Commissioner of Labor, 1898, Hand and Machine Labor, vol. 1 (Washington, 1899).

humble homes, why carriages and wagons clogged roads, and why government arsenals played a major role in the development of industrial technology, and also why factory-made clothing and canned foods were less common and popular. Above all, it suggests what happened to production processes. The introduction of water or steam power led to a complete reorganization of manufacturing, not just to the hiring of additional workers or to a more minute division of labor. Those were the features of the manufactory; the factory was different. Power machinery made conventional techniques and skills obsolete and forced managers and workers to create new techniques and skills.

Though the Lowell mills, the other "Waltham system" plants, and a few other early-nineteenth-century factories suggested the extent of these changes, they also misled. First, the transition to factory production was rarely fast or dramatic. Recent work on nineteenth-century industry has documented the slow diffusion of the factory system; outside the textile industry, the factory system hardly existed before mid-century, and it only gradually embraced many products. Two-thirds of the manufacturing plants of 1890 were artisan shops or manufactories.[3] Major consumer goods industries such as clothing and cigar manufacture continued to rely on hand methods. Second, most nineteenth-century factories were extremely small by later standards. Only 67 of 2500 Cincinnati industrial plants had 100 or more workers in the 1870s; only 45 of 919 Detroit plants employed 100 or more workers in 1880, and only 7 employed more than 300.[4] As George S. Gibb has observed, the transition was often "so gradual that it is impossible to say precisely when 'workshop' was no longer the appropriate name for the enterprise."[5] Third, the day-to-day management of the factory retained a familiar flavor. In textiles the advent of the factory brought a distinct break with earlier practice.[6] But in many industries internal management techniques, particularly those involving relations between factory managers and workers, were not fundamentally different from what they had been in the artisan shop. In practice, managers usually left the operation of the plant to the foremen and the skilled workers. In this respect the factory of 1880 remained a congeries of shops rather than an integrated plant.

During the following decades the manufacturing sector expanded rapidly. In 1880 there were approximately 2,700,000 wage earners in manufacturing; by 1900 there were 4,500,000, and by 1920, 8,400,000.[7] Some of these people worked in manufactories or "sweatshops," but the majority were employed in factories and, to a growing degree, in factories with more than 500 employees. Plant size became a gauge of the complex changes that were transforming the industrial economy. During the last third of the nineteenth century the "average" plant in eleven of sixteen major industries more than doubled in size.[8] In 1870 there were only a handful of large factories, concentrated in textiles. The McCormick plant in Chicago, supposedly one of the nation's largest, had 400 to 500 names on its payroll.[9] By 1900, however, there were 1,063 factories with 500 to 1,000 workers and 443 with more than 1,000 wage earners.[10]

The largest plants were found in a relatively small group of industries, notably textiles, metals, and machinery. Yet there were also important distinctions within these industries. Cotton and worsted mills were generally larger than woolen mills, steel mills were larger than iron mills, and large machinery factories operated alongside small specialty or "job" shops. Within the machinery complex, transportation equipment (locomotives, railroad cars, steamships, bicycles, and automobiles), business machinery (typewriters, cash registers), electrical machinery, sewing machines, and textile machinery were usually made in large plants. There were also large agricultural machinery works, steam engine plants, arms factories, and machine tool works. After the formation of the United Shoe Machinery Company in 1899, the manufacture of shoe machinery was concentrated in a single large plant.

Although the machinery field included many diverse products, there was considerable overlap among them. Because of "technological convergence," the similarity of the processes used in different industries, it was possible to transfer skills and resources from the production of one product to another with little difficulty.[11] Consequently, textile machinery makers also manufactured locomotives and steam engines. Gun makers

Table 2. Wage earners in the Lowell Mills

Mill	1854[1]	1876[2]	1890[3]	1900[4]	1916[5]
Merrimack	2,050	2,700	3,086	3,170	2,900
Hamilton	1,250	1,225	2,121	2,379	1,800
Appleton	520	600	834	987	1,500
Lowell	1,300	—	2,158	—	—
Middlesex	1,305	—	616	786	1,530
					(U.S. Worsted)
Suffolk	500	1,400	1,860	1,618	2,910
Tremont	500				
Lawrence	1,400	—	4,582	3,781	4,200
Boott	1,132	1,875	2,150	2,168	1,900
Massachusetts	1,700	1,475	1,799	2,367	2,800

Sources:

1. Statistics of Lowell Manufactures (Baker Library, Harvard Business School, Cambridge, Mass.), Jan., 1854.

2. Frederick W. Coburn, *History of Lowell* (New York, 1920), 1:351.

3. Massachusetts District Police Chief, *Report,* 1890.

4. Ibid., 1900.

5. Coburn, *History of Lowell,* 2: 417.

made machine tools, sewing machines, and typewriters, and sewing machine manufactures made bicycles and automobiles. E. Remington & Son, a manufacturer of guns and sewing machines, began to make typewriters in the 1870s when the gun business was at a low ebb.[12] Pope Manufacturing, the leading bicycle manufacturer of the 1890s, evolved out of the Weed Sewing Machine Company, which in turn had grown out of a private armory.[13]

Though the large plant appeared with the advent of the factory system in Lowell, Lawrence, Manchester, Fall River, and other New England mill towns, the textile factories showed little tendency to grow after mid-century. As table 2 suggests, there were only small increases in the size of the Lowell Mills in the latter half of the nineteenth century. With the exception of the Amoskeag Mills at Manchester and the Pacific Mills at Lawrence, the textile plants of the Merrimack Valley towns expanded slowly between 1880 and World War I. Moreover, only a handful of other mills, such as the Fall River Iron Works Company and Durfee Mills of Fall River, the Wamsutta Mills of New Bedford, and the Dan River Mills of Danville, Virginia, ever rivaled the largest Merrimack mill in plant size. The shift of the industry from northern New England led to the construction of smaller, not larger, factories.[14]

By the late nineteenth century iron and steel mills had usurped the position of the textile companies. In 1860 only the Montour, Cambria, and Phoenix iron works employed more than 1,000 workmen.[15] By the early

1870s the Cambria and Bethlehem Iron Companies had more than 2,000 employees each at their Johnstown and South Bethlehem plants. The introduction of the Bessemer process and the business recovery of the late 1870s led to the expansion of the existing mills and the construction of new ones. In 1880 Cambria had 4,200 employees, Lackawanna Iron and Steel 3,000, Bethlehem Iron 2,900, Pennsylvania Steel 1,600, and Carnegie's Edgar Thompson works 1,500.[16] Outside the textile industry only the Baldwin Locomotive works, with 2,600 employees, was of comparative size.

The steel plants remained the largest American factories for more than 30 years. Their dominance is shown in table 3, which lists the largest plants of the Northeast and Midwest in 1900.[17]

Only with the rise of the auto industry did new rivals appear. As early as 1910 the Packard plant employed 4,640 workers and the Buick factory 4,000. The Ford Highland Park plant had nearly 13,000 employees in 1914, 19,000 in 1915, and 33,000 in 1916. In 1924 it had more than 42,000 workers, and the Ford River Rouge plant, which later became the largest manufacturing plant in the United States and probably in the world, employed 68,000.[18] By that time the automobile factory had become the universal symbol and stereotype of the large manufacturing plant.

Yet the trend toward larger plant size was not confined to the auto industry. Cambria had nearly 20,000 employees at Johnstown in 1909; General Electric had 15,000 workers at Schenectady and 11,000 at Lynn in 1910. Pullman had 15,000 at its Chicago plant in 1913, and International Harvester had 15,000 at the old McCormick plant in 1916.[19] The war boom, however, made even these figures seem small. Bethlehem Steel's South Bethlehem works employed 6,800 workers in 1910 and more than 13,000 in 1915 before the war orders began. By 1916 it had 24,000.[20] Bethlehem's Fore River, Massachusetts, shipyard employed 3,700 in May 1917; 10,253 in December 1917; and 15,000 in July 1918.[21] The DuPont powder works at Carney's Point, New Jersey, Hopewell, Virginia, and Nashville, Tennessee, all employed 15,000 to 20,000 workers during the war, as did the Remington Arms works at Bridgeport and the Winchester plants at Hartford.[22] The federal government's Hog Island shipyard near Philadelphia and the Submarine Boat Corporation's Newark, New Jersey, shipyard had 34,000 and 14,000 employees respectively in 1918.[23] The Goodyear Tire & Rubber Company employed 15,500 men and women at its Akron, Ohio, plant in 1915 and 33,000 in 1920. Firestone, its principal rival, employed 19,800 in 1920.[24]

Apart from the economic and technological changes that it symbolized, the large factory created immediate practical problems that had not ex-

Table 3. Largest United States manufacturing plants, 1900

Name	Location	Product
8,000–10,000 wage earners		
Cambria Steel	Johnstown, PA	Steel
Carnegie Steel	Homestead, PA	Steel
Jones & Laughlin	Pittsburgh, PA	Steel
Baldwin Locomotive	Philadelphia, PA	Locomotives
6,000–8,000		
General Electric	Schenectady, NY	Electrical machinery
Armour	Chicago, IL	Meat packing
Deering Harvester	Chicago, IL	Agricultural machinery
Illinois Steel, South Chicago plant	Chicago, IL	Steel
National Tube	McKeesport, PA	Pipe
Westinghouse Electric	Pittsburgh, PA	Electrical machinery
William Cramp	Philadelphia, PA	Ships
Newport News Shipbuilding	Newport News, VA	Ships
Amoskeag Mills	Manchester, NH	Textiles
Pennsylvania Steel	Steelton, PA	Steel
4,000–6,000		
Pullman Palace Car	Pullman, IL	Railroad cars
Singer Sewing Machine	Elizabeth, NJ	Sewing machines
Alexander Smith	Yonkers, NY	Carpets
Swift	Chicago, IL	Meat packing
McCormick Harvester	Chicago, IL	Agricultural machinery
Western Electric	Chicago, IL	Electrical equipment
General Electric	Lynn, MA	Electrical equipment
Pacific Mills	Lawrence, MA	Woolens
3,000–4,000		
Arlington Mills	Lawrence, MA	Textiles
Western Electric	New York, NY	Electrical equipment
Nelson Morris	Chicago, IL	Meat packing
Illinois Glass	Alton, IL	Glass
Pressed Steel Car	McKees Rocks, PA	Railroad cars
Bethlehem Steel	S. Bethlehem, PA	Steel
Merrimack Mills	Lowell, MA	Cotton
Lawrence Mills	Lowell, MA	Cotton
New York Shipbuilding	Camden, NJ	Ships
2,000–3,000		
Waltham Watch	Waltham, MA	Watches
Hamilton Mills	Lowell, MA	Textiles
Massachusetts Mills	Lowell, MA	Textiles
Bigelow Carpet	Lowell, MA	Carpet
Boott Mills	Lowell, MA	Textiles
Lowell Machine	Lowell, MA	Machinery
Fall River Iron	Fall River, MA	Textiles
Wamsutta Mills	New Bedford, MA	Textiles
American Steel and Wire	Worcester, MA	Cable, Springs
Pepperell Mills	Biddeford, ME	Textiles
Cheney Silk	So. Manchester, CT	Textiles

Table 3. Largest United States manufacturing plants, 1900 (*continued*)

Name	Location	Product
2,000–3,000		
Winchester Repeating Arms	Hartford, CT	Guns, ammunition
J. A. Roebling	Trenton, NJ	Wire
Standard Oil	Bayonne, NJ	Oil
Schenectady Locomotive	Schenectady, NY	Locomotives
Solvay Process	Solvay, NY	Chemicals
D. M. Osborn	Auburn, NY	Agricultural Machinery
Harmony Mills	Cohoes, NY	Textiles
Brooks Locomotive	Dunkirk, NY	Locomotives
Maryland Steel	Sparrows Point, MD	Ships
Midvale Steel	Philadelphia, PA	Steel, machinery
Henry Disston	Philadelphia, PA	Saws
Reading Iron	Reading, PA	Iron, steel
Lackawanna Iron	Scranton, PA	Steel
Pressed Steel Car	Allegheny City, PA	Railroad cars
Carnegie Steel	Braddock, PA	Steel
National Tube	Pittsburgh, PA	Pipe
Oliver Iron	Pittsburgh, PA	Steel
American Shipbuilding	Cleveland, OH	Ships
Lorain Steel	Lorain, OH	Steel
Republic Iron	Youngstown, OH	Steel
B. F. Goodrich	Akron, OH	Rubber products
National Cash Register	Dayton, OH	Cash Registers
Michigan Peninsular Car	Detroit, MI	Railroad Cars
American Car and Foundry	Madison, IL	Railroad Cars
Crane	Chicago, IL	Plumbing Supplies
Elgin Watch	Elgin, IL	Watches
National Enameling and Stamping	Granite City, IL	Steel
Illinois Steel	Joliet, IL	Steel

Sources: Most firms were assigned to specific groups on the basis of information in the following: Illinois, Factory Inspectors, *Eighth Annual Report,* 1900; New York, Factory Inspectors, *Fifteenth Annual Report,* 1900; New Jersey, Inspector of Factories, *Eighteenth Annual Report,* 1900; Ohio, Workshops, Factories, and Public Buildings, *Seventeenth Annual Report,* 1900; Pennsylvania, Factory Inspector, *Eleventh Annual Report,* 1900; Massachusetts District Police Chief, *Report,* 1900; Connecticut, Inspection of Factories, *Fourteenth Annual Report,* 1900. Shipbuilding companies were assigned on the basis of U.S. Bureau of Navigation, *Annual Report of the Commissioner of Navigation,* 1901 (Washington, 1901), 19–20.

isted or had been less serious a half century before. The new plants covered so much space and encompassed so many different activities that no individual could conveniently visit each area in a day, much less personally oversee their operations. Growing distances also complicated the scheduling of production and the coordination of flows of materials, regardless of the diligence and energy of the managers. Breakdowns and interruptions were costly in small plants; they were potentially disastrous in the fragile organizational environment of the giant factory. The armies of employees required to operate the large plant posed other challenges. Recruiting, training, and motivating them in the traditional, ad hoc manner was at best hazardous. Dealing with their problems and complaints in customary fashion was even more dangerous. Finally, the sheer presence of the large plant, its conspicuous presence in the community, created public relations challenges that had not existed or had been less important earlier. Thus, the transformation of production invited concomitant changes in organization and policy, the social infrastructure of manufacturing.

Whether manufacturers viewed these changes in positive or negative terms, their responses were similar. They continued to emphasize technical change and increased specialization of function. They devoted more attention to the relationship between technological innovation and the "efficiency" of the plant and its labor force. And they gradually substituted managerial direction and controls for the informal, ad hoc methods of the past, particularly those that relied on the judgment of the supervisor and worker. While the operation of these three interrelated dynamics— the technological, the managerial, and the personnel—became clearer in the 1920s and 1930s, the distinguishing features of the twentieth century factory system were apparent by the end of World War I. The legacy of the artisan shop had ceased to be an important force in factory management.

2 The Factory Environment

The vast number of our industrial works are anything but inviting to the eye, or indicative of care on the part of their proprietors with the happiness and the health of their workmen. ["A Model Manufacturing City," *Scientific American* 45 (July 23, 1881): 52]

The raw materials are delivered at one end . . . while the finished product comes out at the other, two miles away. ["The Jones & Laughlin Aliquippa Works," *Iron Age* 91 (January 2, 1913): 26]

The history of the world's industries affords no encouragement that working conditions will be spontaneously and vitally improved by the mass of employers, unless the latter can see profit in the change. [Leicester Allen, "The Economy of Heating and Ventilating the Machine Shop," *Engineering Magazine* 21 (April 1901): 78–79]

The most obvious feature of the large manufacturing plant was its physical presence. The size, concentration of men and equipment, and complex operations of the late-nineteenth-century factory amazed contemporary observers.[1] But it also had a profound impact on the men and women who worked in it. The factory environment was the milieu in which they spent more than half their waking hours; it set and limited their range of personal contacts, and it was an important determinant of their attitudes toward the firm, their jobs, and each other.[2] In countless ways the changing physical setting of the factory impinged upon their lives.

THE FACTORY EXTERIOR

Of the unheralded aspects of nineteenth-century industrialism, the emergence of the factory as an identifiable architectural form was among the most important. At the beginning of the century the manufacturing plant as a specialized structure was virtually unknown. Even the mills that dotted river banks were largely indistinguishable from barns or other agricultural buildings. The advent of more complex machinery and larger groups of workers did not make an immediate difference in most industries as manufacturers adapted existing building to their needs.

Samuel Slater, the early textile manufacturer, for example, first installed his machinery in an old fulling mill and later built a wooden structure that "did not differ essentially from a large barn or farmhouse of the same period."[3] As late as 1888 the commissioner of labor reported that many manufacturing plants were "converted dwellings, stores or warehouses . . . ill-adapted for use as factories."[4]

A major reason for this was the typical manufacturer's view of factory buildings as "places to house machinery."[5] In many cases the manufacturer commissioned a new structure by marking the "four corners of a building with his cane" and saying to the contractor, "'Build me a 5-story building in this space for about $10,000.'"[6] Gradually, however, general ideas about how a particular type of factory should look developed. In part these ideas were the product of necessity; it was impractical to house a rolling mill or iron foundry in a multistory building. In part they were the product of trial and error. The proper procedure for building a foundry, a leading journal advised, "is to visit the best foundries within a reasonable distance . . . as well as to search all the available books and literature."[7]

The degree of sophistication achieved in this process depended on the industry and the activities that were undertaken in specific buildings. In the textile industry the proliferation of machines and the presence of many identical machines in a single plant dictated large, well-organized factories. As a result textile manufacturers developed standard building designs at an early date.[8] Professional "mill doctors"—engineer-designers—appeared by the 1830s, and textile machinery firms offered free building plans to their customers. By mid-century the mill "in a package" was commonplace; by the 1880s, when the southern boom began, competition among mill engineers had become intense.[9]

The most striking characteristics of textile buildings were their length and height. Water or steam power and millwork, the shafts and belts that transmitted power from the engine to the individual machines, encouraged narrow, rectangular, multistoried buildings; dimensions of 300' to 600' by 50' or 60' and heights of five to seven stories were not uncommon. Since the walls, made of timber and brick or granite, bore the weight of the mill, the windows were generally small and the interiors gloomy. A distinctive feature of early mills was the gable roof, often accentuated with monitors or cupolas.[10] Many also had one or more towers, which contained stairways and offices and later elevators and toilets. Huddled closely together along the Merrimack or other New England rivers, these "dark satanic mills" were a formidable sight to nineteenth-century observers.

While the textile mill changed little in appearance from 1840 to 1920, manufacturers and architects made a number of important, though often inconspicuous, alterations in the standard design. The most obvious modification, introduced in Fall River in the 1870s, was the substitution of the flat for the pitched roof in an effort to prevent attic fires.[11] Other changes, similar in objective, resulted from the work of the New England mutual fire insurance companies—perhaps the dominant innovative force in mill construction after 1850. Led by Edward Atkinson, president of the Boston Manufacturers mutual from 1878 to 1905, the insurance companies insisted on the installation of automatic sprinklers and the "slow-burning" type of mill building.[12] Frank Cheney, a Connecticut silk manufacturer, described their methods: "You are subject to a rigid inspection. They come around and insist upon having sprinklers everywhere—fire hose, buckets, and apparatus. If everything is not right, you are told what is not right, and that it must be fixed."[13] By lowering the premiums of manufacturers who met their standards, the mutuals had the all-important power to make change profitable.[14]

The New England mutuals also promoted another important innovation in the factory environment: the one-story mill. Until the 1880s virtually all large plants in the light manufacturing industries were multistoried. The limited land available at mill sites and the need to transmit power in straight lines dictated this configuration. Steam power enabled manufacturers to move away from river banks. Soon they—with the encouragement of the insurance companies—began to consider the advantages of single-story construction: lower building costs; improved internal transportation, layout, and supervision; and reduced fire risks. In 1881 the Willimantic Linen Company built a large one-story plant. The new design made it possible to increase the size of the windows and to place the shafting in the basement, thereby avoiding the vibrations characteristic of multistoried plants and giving "to the women employed sure freedom from the trying physical ailments of their sex which result from standing on vibrating floors."[15]

With the one-story mill also came an English invention, the sawtooth roof.[16] Though expensive and prone to leaks, the sawtooth design permitted uniform natural lighting throughout the shop. Most of the large textile mills built after 1900, such as the Nashawena Mills at New Bedford and the new Naumkeag Steam Mills at Salem, combined this type of weave shed with a multistory spinning mill.[17] The sawtooth roof also became popular for machine shops and other industrial buildings where good lighting was essential.

Although textile companies created most of the precedents for nineteenth-century, factory architecture, machinery makers, whose space requirements were similar, were quick to adopt their innovations. The Lowell and Amoskeag machine shops adjoined the textile factories and were indistinguishable from them. The Whitin shops, built between the

1840s and the 1890s, resembled a large textile plant. Colt's Armory, one of the largest and best-known mid-century machine shops, consisted of two four-story stone buildings joined by another at right angles.[18] The Singer Sewing Machine factory at Elizabethport, New Jersey, the Elgin Watch works at Elgin, Illinois, the Brown & Sharpe plant in Providence, and the McCormick factory in Chicago did not differ significantly in their appearance from the Lowell or Lawrence mills.[19]

One other similarity between textile mills and machinery works was the use of decorative towers. From the time of the early Slater mills, manufacturers had added cupolas to their plants. In the 1840s and 1850s the Stark, Manchester, and Amoskeag mills at Manchester added imposing towers to their buildings which "formed a handsome echelon of masses, very impressive in the narrow mill yard."[20] A number of the Lowell mills added corner turrets in the 1850s, and the Merrimack Company built an elaborate six-story tower in the 1860s. The Harmony Mills plant at Cohoes, New York, a six-story "brick Louvre" built shortly after the Civil War, was the premier example of decorative textile architecture. Not to be outdone, machinery makers added elaborate towers and exterior frills, the most famous of which was Colonel Colt's blue-spired dome, the distinguishing characteristic of his Hartford works.[21]

In later years, as industrial architecture became more severe and utilitarian, the ornate clock tower became a last outlet for the manufacturer's artistic energies. The huge clock tower of the Ayer mills at Lawrence, built after the turn of the century, stood in dramatic contrast to the drab mill buildings. The less imposing but equally elaborate clock towers of the John B. Stetson Company of Philadelphia and the Goodyear Tire and Rubber Company of Akron were equally incongruous amid their surroundings.

In industries where the manufacturing process emitted heat or smoke or required a sequence of steps that made the conventional brick and timber structure inappropriate, the factory form more clearly reflected its function. Iron and steel mills were the most obvious and formidable nineteenth-century industrial plants. The practice of providing a water wheel or steam engine for each major machine or cluster of machines, together with the heat and fumes, necessitated one-story structures covering large areas. The integration of smelting and rolling operations at mid-century encouraged the systematic placement of buildings, and the advent of mass production in the 1870s and 1880s led to a new generation of "greenfield" mills, meticulously organized to facilitate new, more mechanized and capital-intensive operations.[22] Yet the individual factory was often simply a "shell enclosing a hall-like space adapted for heavy manufacturing."[23]

Many steel mill buildings

> constructed prior to 1895 had uneven dirt floors. . . . The roofs were low, and were for the most part either without adequate ventilation or were so loosely constructed as to afford inadequate protection against rain and wind. In the original plans of the mill buildings no attention had been given to the possibility of future enlargement, and as a consequence the additions made to the buildings were most frequently roughly constructed, shed-like structures, which at best gave only partial protection to the workmen.[24]

Foundries and glass factories, which employed somewhat similar processes, were also known for their dilapidated appearance and inhospitable working conditions.[25]

Perhaps the best indication of manufacturers' attitudes toward factory construction was their response to the introduction of structural steel and reinforced concrete, two important technological innovations of the late nineteenth century. In both cases there was a substantial lag between the time when the materials became available and the time when they were widely used, despite their advantages—greater flexibility in plant design and improved lighting—over slow-burning construction. One of the principal aims of the fire insurance companies (and the state factory inspectors) was to convince employers that a more modern (and hence a cleaner and safer) plant was also a more profitable plant.

The use of iron in industrial buildings began in the 1850s but did not become prevalent for another two decades.[26] One reason for the delay was the success of conventional slow-burning construction in reducing fire losses. But by the 1870s and 1880s builders were adding iron columns to slow-burning construction because of the added strength they gave the structure and were using iron and steel materials for foundries, rolling mills, and other buildings that required open work areas. By the turn of the century most manufacturers selected steel framing for multistoried brick buildings; a leading engineer reported in 1907 that only "conservative" businessmen still insisted on brick and timber construction.[27]

Reinforced concrete had a similar history. Although European builders introduced it in the 1870s, American architects and manufacturers did not use it until 1887, when E. L. Ransome built a concrete factory for the Pacific Borax Company of Alameda, California.[28] Before 1900 reinforced concrete was generally used for warehouses where flammable goods were stored. But after the turn of the century, architects recognized its advantages for other types of buildings and widely employed it for factories of all types. A book on concrete factories and warehouse's published in 1911 listed 235 reinforced concrete buildings in thirty states.[29]

Reinforced concrete had many advantages for factory building. Though difficult to work with, it was relatively inexpensive and, if properly applied, as strong and durable as any other material. Its strength permitted much larger windows. "A concrete building can have as much as 80 per cent of its outer wall area devoted to lighting, as against a maximum of about 50 per cent in mill construction."[30] Moreover, a concrete building did not vibrate and was easy to keep clean. And, unlike a brick and steel structure, it was distinctive in appearance.

The first major factory built with reinforced concrete was the United Shoe Machinery plant at Beverly, Massachusetts, in 1903–1904. The United Shoe Machinery plant consisted of three parallel four-story concrete buildings (820' by 60' in 1907), smaller buildings that connected the main structures, and a foundry and forge shop. Windows covered nearly the entire wall space of the three main buildings.[31] The Beverly factory attracted widespread attention and started a trend that spread to other industries in the following years. Textile firms, for example, often employed concrete for one-story weave sheds. But it was the machinery makers, above all the automobile manufacturers, that made the most extensive and spectacular use of reinforced concrete in the pre–World War I years.

The era of the concrete auto factory began in 1905 when Henry Joy, president of the Packard Motor Company, commissioned Albert Kahn, a young Detroit architect, to design a reinforced concrete building for the Packard Company. Shortly thereafter the George N. Pierce Company selected Kahn to design its Buffalo plant, and Joy commissioned Kahn to erect another Packard building in Detroit. The results—concrete, brick, and glass structures with remarkably large windows for the time—drew wide acclaim. Joy reported in 1911:

> While our factory is not primarily a show institution nor at all decorative in its architecture or equipment, its sensible construction and arrangement have probably made it more widely influential in establishing the type of factories for similar lines of work than any other American plant.[32]

The Pierce plant had an additional feature: it was all on one floor. Kahn thus introduced the "one-story, roof-lighted, wide-span format of unlimited horizontal dimensions" to the auto industry, accelerating a trend that would eventually dominate all large-scale manufacturing.[33] The immediate consequence of these successes was Kahn's most important assignment, the Ford Highland Park plant. Starting in 1908 he worked for two years with Ford engineers on the new factory. The result was similar in appearance to the Packard plants except for an enormous glass-topped craneway that ran the length of the building and substantially reduced the time required for unloading railroad cars. But the size (the main concrete building was 865' by 75') and unprecedented coordination of factory layout and architectural form made the "Crystal City" the most famous factory in the country.[34]

Highland Park was the culmination of a trend that dated from the time of the mill doctors and early factory mutuals. Generally oblivious to plant design, manufacturers gradually realized (or were made to realize) the potential economic benefits of planning and the use of new materials. As a result there were alterations in the shape and appearance of the large manufacturing plant that generally improved the interior environment as well. Even if there had been no other changes, the typical factory of 1915 would have been far safer and better lighted than its nineteenth-century predecessors. By the beginning of World War I the "dark satanic mills" associated with the initial phases of American industrialization were rapidly disappearing.

THE FACTORY INTERIOR

Whatever the virtues of a modern factory building, most late-nineteenth-century manufacturers believed that the surest way to increase output and efficiency was to introduce more and better machinery. Acting on this assumption they mechanized hand work whenever possible and refined and specialized machine operations. Their activity, which long antedated 1880 and varied in its details from industry to industry, is largely beyond the scope of this account.[35] At the same time, many manufacturers introduced more basic innovations that often reinforced the effect of machine developments and were important factors in the changing physical environment of the manufacturing plant.

The Technical Organization of the Plant

Two elements were of special significance in the technical organization of the plant. First, the source and distribution of power set general limits on the manufacturer's activities. The use of water power required the factory to be located near a water source, which in turn forced the manufacturer, millwright, or mill doctor to adapt the building to the terrain of the mill site. The application of steam power to manufacturing at mid-century freed manufacturers from these locational difficulties, but within the plant the situation did not change. By mid-century the standard method of distributing power was by wrought-iron shafts, pulleys, and leather belts. In workrooms, whirling shafts, usually attached to the ceiling, turned belts that powered individual machines. This system encouraged manufacturers to build the rectangular multistoried structures that remained popular until the end of the century. It also meant the machinery was often arranged in lines parallel to the shafting. "In other words," one critic noted, "the tools must be installed with first reference to the application of power and not, as should be the case, with reference to handling the work to best advantage."[36]

It is easy, however, to exaggerate the inflexibility of the system. Manufacturers often showed remarkable ingenuity in adapting it to their needs. By the late nineteenth century it was common to find multiple lines of shafting within a department or room, counter shafts to reach areas outside the range of the main shafts, and one line of shafting that ran machinery on two stories by means of openings in the floors. A large plant, such as the Harmony Mills No. 3 plant at Cohoes, had several miles of shafting, thousands of pulleys, and ten miles or more of industrial belting.[37] Frederick W. Taylor's detailed study of belt use, published in the 1890s, eliminated much of the uncertainty that had characterized power distribution via belts.

The quality of the shafting also improved substantially during the nineteenth century. A well-known engineer noted in 1892 "how perfectly the [manufacture of shafting] . . . has been systematized and reduced to a condition of regular manufacturing processes."[38] A single line of shafting at the Amoskeag Mills drove 33,000 spindles; indeed, it worked so well there that water power was used for many years after the company installed electric lighting.[39] The fact that most manufacturers first used electric motors to drive shafting (the so-called "group" drive) rather than individual machines suggests that in many industries the mechanical system was no more than a marginal handicap.

The ability of manufacturers to make the best of these limited arrangements emphasizes the importance of the second factor, the sequence of operations, in determining the physical organization of the factory. Presumably even manufacturers who gave little or no thought to machine layout when building a plant did, at some point, consider the work flow and the possibility that certain alternatives were better than others. And although direct evidence is rare, most nineteenth-century manufacturers probably paid more attention to the subject than later reformers suggested. In industries where the sequence of operations was complex, where handling costs were a high percentage of total costs, and especially where a final assembling or "erecting" operation was necessary, managers could hardly disregard the flow of work.

Textile manufacturers confronted few of these challenges. In cotton mills a standard layout soon emerged: "The first floor is used for weaving and drawing in, and the second for carding, drawing and speeding. The third floor is used for frame spinning, spooling and warping, and the fourth for mule spinning."[40] The determinants were the weight of the machinery and a desire to minimize vibration. Thus the heavy looms were placed on the lower floors, the lighter spinning machines on the upper stories. Since mills typically produced only one type of cloth and since the product was relatively light, there were few problems of routing or transportation. In fact, some manufacturers disregarded these matters entirely.[41]

A frequent grievance of women employees was that they had to carry their finished work to the next department.

As a result of this relatively simple organization, the larger plants, such as those of northern New England, consisted of numerous buildings, most of which were self-contained and operated independently of the others. The Merrimack Company, for example, had forty-one buildings in 1919.[42] At its peak the Amoskeag mills had sixty-two cotton manufacturing departments (thirteen devoted to carding, eleven to spinning, twenty-eight to weaving, and ten to dressing) plus two dye houses, a bleachery, a laboratory, and a cloth room; twelve worsted manufacturing departments (five preparing, four spinning, three weaving) plus a dye house, two other finishing departments, and a cloth room; nineteen mechanical repair departments; five electrical departments; seven steam and water power departments; and eight miscellaneous departments.[43]

When bottlenecks did arise they usually appeared in the finishing departments. In bleacheries and dye houses production processes were more complex; the equipment was more varied, and the product had become, by the time it reached this stage, heavier and more unwieldy. Textile manufacturers who attempted to "systematize" their operations almost invariably began with the finishing departments.[44]

A shoe factory was similar in many respects to a cotton mill. By the late nineteenth century the typical plant was a long, narrow, four-story structure.

> The sole leather department occupies the first or basement floor. The upper leather and stitching departments occupy the fourth or upper floor. The making department occupies the third floor. The finishing, packing, and shipping departments are upon the second floor. . . . Shoes in process of making pass downward continually to the packing and shipping rooms.[45]

Perhaps because of this obvious arrangement few shoe manufacturers made any effort to facilitate the flow of work, and there were frequent delays and shutdowns. "Few shoe factories have made even an approach to the methods which have prevented such waste."[46] A proper layout alone did not guarantee success.

In the iron or steel industry the manufacturer's principal objective was to insure that nothing interfered with the natural progression of the work. Open hearth and rolling mill buildings were "usually two or three times as long as they are wide, in order that the material may pass through the mill directly in a straight line and thus avoid side transfers, which waste time and require expensive machinery."[47] Because of the enormous weight of the material, iron and steel makers were forced to use railroads, cranes, and other conveying devices. The typical mill yard was "honey-combed with railroad lines, continually in use."[48] A large open-hearth department in 1890 contained two or more ladle cranes, a dumping crane, and several hydraulic ingot cranes.[49] By the turn of the century, outsiders had trouble distinguishing steel production from the operations of a continuous-process plant.[50]

In the food-processing industries the desirability of a continuous work flow also determined the shape and organization of the plant. Oliver Evans's elevator and conveyor, used by the Brandywine flour millers in the 1790s, and the "disassembly" line, introduced in the Cincinnati packing houses as early as the 1830s, were precursors of an approach that dominated more and more industries in the late nineteenth century.[51] In the 1880s, continuous-process machinery—machines or integrated groups of machines that processed materials automatically—revolutionized the manufacture of flour, cigarettes, soap, matches, and bottled and canned goods. The distinguishing feature of this type of mass production was the virtual disappearance of the production worker. Though the Minneapolis flour millers dominated a major industry, they were not important employers.[52] Continuous-process plants, regardless of product, more closely resembled refineries than textile or steel mills.

In other industries the character of the work or the strategic role of the skilled workers made the arrangement of the factory more difficult. Machine shops and foundries engaged in job or repair work were necessarily unspecialized. An iron shipyard consisted of structures "of every shape and size scattered about the inclosure in apparent confusion."[53] Railroad shops were notoriously chaotic, and stove foundries were usually organized in a haphazard fashion.[54] In potteries and in glass bottle plants, the manufacturer created "shops" within the plant. In the typical bottle factory each shop worked independently under the skilled blowers. The product was transported by the blowers' young helpers.

> The shop boys get into a regular swing or "gait" . . . and when these semi-automatic movements are once acquired boys can pass each other to and fro in an extremely small space, and even regularly jostle their bodies against each other without much danger of striking one another with hot tools or hot glass. The constant changing of "small help," however, is continuously thrusting green boys into the shop, in which case there is real danger until all engaged in the "team" work get into a harmonious swing.[55]

In the last analysis, however, even the difficulties of organizing and co-ordinating a pottery or bottle plant were relatively simple compared to those of planning and operating a sewing machine, locomotive, or automobile factory. Unlike most manufacturers the machinery producer had to incorporate a variety of functions within the plant, provide for the handling of heavy materials, and manage a complex assembly process. As a result he was often more concerned than other manufacturers with production problems and with innovations that promised to solve those problems.

One sign of this concern was the appearance of debates in the technical journals over the best plan for a machinery works. Engineers discussed the virtues of the hollow square, the H, and the L forms; the multifloor versus the single-floor machine shop; and the "group" versus the "output" plan of machine layout. The appropriate location of the foundry, the smith-shop, the drawing room, and the foremen's offices was a source of continuing controversy. In general the trend was from the hollow square to the other forms, from the multistory shop to the single-story plant, and from the "group" to the "output" (emphasizing product rather than machine function) plan. Most observers and manufacturers also concluded that the foundry and blacksmith shops ought to be segregated from the rest of the plant because of the heat, smoke, and dirt that emanated from them.[56]

The results of this interest in plant organization were often striking. Although little is known about the performance of the "average" machinery manufacturer, the "best" practices received much publicity. Of the large mid-to-late-nineteenth-century plants the Colt Armory in Hartford and the Brown & Sharpe Company works in Providence were probably the best known. Colt was apparently one of the first manufacturers to abandon the hollow square for the H form. This plan of organization "gave more floor-room than a hollow square form on the same ground area, was equally well lighted, had shorter lines of work-travel and official travel, and gave detached work-rooms."[57] The Brown & Sharpe works, which expanded from one large building in the 1870s to more than three city blocks by the 1900s, retained the hollow square pattern. By the latter date the machine shops and blacksmith shops occupied one square, a large foundry and machine shops another, and additional foundries the third. The factory was the "best constructed, arranged, and equipped of any kind in the world."[58]

Though most machinery makers left the actual routing of materials and components to the department foremen, they did what they could to expedite the flow of work, often with marked success. At the Pullman works, for example,

> all the timber is taken in in lengths at one end and is never turned around until it finds its proper place in a completed freight car, being carried constantly from one process to another in a direct line from its reception at one end to its utilization at the other.[59]

The manufacture of locomotives at the Altoona works of the Pennsylvania Railroad was compared to the "passing of an earnest student from class to class":

Upon completion the boiler goes into the erecting shop, the end of which is directly opposite that of the boiler shop. The blacksmith shop is beside the latter. From the former the frames and forgings enter the machine shop, which occupies the same relative position to it as the erecting shop does to the boiler shop. The lay-put of the machine shop is such that the forgings are finished as they pass through without going over the same path twice, and they reach a completed stage at about the center of the building. The cylinders and other castings enter the machine shop from the opposite end, and after going through the various machining operations they reach a completed stage where they meet the frames and other forgings.

From this point the parts go in company through a side door to the erecting shop, and are there met by the boiler which has come in from the boiler shop.[60]

The advent of electric power—probably the single most important stimulus to change in the layout and operation of the large factory— greatly facilitated these efforts. In the early 1880s manufacturers began to replace gas or oil lights with arc and then incandescent bulb lights. Electric lighting proved so superior that by the 1890s it had made gas lights obsolete. But electric lighting was also the "spark plug" that led to the use of electricity for other purposes.[61] By the turn of the century electric traveling cranes, railroads, and other materials-handling equipment had eliminated the most serious bottlenecks in the old-time shop. Together with the transformation of factory architecture and the rise of systematic management, electric power made the typical manufacturing plant of 1900 or 1910 a far different place from what it had been in 1880.

The introduction of electric motors to drive machinery proceeded at a slower pace because of the high initial cost of the electrical equipment and the problems of refitting a plant designed for water or steam power and shafting. The first important application of electric power to drive machinery occurred in 1890 when the Baldwin Company remodeled its erecting shop and installed electric motors.[62] In 1893 the Ponemah Mills at Taftville, Connecticut, and the Columbia Mills at Columbia, South Carolina, introduced electric driving in the textile industry. Thereafter the use of electric machinery, particularly in the southern mills, spread rapidly.[63] Meanwhile other manufacturers adapted their lighting systems to solve other problems, such as the operation of cranes. Supposedly, Building No. 60 of the General Electric Schenectady works, with thirty-five electric cranes and one thousand motor-driven tools, was the first machine shop to dispense with shafts and belting altogether.[64] By the World War I period manufacturing was "the largest electricity using sector in the economy."[65]

The potential effects of these innovations on the factory setting were almost limitless. Electric power greatly reduced transmission costs. With the growth of electric utilities and the shift from "group" to "unit" drive (the installation of motors in each tool or machine), it also eliminated the expense of maintaining steam engines, shafting, and belts. By freeing manufacturers to build plants in any shape, it undoubtedly speeded the adoption of new construction technologies. By permitting use of the most advanced cranes, conveyors, railways, and other transportation devices, it facilitated the handling of materials. It improved factory illumination and, by allowing the removal of the maze of belts found in most shops, permitted natural lighting to an unprecedented extent. Its effects on working conditions notwithstanding, electric power gave the manufacturer the ability to control the factory environment to a greater degree than ever before.[66]

The changes that had occurred by the turn of the century were apparent in the "model" factories that appeared at that time. Just as the Colt, Brown & Sharpe, Sellers, Baldwin, Pullman, and McCormick factories represented the best in late-nineteenth-century shop construction and organization, so the Westinghouse Electric and Manufacturing Company works (1895), the National Cash Register plant (1896), the West Allis factory of the E. P. Allis Company (1902), the United Shoe Machinery plant (1904), the U.S. Steel Gary works (1906), and the Detroit auto factories (1903–1910) were among the best examples of the new generation of plants. And though these factories were the products of the specific changes described above, it would be impossible to pinpoint the impact of each change. The innovations that brought about the transformation of the factory were interdependent and, as applied in the new plants, inseparable.

The most obvious characteristic of the new factories was their immense size relative to the largest plants of the 1880s. Most of them consisted of a series of interrelated buildings rather than a single large structure. Moreover, most were located in suburban areas where ample land was available. The manufacturers often made specific provisions for expansion. This involved a degree of prior planning that had seldom existed in earlier years. Not only was the purpose of the building considered beforehand, but the flow of work between departments became another important factor in building design.[67]

A second characteristic of the new factories was the extent to which they escaped the technological constraints that had plagued earlier manufacturers. Steel and brick or reinforced concrete construction and electrical power permitted far more flexibility in arranging the plant and the manufacturing process than progressive engineers and manufacturers of the previous generation had ever imagined possible.[68] Observers agreed that the new shops were well lighted, well ventilated, and unusually clean.

Of all the new plants the auto factories were by far the most advanced. The seemingly insatiable market for automobiles and the fact that the auto factory, unlike the steel, locomotive, or other heavy machinery plant, was not limited by the bulk or weight of the materials or product allowed "bold flights of invention in planning and designing the best possible factory building."[69] As a consequence the auto makers assimilated the best current thinking on shop layout, routing, specialized tools, and assembly techniques and often devised new methods for moving parts. The Olds, Packard, White, Lozier, Cadillac, Pierce-Arrow, and Willys-Overland plants won acclaim for their innovations.[70]

Yet contemporary observers agreed that the Highland Park plant represented the outstanding synthesis of progressive thinking in the industry. Built between 1908 and 1910 and extended in the following years, the Highland Park factory testified to the revolutionary effects of electric power and production planning. Henry Ford's first career had been with the Detroit Edison Company, and he had developed a keen appreciation of the value of electricity. Although electric motors were used to drive shafts in the machine shop, the plant was otherwise free of shafts and belts. The first floor of the main, four-story building and the adjoining one-story machine shop were devoted to heavy machine work and the assembly of the engine and chassis. The sawtooth roof on the machine shop admitted ample light despite the belts. Workmen assembled the car bodies on the top three floors of the main buildings: the metal and upholstery work took place on the fourth floor, wheel and lamp production on the third, and the body assembly on the second. Except for cars that were to be sold locally, the chassis and body were packed separately and assembled at their final destination.[71]

Although the Highland Park plant was a substantial achievement, the phenomenal success of the Model T encouraged Ford to reorganize production and introduce mass production between 1910 and 1913. The most significant of the Ford innovations occurred in the massive machine shop, where Ford engineers refined the practice of interchangeable parts manufacture, introducing a remarkable array of special-purpose machine tools.[72] By manufacturing more of the car at lower cost, they were able to undercut competitors and expand their market. To take full advantage of this strategy, they sought to speed the movement of parts in and out of the machine shop. As noted earlier, one of the distinguishing features of the Highland Park plant was the long, glass-topped craneway, which allowed the rapid movement of materials between floors. Individual departments also had smaller cranes, and rail lines crisscrossed the yard. But the large number of parts needed to build an automobile posed additional problems. The Ford engineers first installed metal gravity slides that moved parts from one worker or group of workers to another and employed hundreds of men to push or carry materials through the plant. From this point it was only a short step to the ultimate achievement in pre–World War I materials-handling technique, the moving assembly line.

Although the Ford assembly lines of 1913 have been described in detail elsewhere, several points deserve emphasis.[73] First, they were an important breakthrough in an area that manufacturers had often neglected. Despite an increasing recognition of the importance of shop layout and routing, manufacturers apparently devoted relatively little attention to assembly methods. The standard procedure of bringing the necessary parts to a central location and depositing them at a number of erecting sites was unchallenged in most industries before World War I. Even some progressive auto makers retained this method after Ford demonstrated the efficacy of his approach.[74] The problem in most industries was, of course, the variation in the product. In the tire industry, which embraced mass production after 1910, assembly methods remained labor-intensive. Even when special-purpose assembly machines became available, traditional methods prevailed. The multiplicity of tire sizes and styles and the constantly changing product mix defied the mechanization and standardization of this critical step in the manufacturing process.[75]

Second, the moving assembly line soon became an ambiguous and often misleading symbol of the new environment of the twentieth-century factory. Insofar as it implied the use of mass production technology and the managers' efforts to control the technical organization of the factory, it reflected the developments of the pre–World War I period. But to many observers it also signaled—inaccurately—the triumph of machines and machine-paced work in twentieth-century factories. Impressive though Ford's achievements were, they did not create a continuous-process plant. Even with moving lines, auto assembly depended on human effort. Chassis line employees were expected to work at a uniform pace, but they were not automatons. General Motors, among others, long used group bonuses to encourage cooperation among assembly line workers.[76] Body assembly remained even more labor intensive, and assembly lines did not appear in body plants for another twenty years. In auto manufacturing as in other industries, human labor remained indispensable to success. This fact largely accounted for other features of the new factory system, notably efforts to improve shop management and to enhance the quality of the factory labor force. It was also related to another aspect of the manufacturer's effort to control the factory environment: the improvement of working conditions.

Working Conditions

Although new methods of factory construction, machine utilization, power distribution, and materials handling appear, in retrospect, to have revolutionized the physical setting of the large manufacturing plant, their impact was much less obvious to contemporaries. A worker who began his or her career in a small dingy mill might end it in a large modern factory, but the change would occur over a number of years and probably involve a series of job changes.[77] Moreover, many plants that dated from the initial phases of the factory system remained in operation in 1920, so new techniques did not seem to supersede the old but rather to complement them. The gradual diffusion of the broader changes suggests the importance of a third aspect of the physical setting to managers and workers before 1920—the shop conditions that influenced the performance of particular jobs. When workers agitated for changes in the factory environment, they seldom demanded a new plant or the introduction of electricity. They did, however, call for better heating or ventilation, clean rest rooms, and security against accidents.

The preceding pages make several general distinctions that help categorize working conditions in the pre–World War I plant. Because of the technological changes that transformed the factory after 1880, large plants were likely to be superior to small plants, new plants to old, and those in the Midwest and South to those in the East. Observers were virtually unanimous in their opinion that large factories were cleaner, safer, and healthier places to work than small factories. State inspectors often noted the progressive attitudes of managers of large firms. An investigator who studied the reports of the Massachusetts health inspectors concluded:

> From the data thus collected, manufacturers may be classified in two general groups. There are, on the one hand, those who concern themselves but little with the health and welfare of their employees. . . . To this class belong, in the main, the smaller industrial establishments which need considerable looking after in order that they may be kept in reasonably good sanitary condition. . . . The second class of manufacturers represents principally the larger industrial establishments. . . . These employers recognize that money invested for the maintenance of sanitary and healthful conditions in their establishments is a profitable investment.[78]

The clearest contrasts were in the tobacco and clothing industries, where the largest plants, those of P. Lorillard & Company or Joseph & Feiss, for instance, were models of good working conditions while the smallest plants—the classic sweatshops—epitomized the opposite extreme.[79]

Newer establishments also had natural advantages. A post-1900 factory was more likely to be better lighted and cleaner because of improvements in building techniques and power distribution. "Most of the [southern] cotton manufacturing establishments," a U.S. Bureau of Labor report noted, "were handsome new buildings, well ventilated and lighted.[80] Even Florence Kelley, the outspoken Illinois factory inspector and reformer, admitted that "there is a certain advantage in the West . . . in the matter of modern construction of factories."[81]

But in every region and city and even in multiplant firms, there were marked variations between factories.[82] At Standard Oil's Baltimore refinery, for example, workmen "had to improvise their own washing facilities," while at the Bayonne works the company supplied toilets, washrooms, and lockers.[83] U.S. Steel executives faced the most severe challenge in attempting to establish minimum standards for their many plants and, despite their claims, were probably only partially successful. There was some truth to a contemporary judgment that the workers' lot seemed to depend "upon the particular employer they happen to get; in practically every industry both extremes [are] found."[84]

Data on the mortality and morbidity of factory workers do little to clarify the situation. Aside from underlining the risks of an unhealthy work environment, they merely emphasize the dangers of particular occupations. Thus factory employees who were occupied for prolonged periods where the air was dusty or otherwise polluted—textile and tobacco workers, printers, machinists—were susceptible to respiratory diseases. Others who were subject to rapid temperature changes—foundry and steel workers—often contracted pneumonia. And operatives who were engaged in strenuous physical labor and who required refreshment, either at the communal water bucket or at the neighborhood saloon, ran a high risk of death from typhoid fever or alcoholism.[85] Yet critics of the factory system were never able to establish a conclusive relationship between ill health and factory work per se, for even with a work week of sixty hours or more, wage earners still spent most of their time outside the plant, often in surroundings that were even less conducive to good health.[86]

Though there were simply too many variations to permit sweeping conclusions about plant conditions, one additional distinction is helpful in identifying areas where significant changes occurred. Working conditions that were technologically determined, that developed out of the nature of the manufacturing process, were subject to different imperatives than conditions that were largely the product of managerial discretion. Obviously there was no fixed boundary between the two spheres, but there were different categories of decision making. The factory owner or manager in most industries had a strong incentive to adopt at least some of the techniques of the industry leaders. This meant that most manufacturers in a particular field undertook roughly the same operations. Conversely, there were other areas unrelated to the process or the product of the plant where managerial prerogatives were all-important.

All production workers were subject to technically determined working conditions to some degree. This was inherent in the nature of the factory and affected the relationship between the supervisor and the worker, the social organization of the plant, and other aspects of the general factory setting. But in some cases the exigencies of production had a particular identifiable impact on the worker. Invariably this impact was adverse in that it required unusual physical exertion or created an unhealthy work atmosphere. Often it was so marked that it became the distinctive feature of the occupation or craft.

In the textile industry the mills were generally clean, and most jobs required neither brains nor brawn; the most frequent complaints were that the operatives had to stand and that the work produced "a lassitude in anyone who performs it."[87] But there were two additional, more serious liabilities that were particularly evident in cotton mills. The first was the cotton lint that permeated the air and was a major cause of lung disorders.[88] The second, which compounded the first, was the necessity of maintaining a humid atmosphere to prevent the cotton or wool fiber from breaking. The desirability of moisture-laden air was one reason the industry shifted from the Merrimack to Fall River and New Bedford in the 1860s and 1870s. In most mills it meant that the windows were never opened and that various devices were used to increase the moisture content of the air. The most common method was to force steam through pipes into the spinning and weaving rooms. The heated air was often a source of extreme discomfort. At a Holyoke, Massachusetts, mill the state factory inspector found the atmosphere so oppressive that he was forced to leave.[89] Although some mills used cool water in the summer, many did not, and it was not until the introduction of mechanical humidifying devices, notably the Sturtevant system, in the 1880s that the situation improved. By World War I most mills had abandoned the use of steam.[90]

Iron and steel mill employees encountered nearly every conceivable adversity. Their work was hot, dirty, and physically exhausting.[91] Yet the shift from iron to steel in the 1870s and the subsequent introduction of electric cranes and railways eliminated the most difficult work. The Bessemer process required less physical labor than puddling, and the open-hearth process required even less. In the fabricating departments the replacement of "hand" by "mechanical" mills reduced the need for human labor. "Almost without exception every genuine advance in the art of steel making has improved the physical conditions under which the men work."[92]

The same problems often existed in a machinery factory where the work, by its nature, exposed the men to dust, heat, and smoke. There was a "belief that machinists, boiler makers, moulders, and blacksmiths must be coarse and brutal to be effective workers."[93] Some workers, such as grinders and buffers, faced special health hazards due to dust or poisonous gases, but they seldom suffered the fate of the foundry employee. The foundry was often the least hospitable part of the plant; it was invariably dirty and damp. When a large casting was poured "the interior . . . is an inferno of smoke, flame, and coruscations."[94] Equally serious was the constantly fluctuating temperature. Foundries were often unheated and drafty, but the molder's work exposed him to intense heat. "In the winter morning it is bitterly cold, and the men's feet and fingers suffer in the wet raw sand. . . . In the afternoon, at casting time, the place becomes insufferably hot, from which atmosphere the men go home through raw frost or snow."[95] A 1912 study of 153 foundries in New York state concluded that 39 percent were poorly ventilated, 32 percent were poorly lighted, 43 percent were poorly heated, and 73 percent had inadequate washing facilities.[96]

Technological advances improved the lot of the machinery worker to some extent after the turn of the century. Modern factory buildings aided machinists and assemblers in the machinery industries; molding and forging machinery lightened the work of the molder and blacksmith; exhaust systems reduced the dangers to the buffer and grinder; and heating and ventilating apparatus was a boon to employees in the large and more progressive foundries.[97] But in general the metal trade worker's environment remained an unpleasant one.

Steel mills, forge shops, and foundries, however, had no monopoly on dangerous or unappealing working conditions. The typical glass factory was hot and drafty, the air in the "shops" often polluted with glass particles. Meat-packing plants were cold and wet; in one not atypical room the "slime and grease were so thick that a foothold was hardly possible."[98] Tobacco factories, woodworking plants, and potteries were invariable dusty, and rubber manufacture exposed the worker to poisonous chemicals.[99] Although technological innovation tended to eliminate the worst of these conditions, a wide disparity remained between the "best" and the "average" plant.

In the second area, where managerial discretion rather than technological or engineering considerations was paramount, the situation was different. The improvement—or at least the alteration—of the factory environment was the manufacturer's objective, not a secondary consequence of other activity. As a result, factories varied more in some areas than others. Few employers, for example, disputed the contention that electric lighting was both conducive to greater productivity and better for the worker than gaslight. Nor did they usually question the arguments that skylights, monitors, and large windows were desirable for the same reasons. The contrast between the old and the new in both cases was so dramatic that objection was unrealistic. There was less consensus on the value of forced-air heating versus the older method of running steam pipes along the ceiling or around the walls. Yet by 1900 most large plants and virtually all new ones were using the forced-air system, as well as electric lighting and improved methods of ventilation.[100]

On the other hand, there were wide differences of opinion on the desirability of amenities for workers. A few firms, such as Brown & Sharpe, provided washrooms with modern lavatories, toilets, and lockers long before proponents of "welfare work" began to emphasize the relationship between pleasant surroundings and employee morale.[101] But many otherwise progressive manufacturers continued to believe that "good work and great production at low cost can be secured without much consideration of fatigue, accommodations for meals . . . or cleanliness of workmen."[102] Few gave any consideration to the location of toilets or even to the provision of washrooms or drinking water. In the Lowell mills "the water closets are badly located in the center of the room. . . . The effluvia from them are sure to pollute the air of the rooms."[103] In the Wood Mill at Lawrence there were "no special comforts for employees."[104] As late as 1910 many textile mills did not provide dressing rooms or lockers for female workers.

> When time for the noon hour comes, the women take a wooden pail which they keep beside their machines, fill it with water at the sink, and bring it back again. They have soap, cloth, and towel, and perform their toilet while watching their machines, even to taking down curl papers, combing their hair, changing shoes or waist if they wish, donning skirt, hat and coat while work is going on, the only privacy being the shelter of the machinery.[105]

Most manufacturers apparently paid even less attention to industrial accidents. Though they were not oblivious to the human costs of injuries, they invariably viewed accidents as an inevitable product of factory work, a problem that was "without remedy."[106] A concomitant to this view, expressed by a Pittsburgh mill manager, was that "95 percent of our accidents are due to the carelessness of the man who gets hurt."[107] Yet as investigators accumulated data on injuries, it became apparent that this attitude was not only incorrect but responsible for thousands of injuries.[108] If only one-quarter of the workers killed in Pittsburgh bore any responsibility for their misfortune, as the Pittsburgh Survey indicated, there was obviously room for remedial action.[109]

Government statistics revealed that accident rates varied widely between industries and, more important, between occupations in specific industries. In textiles the overall rate was relatively low, but workers in picking and carding departments had injury rates comparable to those of operatives in more hazardous industries.[110] In the machinery industry workers engaged in ship and locomotive building were more prone to accidents than those in electrical apparatus or machine tool manufacture. Yet there were also marked variations between trades: boilermakers, cranemen, erecting shop workers, and yard laborers had higher accident rates than machinists or molders, whatever their industry. Night workers in all occupations had higher injury rates than day workers.[111]

The most hazardous of all manufacturing industries was iron and steel making. As late as 1909–1910 nearly one-quarter of the full-time workers in 155 plants suffered some type of injury.[112] And, as in other industries, there were wide variations between occupations. Blast furnace, Bessemer, and open-hearth employees suffered more injuries—and far more severe injuries—on the average than fabricating, mechanical, and yard workers.[113]

Yet until the 1890s most employers dealt with each case on an ad hoc basis, as if it were a unique occurrence.[114] The superintendent would "look at the case upon its merits in reference to the man's condition."[115] Many paid the employees' hospital bills and funeral expenses or assisted "mutual benefit" or "relief" associations—plant insurance organizations to which the employees contributed. In 1908 the Commissioner of Labor published a study of 461 of these associations. Nearly three-quarters began operations in the 1890s or afterwards. Over 400 provided death and temporary disability benefits, but only 54 provided permanent disability benefits, and only 5 offered old-age pensions.[116] The 1908 study concluded that

> the workingman usually receives but scant compensation for disabling injuries received in the course of his work, and especially when he suffers the loss of a part of the body, or some other permanent disability. The investigation shows further that by far the greater part of the compensation received comes from the workman rather than from the industry that presents the hazard.[117]

A few manufacturers maintained infirmaries; others, like the Phoenix Iron Company, depended on the local hospitals with varying results. "When the ambulance is needed . . . [the nurse] calls the Hospital, the Hospital 'phones the Phoenix Hotel, the Phoenix Hotel 'phones the Livery Stable and the Livery Stable hunts up a driver."[118] Some firms also presented a gift to the widow, allowed the family to live in a company-owned house, or supplied coal without charge.[119] In 1907 the Jones & Laughlin Steel Company paid benefits to eleven of twenty-eight families of fatality victims; the Pressed Steel Car Company to four of ten families; and the National Tube Company, to seven of thirteen.[120] Moreover, by the turn of the century many firms carried liability insurance, which protected them against the workers' legal claims and often foreclosed even these modest philanthropic gestures. As a consequence, perhaps as many as half of all accident victims and their families received no financial compensation, while another quarter received only meager settlements. A 1917 comparison of employers' grants and workmen's compensation payments to families of accident victims in three states found that the former averaged less than one-fourth the compensation payments.[121]

The accident records of two major Massachusetts textile firms, the Lawrence Manufacturing Company of Lowell and the Dwight Manufacturing Company of Chicopee, illuminate the informal method of handling accident cases. Though both firms carried liability insurance, the agents or superintendents settled most of the claims. In a few instances they were surprisingly generous. The Lawrence agent sent an operative with a weak claim to a hospital free of charge; the Dwight agent granted "allowances" to an employee in "straitened circumstances" and gave money to another who had "no friends in this locality."[122] Usually, however, they acted on the assumption, expressed by the Dwight agent, that "the people about here seem to think that the . . . Company is a charitable institution" and were niggardly at best.[123] When an employee did have a strong case against the company, the respective agent attempted to persuade the victim to settle out of court for as little as possible. In one case the Dwight executive reported that he had sent his plant superintendent to make a "casual" call on the injured operative

> so that it would not appear that I was too anxious to settle but really to find out what she would settle for. . . . After talking and sympathizing with her for a while he suggested that she call at his Office, and see what arrangements I could make with her. . . . He told her it would be much better for her to settle now and avoid paying large lawyer's fees, that she would receive but little of it, should they win the case, and that your company would fight it to the bitter end, etc. After talking with her for quite a while, he thought she would be inclined to settle for from $400 to $500. He told her that it would be best for her to come in and see me, at the same time giving her the impression that he was urging this without my knowledge for her sake, etc.[124]

Most of the time the agents were successful. A Lawrence employee who lost a hand received $50; another worker who lost an arm was awarded $66.71, including $15.71 to pay his hospital bill and $1.00 to buy new overalls and a jacket.[125]

Most manufacturers operated like the Lawrence and Dwight agents, but there were exceptions. Some firms, like the E. P. Allis Company and the Cramp Shipyard, paid their employees' wages when they were injured.[126] Others, principally iron and steel producers, reacted against the liability companies' "heartless" approach, as well as their high premiums, by establishing their own insurance departments.[127] In many cases firms also sought to reduce payments to victims by providing up-to-date medical facilities. The Illinois Steel Company, for example, built modern hospitals for its employees on the premise that first-class medical attention would speed recovery and make the worker "ashamed" to ask for a cash settlement.[128] Gradually the managers of these companies began to consider the possibility that accidents were another managerial problem to be studied and solved. From this point it was only a short step to the idea that accident reduction increased profits and to the organized safety movement.

The safety movement supposedly began in 1906–1907 when the

American Museum of Safety was founded and U.S. Steel took its first steps toward a safety program.[129] The former, financed largely by steel executives and headed by William Tolman, an ex-minister who had earlier devoted considerable energy to publicizing welfare work, was the first major safety propaganda organization.[130] U.S. Steel promoted safety work and created a model program. It called for a safety organization headed by executives to indicate top-level concern, shop committees to involve the foremen and workers, prizes and publicity to generate interest, full-time inspectors to find and correct potential sources of injury, warning signs and pictures, installation of the latest mechanical devices, and medical services to minimize the seriousness of injuries.[131] It was highly successful in reducing injuries and was copied by many other manufacturers. The popularity of U.S. Steel's safety program symbolized the remarkable change that had occurred in the employer's conception of what could be done to change the physical environment of the plant.

It would be a mistake, however, to exaggerate the success of this movement before World War I. A few large firms that undertook extensive safety campaigns reduced accident rates by 50 to 75 percent, but most companies continued to do little or nothing.[132] Even in the iron and steel industry there were laggards. In 1910 John Fitch wrote, for example, that the Jones & Laughlin Company had "manifested considerable indifference" to accident prevention.[133] There was no evidence of reduced accident rates in the machinery industries until 1912.[134] Substantial progress in lowering the number of industrial accidents came only after World War I, when the spread of the safety movement and workmen's compensation legislation virtually forced managers to consider the benefits of accident prevention. Nevertheless, by 1910 a growing number of manufacturers were awakening to the economic advantages of reforming traditional activities, a realization that stimulated changes and enlarged the manager's functions.

Whether viewed from the perspective of the factory exterior, the internal operation of the plant, or working conditions, the factory environment changed substantially between 1880 and 1915. In many cases innovations derived from major inventions or technological trends of long standing and were initially unrelated to the growth of a new managerial role in the factory. In others—such as the safety movement—the factory environment changed in response to the managers' increased sensitivity to the economic importance of internal operations. But in either case the effect was to alter—indeed, to transform—the factory. As the preceding pages suggest, this was a continuous process that had no beginning or ending dates. Moreover, at every stage old, seemingly obsolete plants operated alongside modern factories. Yet if the operation of the technological dynamic is impossible to pinpoint, it is clear that it interacted at many points with the more conscious and deliberate efforts that led to changes in management practices. Appropriately, the age of concrete and steel construction, electric power, and safety campaigns was also the era of systematic and scientific management.

3   The Foreman's Empire

In the first place, most managers are reluctant, except under the compulsion of circumstances, to undertake revolutionary improvement; in the second place, because of natural basic conditions of prosperity in America, there has not been general compulsion toward ideas and methods marking a radical departure from opportunism. [Morris L. Cooke in Harlow Person, ed., *Scientific Management in American Industry* (New York, 1929), p. 11]

The reason why coercive "drive" methods have prevailed in the past has been that the central management has been indifferent to the methods pursued by foremen in handling men but has insisted rigidly upon a constantly increasing output and constantly decreasing costs. [Sumner H. Slichter, *The Turnover of Factory Labor* (New York, 1919), p. 375]

The higher the organization of the factory, the more nearly the factory approaches the condition of automatic plant equipment. . . . Men may be brought to clock-like regularity of action during their hours of factory service, and may gladly and happily meet every factory labor requirement, without the slightest loss of self-respect, or the slightest consciousness of surrender of independent volition. [Horace L. Arnold, *The Factory Manager and Accountant* (London, 1910), p. 10]

If the nineteenth-century factory was an assemblage of buildings and machinery, it was also a complex social organization, encompassing hundreds, often thousands, of individuals. Yet it was a fragmented, decentralized organization, for the typical manufacturer entrusted most aspects of the day-to-day operation of the large manufacturing plant to the first-line supervisors and skilled workers. The exact implications of this practice differed among industries and shops, but one point is clear: the technicians, clerks, and other staff specialists—not to mention the union representatives—who dominate the present-day manufacturing plant were unknown in the late-nineteenth-century factory. By modern standards the foreman's empire was a formidable realm.[1]

THE HIERARCHY OF AUTHORITY

The relationship between the management and the first-line supervisor in the late-nineteenth-century plant was seldom clearly defined.

There were discussions of what constituted good foremanship at trade association and technical society meetings but few efforts to define the foreman's responsibilities in a precise and explicit way or to "professionalize" the job before World War I.[2] As a result, the factor that most often determined the foreman's authority was the "technological system designed by the company to organize the work process."[3] Ultimately the method of production delimited the scope of the foreman's empire.

The Management and the Foreman

To understand the foreman's power vis-à-vis the management in the late-nineteenth-century factory it is helpful to visualize a continuum of industrial technologies ranging from unit or small-batch production at one extreme to continuous-process production at the other. At one end the firm manufactures relatively small quantities of a particular product, often on order; precision work is necessary, and skilled workers who set their own pace are a high percentage of the labor force. At the opposite end are volume producers that depend on chemical processes or automated machine operations; production workers have diagnostic skills but work at the pace of the machines they manage.[4] In general, late-nineteenth-century foremen had the greatest power in industries that used unit and small-batch techniques and fewer prerogatives in industries that relied on continuous processing.[5]

It is hardly necessary to add that this categorization disregards many important distinctions. There were, on the one hand, a number of industries that defy classification. The arms makers, for example, were among the first to embrace the goal of a standardized product made with interchangeable parts—a particularly fertile approach to volume production—but among the last to abolish the internal contract system, which placed great power in the hands of the contractor, a substitute for the foreman.[6] In other industries, the prevailing methods of manufacture were revolutionized between 1880 and World War I. This was the case in flour milling; steel, match, and cigarette making; petroleum refining; and some forms of food canning, where continuous processing became the rule. It was also true in the auto-related industries, including auto, tire, and glass manufacture, and in the machinery industries, where other forms of mass production were introduced, with a resulting deterioration in the foreman's status. Even in foundries, supposedly the most tradition-bound of all enterprises in the metal-working field, the introduction of molding machinery made possible dramatic increases in the production of standard products and a decrease in the formerly all-powerful foreman's authority.[7]

Assuming, however, that these ideal types have some validity, the questions still remain: What powers were in contention? What functions did a "typical" foreman perform? How much variation did in fact exist? In general it appears that the range of the foreman's possible responsibilities spanned three basic areas of decision making. First-line supervisors determined the manner and timing of production, had responsibility for the cost and quality of the work, and had virtually complete authority over the man or women in their departments or areas.[8]

The foreman's actual powers in the areas of production management, cost accounting, and quality control varied from industry to industry depending on the particular production methods in use. Even before the inroads of "systematic" or "scientific" management there was a tendency in most large manufacturing plants to relieve first-level supervisors of their responsibilities in these areas. This trend derived from the exigencies of manufacturing in a rapidly growing economy rather than from any internal considerations.[9] The process, however, was generally a gradual one; in most industries the foreman's position remained secure well into the twentieth century.

The nineteenth-century supervisor's authority was probably greatest in machinery factories of the New England and the Middle Atlantic states, where the work involved, as an 1880 source put it, "the fabrication of a multitude of distinct parts."[10] In these plants the internal contract system of manufacturing remained an important form of industrial organization until the World War I period.[11] Under it highly skilled workmen became managers as well as workers. The firm provided materials, tools, power, and a factory building. The employees—"contractors"—in turn agreed to manufacture a particular object or component in a given quantity at a designated cost and by a specific date. Otherwise they retained virtually complete control over the production process. The contractor was thus an employee working for a day wage and an independent businessman working for an anticipated profit.

The benefits that contracting offered machine builders are apparent from an examination of the areas in which it retained its hold longest. No firm placed all its operations under the contract system. Usually the contractors made components that were designed, inspected, and assembled by other, noncontract employees. In the gun factories, for example, contractors made barrels, stocks, and screws but did not assemble the finished product. At the Winchester Company no more than half the total employees were ever under the contract system at one time.[12] In the arms industry, as in others, jobs assigned to contractors involved difficult precision work and demanded highly skilled workers and close supervision.

Above all the contract system was popular because contractors kept their costs low. Even with the contractor's profit and that of his "subcontractors" if he further divided the job, production costs were lower than on work performed under the foreman system. As manufacturers recognized, contracting provided a powerful stimulus for cost reduction through technological innovation and careful management. The extent of this incentive is clear from the fact that the contractor alone reaped the rewards of the system. The men who worked for him ordinarily received day wages and often bore the brunt of the downward "adjustment" in the contractor's price. Although the social relations that frequently existed between the contractor and his "employees" may have protected the workers, the contractor was naturally reluctant to reduce his profit margin. For these men the supposed psychological advantages of the artisan proprietorship were present in a factory setting.

The inside contract system was thus a useful expedient for nineteenth-century American machine builders. It became less useful as manufacturers increased their output to take advantage of growing markets. In firms that expanded slowly and continued to require highly skilled shop workers at crucial points, the system was retained, often into the twentieth century. In other companies that increased output more rapidly or introduced mass production technologies, the contract system soon fell into disfavor. The Singer Sewing Machine Company, for instance, introduced contract work in 1863 after its foremen had encountered many difficulties in making precision parts. The contractors worked diligently, improved the product, and made high profits. But the management, apparently learning from the contractors' experiences and unhappy at their profits, replaced the system in 1883 with salaried foremen. For Singer, contracting had become unnecessary to maintain product quality or work incentives. "Experience has shown that, with a wise and liberal policy pervading the establishment, and with a good system of accounts, the heads of departments will have sufficient ambition to make a good showing."[13]

A variation of the contract system continued in many machine shops even after World War I. Under this arrangement the skilled employees working under a foreman bid on a specific job. The foreman selected the contractor, who in turn recruited his workers from among the men already employed in the department. When the contractor completed the job, he resumed his position as a regular shop employee, and other men, who had served as "employees," bid on new work. The contract jobs under this modified approach were all similar: they were special in nature and difficult to perform, and they required the attention of one or more competent technicians. Officials of the Winchester Company and the Baldwin Locomotive Works maintained that this method was highly successful in producing accurate, low-cost work.[14]

In industries where it was retained the contract system offered supervisors the greatest opportunity for initiative and influence. The basis of the system was, of course, the contractor's virtually unlimited authority. After the contract had been negotiated, the manufacturer's most important function was to provide an able force of inspectors. The contractor, on the other hand, made virtually all the important decisions relating to what, when, how, and by whom the product would be made. In addition he alone knew—or at least had the opportunity to know—the actual production costs. One writer has described the contract arrangement as a substitute for cost accounting.[15] Finally, the contractors had nearly complete control over the factory labor force. In many firms the management did not even know how much the contractor's "employees" were paid.

The power and independence of the contractors ultimately led to the abandonment of the system, even in firms where it remained an effective method of reducing costs. For example, at the turn of the century the Whitin Machine Works, the nation's largest textile machinery producer, had four or five contractors with more than fifty "employees" and several with more than one hundred.[16] Horace L. Arnold reported that the "management of the labor was without even the faintest trace of a defined policy."[17] But the Whitin managers became increasingly apprehensive at their ignorance of the contractors' activities. After 1900 they gradually increased their control, and the last of the contractors retired in 1911.[18]

The experiences of other firms apparently differed only in detail. Either the management found it expedient to pay—and perhaps to hire—the workers directly or the employees protested over wage reductions after the contractor's price had been cut. In 1904 a government study reported the rise of a "sweating system in the factories" where the contract method still operated.[19] When contractors lost the allegiance of their workers, the advent of salaried foremen was only a matter of time.[20]

As important, then, as any inherent defect of the contract system itself was the fact that it seemed anachronistic—out of step with the developing management movement, whatever its effects on costs. Perhaps the most visible indication of this was the social status of the contractors. In many firms the contractors' earnings far exceeded any foreman's wage, as well as the salaries of many company officers. The contractors were consequently influential figures inside and outside the shop. In many New England communities an ambitious boy turned to factory work rather than a clerical position. In 1880 the contractor's status may have seemed commensurate with his contribution, but by 1900 or 1910 it suggested a confusion of priorities to the growing number of white-collar workers.

While inside contracting apparently prevailed only in the machinery factories of the Northeast, other manufacturers who relied on highly skilled workers to perform some part of the production process often used the helper system, which bore many similarities. The skilled employee hired his assistants, or "helpers," and paid their wages from his earnings. In most cases the company paid the worker for his output, and he in turn paid the helper a fixed rate. The skilled employee's other managerial functions, however, were somewhat limited: often he worked under a foreman, was allotted only set amounts of raw materials, and played only a minor role in the firm's cost-keeping system. Seldom did he have more than half a dozen helpers, often boys serving an informal apprenticeship. Mule spinners, for example, often "employed" their sons as helpers.[21] In the South, mill managers perpetuated a variation of this arrangement by allowing children "to come in and 'help' their parents or older brothers and sisters. The manager calmed his conscience by declaring that he did not hire them."[22]

In the pottery, glass, and iron industries skilled workers regularly employed boys or women to assist them or perform secondary operations connected with their work. English potters brought the helper system first to Trenton, New Jersey, and then to East Liverpool, Ohio. Their procedure was similar to that of other highly skilled workers. They received a set price from the manufacturer for every acceptable finished piece and hoped to make a profit by paying their subordinates a lesser amount. Occasionally when the manufacturer "saw he had the shop going to suit himself," he offered the helpers positions as regular employees, but the helper system continued at least until World War I.[23] Glass blowers similarly hired and supervised their furnace boys.[24] Yet neither of these skilled groups had the power, the functions, or the managerial perspective of the true contractors. Their influence was a reflection of their skills rather than their supervisory responsibilities.

Puddlers and rollers were also basically workers rather than managers:

> A puddler usually has a helper and sometimes two helpers. . . . The helper proper gives the journeyman a spell. He takes hold of the paddle when cinder is put in to "thicken it up," that is, to make the flux. The second helper— commonly known as a "third hand," or "green hand"—generally breaks down the pig when it begins to melt, chocolate-like. He gives a "push" or a "shove" in drawing the heat, and does similar work that requires little knowledge or skill. The work of each "underhand" is so clearly understood by custom, that it is usually unnecessary to have specific rules refining it.[25]

The head roller bossed his own crew and had nominal control over the night crew as well. In some cases his profit (the difference between his rate and the wages he paid the crew) was comparable to the earnings of the most successful machinery contractors.[26] Yet he acted primarily as a production supervisor and employment agent. Many rollers were undoubtedly skilled metallurgists, but technical and organizational innovation in the iron and steel industry came from other sources.[27] In any event the power of the rollers won them the enmity of the Amalgamated Association of Iron, Steel, and Tin Workers, which succeeded in abolishing the helper system in most rolling mills by the early 1890s.

In the stove industry molders hired and paid their "berkshires" from their earnings. While this arrangement enabled them to control their helpers, it was also, they argued, a way of reducing their pay and an insidious method of training (at their expense) low-paid molders and strikebreakers. The Molders Union, like the Amalgamated Association, made the abolition of the helper system a prime objective and by the turn of the century had succeeded in eliminating it from unionized foundries.[28]

In their relations with the management, skilled workers in the textile, glass, pottery, and iron industries thus occupied a position considerably inferior to contractors of the New England machine shops. Like the contractors they were their own bosses, made high wages, and enjoyed an enviable social position in and out of the shop. But they had fewer helpers, did more of the actual work themselves, and had fewer strictly managerial responsibilities. And they saw themselves as workers rather than managers. Whereas the contractors considered themselves important company officials and long remained a bulwark against unionism, the mule spinners, glass blowers, potters, puddlers, rollers, and molders formed the most powerful labor unions of the manufacturing sector.[29]

In general, the salaried foreman also occupied a less important position in the shop than the contractor. He seldom had the same degree of independence or responsibility for production costs. Whereas the contractor set the manufacturer's direct labor and materials costs, the foreman only promised to keep costs low. In many shops he also collected cost data and, before the introduction of automatic time clocks and card systems of cost keeping, acted as timekeeper. It is not surprising that many factories had no formal system of cost accounting or used a variety of formulas to approximate costs the foreman failed to obtain directly.

In other respects the foreman's responsibilities did not differ significantly from the contractor's. In many industries he made most of the decisions about how the job was to be done, the tools and often the materials to be used, the timing of operations, the flow of work, the workers' methods and sequence of moves. In all industries he was held accountable for what, in fact, the workers did. Finally, in personnel matters—the hiring, training, supervising, and disciplining of factory employees—the foreman had virtually complete control. As a result his social standing differed from that of the contractor only in degree. At the Reed & Barton Company, for example, foremen "deported themselves with great dignity and . . . customarily reported for work attired in silk hats, cutaway coats, and attendant accessories."[30] Only where the new management made considerable headway or where strong labor unions became entrenched was the foreman's authority significantly reduced.

Within this framework the actual degree to which the management interfered in the foreman's empire depended on the industry and the production process. On the one hand, in machine shops the first-line supervisor customarily decided the order of work, the tools to be used, and the "speed and feed" of the machines.[31] He might have a clerk or timekeeper and in very large shops one or more subforemen, but in general he did the work himself. At the E. P. Allis Company, for example,

> the workmen . . . obtained the number of the casting or forging verbally from the foreman and gave their job to the timekeeper who posted it on a sheet which covered the entire labor cost on the order. . . . There were no time clocks and no production boards to assist the foremen in knowing the next job to give the workers. The result being that the foreman would let his men run out of work and the men would have to call at the foreman's desk or trail him around the shop to see what the next job would be.[32]

In steel mills and other factories that relied on chemical processes, the engineering staff made most production decisions. The blast furnace foreman, or "head blower," merely supervised the "blowers," who were responsible for two or three furnaces and who in turn bossed the keepers, the heads of individual furnaces. In open-hearth plants a similar kind of organization existed, except that the foreman had charge of three to five furnaces, their crews, and their supervisors, the "first" and "second helpers."[33] In both cases the managers allowed the foremen little discretion except in the handling of the labor force, and the foreman and his assistants were under constant pressure to maintain or exceed a predetermined schedule.[34]

In the cotton textile industry the overseer, like the steel mill foreman, was subject to continuous supervision. It was customary for an overseer to head a department or several similar departments in different mills. Though he might thus be responsible for a large number of machines and several hundred workers, including subforemen called "second" and "third" hands, his managerial prerogatives were distinctly limited. He did not decide what to produce, how much to produce, when to do it, or even at what speed. Specialists repaired or adjusted the machinery and, except for men in the finishing departments, there were few technical skills or "trade secrets" to make him indispensable.[35] At the Amoskeag Mills "the overseers are limited as to the amount of wages they shall pay, the number of people they shall employ, and in other directions, but they are held responsible for the amount and character of the work they shall turn out."[36]

Fortunately, two volumes of communications between the managers and overseers of the Dwight Manufacturing Company have survived, showing the difficult circumstances under which many overseers worked. Although most of the orders were routine, a minority were of a different character. When quality declined the agent demanded to see "an improvement in this line at once." On another occasion he urged: "Push it for all you are worth, and weave it decently." When production slackened he warned: "This of course is under your own immediate management . . . and I am helpless unless I go in and do your work. I give you notice now that if this continues we shall have to part." When trouble developed in another department he summarized his relationship with the supervisors: "These goods must be made better or there will be 'grief' ahead."[37] These statements help explain why, in dealing with their subordinates, foremen and overseers were often equally harsh and demanding.

The Foremen and Workers

Although the managers and foremen set goals for the organization and judged the effectiveness of the group in meeting those goals, their decisions were implemented through a second set of relationships involving the foreman and the workers. And though the foreman's position in the managerial hierarchy varied from plant to plant, his status vis-à-vis the worker was remarkably similar whether he bossed a locomotive repair shop gang or an auto assembly line. Before 1900 and in most factories before 1920 the foreman was the undisputed ruler of the department, gang, crew, or shop.

The foreman's authority constantly reminded the workers that technical skill was the key to power. The foreman had invariably worked his way up: he had achieved his position because he knew how to do the work in his shop better than anyone else. To the ambitious newcomer the "promise of mobility" was not an abstraction or a fraud.[38] The factory labor force was "pyramided and held together by the ambition of the men lower down; even a serious break in the ranks adjusts itself all but automatically."[39]

Nor were the kinds of skills necessary for success beyond the reach of most workers. Formal education meant little; mechanical ability and experience were all-important. A government study of foundry work summarized the appeal and the weakness of the traditional system.

> In this and most other plants in the city these supervisors have considerable practical knowledge as to foundry processes. What seems to be most lacking is familiarity with the best principles and practices in systematizing foundry work and an acquaintanceship with the construction, operation, and adaptation of various types of foundry apparatus. Not more skill in shaping molds but more business and technical knowledge is the greatest need of foremen and supervisors.[40]

The convergence of skill and power made foremen conservative men, uncompromising defenders of the status quo. Because of their success they looked askance at anyone or anything that threatened to change the "shop culture" that had rewarded their ability and diligence.[41] Understandably, they were seldom receptive to union organizers or management "reformers" who sought to strip them of their powers.

The foreman performed several important functions relative to the workers. First and most important, he "got the work out," a job that varied from industry to industry depending on the degree of management participation in production decisions. Second, he interpreted the management's policies to the workers, a less onerous task. Finally, the foreman hired, trained, motivated, and disciplined the workers. Although nineteenth-century managers and foremen seldom distinguished these activities from "getting the work out" and enforcing the employer's rules, the foreman's personnel functions later became the responsibilities of experts. This shift was itself a major feature of the new factory system and is considered separately in chapters 5 and 6.

In later years it became popular among critics of factory management to recall the old-time foreman's "rule-of-thumb" methods, lack of "standards," and crude approach to supervision. Although these statements were often exaggerated for the sake of contrast, they contained an element of truth. Foremen undoubtedly relied on experience and memory, expected workers to know their jobs, and were insensitive to good "human relations." But in many cases they were also highly versatile workers who performed their varied functions with remarkable effectiveness.

The basis of their approach and of their success was the "driving" method of supervision, a combination of authoritarian rule and physical compulsion. It was prevalent in industries where the foreman's powers were greatest, as the contractors' experiences suggest. It was also the rule where foremen bossed unskilled workers. As John Fitch, author of a study of labor conditions in the steel industry, explained to a congressional committee:

> MR. FITCH: The foreman of the labor gang is called in the Pittsburgh district the pusher.
> Q: Who does he push?
> MR. FITCH: He pushes the gang.
> Q: Explain how that is.
> MR. FITCH: It is done in various ways, through motions and profanity.
> Q: Rolling-mill English?
> MR. FITCH: Yes. The effort is made to induce the gang to get a move on.[42]

When the employees complained, the foreman's response was invariably the same: "If you don't like it, get out."[43]

But the drive method was most apparent in highly mechanized industries where the foreman's principal responsibility was to ensure that the workers did not reduce the machines' potential. In the Fall River mills, the "agent drives the superintendent, he drives the overseer, and the overseer drives the operative."[44] At the Dan River Mills the second hands were

> variously charged with impurity and profanity, with driving, overbearing, and unsympathetic administration of their power, with discriminating unfairly against their best help because of jealousy. . . . The Superintendents and Overseers are censured for backing up the Second Hands, without due investigation of the merits of every one, so that often gross acts of injustice are committed and allowed to pass.[45]

The president of Goodyear Tire and Rubber Company objected to a charge that Firestone had introduced the driving method in the rubber industry. "It is a Goodyear invention," he insisted.[46]

As long as the foreman succeeded in "getting the work out" he had little to fear from his superiors. Most of the management policies he had to enforce—whether they defined the hours of work, established standards for hiring or shop behavior, or defined the employees' obligations to the firm—did not impinge upon his power.[47] Some had little practical meaning; others could be interpreted to the foreman's satisfaction. With the exception of regulations pertaining to the length of the work day and activities that would be obvious to outsiders (drinking or smoking on the job, for example), the shop rules were largely what the foreman made of them. Historians have too readily assumed that lists of rules reflected the "burden" of industrial discipline without considering the foreman's intermediary role.[48]

Nor did the manager often contradict the foreman's decisions, no matter how arbitrary or unfair they might be.[49] The plant superintendent typically boasted that his door was "always open" to employees, but in practice this was seldom true. Cyrus McCormick, Jr., apparently listened to workers' complaints when he was factory superintendent at the McCormick works; more typical was the superintendent of the Bethlehem Steel plant who discharged five workers in 1910 for complaining about overtime work.[50]

In many plants the supervisor also determined wage rates—in practice if not in theory. Where the operatives were paid by the hour or day the foreman had the power to vary rates for individuals. This was perhaps inevitable as long as he retained the right to hire and fire, but it meant that workers doing identical jobs in different departments frequently received different rates. Wide variations existed even in the textile industry, where jobs were standardized to an unusual degree. During World War I the Amoskeag Mills, prodded by the United Textile Workers, adopted a policy of identical pay for identical work. In one department alone sixty-nine changes were required; the adjustments involved "almost every operation."[51]

Where the piecework system prevailed, the supervisor usually acted as rate setter.[52] This was a delicate assignment, for if the rate was too low the employees objected, and if it was too high the manufacturer was equally unhappy. But the foreman was the ideal man for the job. He knew the work and the employees and presumably could estimate their capabilities. Rate setting was thus a matter of his educated guess, based on his experience and intuitive judgment of what could or should be done. A description of piece rate setting in a boot and shoe factory was probably representative:

> We take all but the very slow . . . and get the average [time] of the lot. Then we deduct about ten percent for loafing and go to some factory in our town that has a piece price on that work. If no one in our town has a piece price we compare it with factories in other towns, and if we are not much too low or too high, we put it in.[53]

Yet the foreman rarely had complete control over the wage system or individual rates. Two major constraints—constraints that ultimately revealed the limitations of his power—reduced his authority. First, because of the obvious influence of labor costs on the firm's total costs, the manager kept a close eye on the payroll and was ready to interfere whenever the workers' pay exceeded the "going" rates for particular jobs in the area.[54] This was seldom necessary when workers were paid by the hour or day. Employers like Henry Ford who violated community norms by paying higher rates were few in number and highly unpopular in employers' circles.[55] Piece rates, however, were a different matter. Whenever piecework was introduced and employees began to receive significantly higher pay than they had under the day wage system, the manufacturer was tempted to cut the rate so that the workers, though producing more, would earn approximately what they had under day work.[56] But as soon as the manager cut the rate the incentive was destroyed; the workers would turn out only enough to make the going wage. Employers who gave this problem serious thought soon came to the conclusion that the solution lay in two areas: more care in rate fixing and a guarantee against rate cutting. By the 1890s many progressive firms, such as Baldwin Locomotive, Brown & Sharpe, and William Sellers & Company, had adopted a policy of guaranteeing rates unless the job changed.[57]

More important was the "common sentiment of the workman . . . against those whose output is materially above the average."[58] The workers' ability to deceive the foreman (who set the rate) and thwart the manufacturer (who cut it) clearly indicated the limits of traditional methods of supervision. Despite profanity, threats, and discharges, the workers established and maintained production limits that were below their potential. Though they often succeeded in preventing overwork (or additional work), their activities evoked substantial concern among manufacturers and engineers. By the 1890s engineers were devoting considerable attention to special bonus plans that substituted financial incentives for the foreman's traditional methods of exacting greater effort from the workers. Although these plans were no more successful than the foreman in eliminating output restriction, they became an important and controversial feature of the management movement. The one that seemed to pose the greatest threat to the status quo, the Taylor differential piece rate, was part of a larger system that eliminated the foreman's power to set piece rates and ultimately the "driving" method itself.

The procedure for restricting production varied from shop to shop. In most plants the regulation of output was a function of the work group. There were numerous stories of new employees who were approached by older, presumably wiser, workers: "'See here, young fellow, you're working too fast. You'll spoil our job for us if you don't go slower.'"[59] If a friendly admonition did not have the desired effect, the newcomer was judged a "rooter" or "rusher," and social pressure, threats, and even violence might follow. Employees sometimes accepted bonuses to be "pace setters' but only at "considerable risk to themselves."[60]

The pattern of output restriction also varied between industries and occupations. Assembly line operatives, for example, had less opportunity to set group goals than team workers. Women employees who expected to work only a few years were supposedly less sensitive to group pressures. In the can-making departments of meat-packing plants, the female employees disregarded "the excessive speed, which to the men . . . becomes the greatest of all their grievances."[61] The workers' behavior also depended on the state of the labor market—whether jobs were hard to find or plentiful—and on the national origin of the worker (English and Welsh operatives were notorious for their restrictions). Yet these distinctions did not obscure the fact that a belief in output limits was "widely prevalent . . . among all wage earners."[62]

More formal constraints on the foremen's powers existed where the workers were members of powerful labor unions. Textile, glass, and metal workers unions attempted to curtail the foreman's authority in numerous ways.[63] They restricted the "driving" method with production standards. Contracts between the iron manufacturers and the Amalgamated Association of Iron and Steel Workers, for example, included "(a) restrictions on the size of the charge and the number of heats per turn in puddling mills; (b) restrictions on the numbers of bars to be rolled per turn in sheet mills; and (c) restrictions on the number of pounds of tin plate to be rolled in tin-plate mills."[64] Union members also compromised the manager's rule-making authority with rules of their own. If successful, they restricted the foreman's power to hire and fire, set wages, and discipline subordinates. By the turn of the century various employers' groups and the Machinists,

Molders, Green Glass and Flint Glass Workers, and Pottery Workers, as well as the Amalgamated Association, had negotiated agreements that applied to all the organized workers in their respective industries. In plants covered by such agreements foremen presumably exercised few of their traditional powers.

Yet only a relative handful of foremen were subject to these restraints. The number of organized workers in manufacturing increased slowly and fitfully, from 4 percent in 1897 to 11 percent in 1915.[65] Most of them were highly skilled workers, in many cases quasi-foremen; they had no immediate "boss" in the sense that semiskilled or unskilled workers did. In many respects their union agreements were legalistic approximations of the informal employment contracts that manufacturers and foremen negotiated. A 1915 government report on the pottery industry summarized the relationships between manufacturers, organized craft workers, and other factory employees: "The union workmen have steadily refused to accede to the manufacturers' demand that a record of their actual hours worked be kept, and the time and earnings of their employees, as they feared that such record would be used to their detriment at the wage scale conference every two years."[66]

Finally, the foremen lost all control over the workers when a strike occurred. If effective, a work stoppage brought production to a halt, threatened the future of the firm, and necessitated decisions by higher authorities. Probably more than any other event, a strike made the managers aware of the workers and their role in the operation of the plant.[67] Unfortunately, the experience rarely enhanced their understanding of the workers' position. Manufacturers were seldom as ruthless or violent in their dealings with strikers as employers in mining, transportation, and forest products, but they differed only in degree.[68] Between 1880 and 1920 they recruited thousands of strikebreakers, a practice that was tantamount to encouraging disorder.[69] In addition they used virtually every antilabor weapon—spies, provocateurs, blacklists, and "yellow dog" contracts—known to other sectors of the economy. The Homestead, Pullman, Standard Oil, American Woolen, Swift, Armour, Pressed Steel Car, McCormick, and Bethlehem Steel plants were, after all, the sites of the best-known labor confrontations of the pre–World War I era.[70]

Though the foreman usually lost his influence during a strike, his displacement was only temporary. At the end of the dispute the manager typically turned his attention to more comprehensible matters and the foremen resumed control of the factory. The recognition of a union or, more likely, the blacklisting of former employees or the introduction of an open-shop pledge for new workers compromised the supervisor's freedom of action, but mostly in minor ways. The real challenge to the foreman's empire derived from the manager's effort to operate in a more rational manner, not from temporary aberrations.

INROADS: THE RISE OF SYSTEMATIC MANAGEMENT

The developments that ultimately led to the destruction of the foreman's empire were diverse in character and in some cases only indirectly related to the internal operation of the factory. Two were of particular importance: the rise of "systematic" management, which resulted in the adoption of management "systems" and the transfer of many of the foreman's ad hoc responsibilities, such as production and cost control, to staff departments; and a growing awareness of the "plight" of the industrial worker, which was a major influence in the introduction of private welfare programs and the enactment of various forms of regulatory labor legislation. A third, the advent of industrial unionism, did not become important until the World War I period. Indeed, the earlier changes, by increasing the management's power over the work force and eliminating some of the most obvious abuses in the operations of large manufacturing plants, often deterred the growth of unions.

Of these challenges to the traditional mode of factory administration, the rise of systematic management—the effort to put "method" into shop management—posed the first and more direct threat.[71] It alone was inspired by an analysis of the internal operations of the large manufacturing plant. It also postulated the most sweeping changes. Yet it was not based on an evaluation of the foreman's role or the relationship between the foreman and the workers. In fact, discussions of first-line supervision (with the exception of wage plans) seldom appear in the management literature before 1900.[72] The proponents of systematic management had a different focus, whatever the results of their work.

Two broad, related trends of the last quarter of the nineteenth-century supplied the impetus for the rise of systematic management. The first and most obvious was the growth of the manufacturing firm in size and function and the increasing complexity of manufacturing operations. The second was the advent of trained engineers who rapidly assumed managerial as well as technical responsibilities.[73] The engineers quickly discovered that mechanization alone did not guarantee success. Initially, the substitution of machines for hand operations had seemed to herald an era of automatic factories, when managerial energy and attention could be diverted to other business problems. But manufacturers gradually awakened to a less pleasant reality: machine operations required more, not less, attention. Competition reduced or eliminated the advantages of mechanization, while machinery created new challenges. Maintenance, production scheduling, cost allocation, depreciation, and a host of labor issues—hiring and training maintenance workers, motivating machine tenders, avoiding unions and strikes that could immobilize the plant—became more critical. In growing numbers engineers agreed with Frederick W. Taylor that the "lack of . . . system and method . . . constitutes the greatest risk in manufacturing."[74]

The technical literature of the late nineteenth century reflected the engineers' growing interest in managerial methods. After a thorough survey, Joseph A. Litterer concluded that there was "little evidence of any literature relevant to management in the United States" before 1870.[75] Only 15 articles appeared before 1880. After that time, however, the number increased rapidly. From 1880 to 1885, 60 articles appeared, between 1885 and 1890, 93, in the next five years, 68, and in the last five years of the century, 185.[76] Included in this list were the pioneering works of Henry R. Towne, Horace L. Arnold, A. H. Church, Hugo Diemer, J. Slater Lewis, and Henry Metcalf. The most important vehicles for their ideas were, appropriately, the *Transactions* of the American Society of Mechanical Engineers, the *American Machinist,* and the *Engineering Magazine.* The last journal was relatively unimportant until 1896, when it published a series by Arnold on "Modern Machine Shop Economics." This, in the words of the publisher, was the "Golden vein."[77] For the next quarter century the *Engineering Magazine* was a leading source of information on the principles and practice of industrial management.

While the management literature was highly diverse, it had several recurring themes. It emphasized that traditional factory management was "increasingly chaotic, confused and wasteful" and that this problem was responsible for the managers' loss of control over operations.[78] The reformers seldom spelled out specific weaknesses; they wrote for men who were well acquainted with the status quo. But they emphasized the lack of coordination between the parts of the enterprise and the need, in Litterer's words, for "organizational recoupling."

In some respects the engineers' critique was highly perceptive. It correctly emphasized the improvised nature of factory administration and the primitive state of mechanisms such as cost accounting that might have enabled the manufacturer to exercise greater control over production. Henry Kendall, a prominent manufacturer, summarized the reformers' views when he contrasted traditional or "unsystematic" management with systematic and scientific management.[79]

But the engineers' assumption that a lack of coordination was synonymous with a lack of system, that "unsystematic" management indicated an administrative vacuum, was patently false at the shop level. When the reformers attempted to eliminate parts of the foreman's empire or revise the workers' activities, they frequently realized the extent of their miscalculation. Complaints of resistance to change, of unyielding conservatism on the part of supervisors and workers, were endemic in the early literature of shop management.

The same strengths and weaknesses were apparent in the engineers' prescriptions for change. Litterer identifies three types of policies that they recommended: cost accounting systems to promote vertical integration; production and inventory plans to facilitate horizontal integration; and wage payment plans to stimulate production and reduce unit costs.[80] In each case the objective was to enhance the manager's control over production, including the foremen and the production workers. What was clearly implied but never stated was that this goal would be achieved at the expense of the foremen's—and ultimately the workers'—autonomy.

The engineers were responsible for major refinements in accounting procedure. Systematic accounting involved more detailed statements prepared quarterly or monthly, together with comparative cost figures. Cost accounting became a tool of management, a device for insuring the adequacy of the selling price and for identifying problems in the production process.[81] By using job cards and time clocks it was possible to allocate prime costs to specific jobs. The cards also provided a convenient system of inventory control. By 1910 prime cost accounting had assumed its twentieth-century form.[82]

More important were new methods of ascertaining and allocating overhead costs. The quantity of writing on this subject after 1885 was itself extraordinary; many so-called management systems were really accounting systems with special attention to the issue of "burden" costs. There were major debates over the types of costs to consider—specifically whether office and selling charges should be included in manufacturing costs—and over the handling of idle time. Probably the most important innovation of the period was the "machine hour" method of allocating costs, a method by which overhead costs were related to machine use. A. H. Church's "scientific production center" plan of 1901, an elaboration of this approach, was the most influential cost plan of the period.[83]

The reformers revealed a similar commitment to order and detail in the acquisition and handling of materials. They centralized purchasing, standardized materials, and insisted that stores be kept in designated areas and dispatched only when requisitioned by the foremen. In better organized plants they assigned a special staff to move materials to and from the storerooms.[84] No longer was the foreman responsible for obtaining the materials that he needed.

Closely related to changes in accounting technique and stores methods were efforts to integrate and control the various steps in the manufacturing process. Most production plans of the 1880s and 1890s used cards or tickets issued by the engineering or production office to convey instructions to the foremen and workers and to elicit information on their activities. These systems became increasingly elaborate. In 1882 Henry R. Towne, president of Yale & Towne, published one of the first descriptions of a production control system. Under his plan the office notified the foremen when it received an order and asked them to estimate completion dates for the work.[85] By 1900 such an approach would have seemed elementary, even simple-minded. The complicated plans of Metcalf, Lewis, Arnold, and Diemer, which had appeared in the intervening years, extended the potential limits of managerial control far beyond anything that Towne had envisioned in the early 1880s. Their systems included specifications of parts and operations, centralized controls over parts and materials and their movement between operations, records of operating costs, and methods of allocating overhead costs to specific jobs.[86] The engineers also advocated the creation of larger clerical staffs to record the data they needed. Factory clerks were an essential accouterment of systematic management.[87]

These plans reduced the foreman's area of discretion and in some cases eliminated auxiliary duties. The acquisition of materials, routing of orders, scheduling of jobs, movement and storage of finished parts, and recording of production costs were either undertaken by other employees or subjected to explicit policy statements in virtually all the plans. The foreman had to work closely with other foremen, managers, and clerks. In short, the supervisor under systematic management ceased to be the all-round manager that he had been in the traditional organization.

Equally important was the engineers' threat to the foreman's relationship to the worker. At the same time the reformers sought to divest the supervisor of his ad hoc managerial functions, they also became interested in ways of stimulating the worker to greater exertion. Their interest was eminently pragmatic and usually did not involve an explicit rejection of the foreman's role. But their method—the incentive wage[88]—led to a further diminution of the foreman's limited ability to regulate wage rates.

The earliest incentive schemes were profit-sharing plans, products of the growing concern over the "labor problem," particularly the strikes and unrest of the mid-1880s.[89] Most were precursors, directly or indirectly, of welfare programs, but there was one notable exception, the gainsharing plan of Henry R. Towne of Yale & Towne. Towne's contribution was part of a far-reaching effort to improve the operation of his plant. In addition to his production control system, Towne introduced a combination cost and time card plan, ran a "first class foundry which is systematically managed" and maintained the building and yards in immaculate condition.[90] Lavatories abounded, and the "use of well-appointed washing facilities is not optional with hands, but obligatory."[91] This requirement, in fact, produced the only strike during Towne's tenure, when molders insisted on using their traditional buckets.

Towne's most noteworthy activities, however, grew out of his efforts to cope with the "labor problem." He wrote that "some readjustment of the relations of labor and capital has got to be made." Yet the proper motive, he argued, was not fear of unions, "philanthropy or sympathy," but the "self-interest . . . of the employer. Some better method of bringing out of the men the best that is in them in doing their work must be adopted."[92]

Towne's solution involved a variety of measures. He ended the contract system, introduced piece rates, which he guaranteed for one year, and established systematic procedures for dealing with grievances. On new work Towne set minimum and maximum earnings levels so that piece rates, if incorrect, would not unduly punish or reward workers.[93] In 1887 Towne introduced the most important feature of the program, the gain-sharing plan. This he defined as "savings sharing" rather than "profit sharing," since it divided part of any cost reduction with the employees who were responsible for the reduction.[94] Though the plan seemed to work at first, Towne soon discovered a serious defect: there was no connection between the individual's effort and the reward. As a result he dropped gain sharing between 1893 and 1895 and introduced an executive profit-sharing plan.

The next important wage system was Frederick A. Halsey's "premium plan." An engineer and later assistant editor of the *American Machinist,* Halsey also was disturbed by the labor turmoil of the mid-1880s.[95] But his answer was quite different from Towne's; indeed, he explicitly rejected profit sharing and other forms of welfare work. The former, he wrote, "is wrong in principle, and cannot be in any large sense a solution of the wages problem."[96] Instead, Halsey devised the premium to induce factory workers to increase their output in return for additional pay. As Halsey instructed the workmen: "According to previous experience this work should require . . . hours. If completed in less time than that a premium of . . . cents will be paid for each hour saved." The premium was lower than the customary piece rate, so that the employer would not become alarmed at escalating wage costs and cut the rate, but presumably high enough to reward the wage earner for faster work.[97]

The premium, Halsey believed, would end restrictions on production and reduce labor conflict, since the managers' interest in lower unit costs would be reconciled with the workers' interest in higher pay. To make the premium attractive to the worker Halsey urged employers not to cut the base rate (usually the traditional piece rate for a particular job) and make the plan "voluntary"—meaning that employees did not have to earn a premium or face discharge—in order to avoid charges of a "speed up." "Surely," he wrote, "a system which increases output, decreases cost, and increases workman's earnings simultaneously, without friction, and by the silent force of its appeal to every man's desire for a larger income, is worthy of attention."[98]

Despite these advantages the premium plan made little progress until the turn of the century. Though Halsey first developed his ideas in 1884 and explained the plan to friends in 1888, he did not publish a description of it until 1891. At that time three firms, including his own, had introduced the premium. Halsey did not publish another account of his plan until 1899, supposedly waiting for independent verification of his own experiences.[99] After the appearance of his 1899 article in the *American Machinist,* however, he began to publicize and defend his approach. The premium became a popular incentive wage plan on both sides of the Atlantic for several decades and the basis for many related bonus schemes.[100]

The premium was similar to the other features of systematic management not only in its designer's primary objective but also in its underlying assumptions about the workers' motives. Halsey believed, as did most proponents of systematic management, that "every man's desire for a larger income" was the key to a worker's behavior and dismissed as romantic nonsense any notion that other factors were involved. Halsey's simplistic view of human motivation resulted in numerous disputes, especially when workers—including the foremen—refused to respond to incentive plans in ways the engineers anticipated.

The conflict began almost immediately, when the metal trades unions, particularly the Machinists, refused to work under the premium. To them Halsey's plan was simply another form of piece work, more insidious because of its unique features. A crucial battle occurred in 1899, when union machinists at the Bickford Tool and Drill Company of Cincinnati struck rather than accept the premium plan. After a conference with the plant superintendent, H. M. Norris, James O'Connell, the Machinists' president, agreed to present the plan to the union convention. He recalled:

> I proposed that Mr. Norris' plan be endorsed temporarily; that it be given a fair trial, and if found to do all that its originator claimed for it, that no organized antagonism from our organization should check its progress or usefulness in the future. Then the storm broke. And it was not an ordinary one—it was a cyclone. When the storm blew over, Mr. Norris' premium plan—or rather the notion to endorse it—was beyond resuscitation.[101]

This reaction, based on a misinterpretation of the purpose of the premium plan, was nevertheless prophetic. To Halsey and most employers who adopted his method, the premium system was merely a corrective to the most obvious defect of piece work. To the employees, however it represented much more. It was an opening wedge, a new front in the broadening attack on traditional methods of factory work and life. This radical difference in interpretation accounted for the frequent complaint of employers that unionists simply would not listen to their explanations of the benefits of the premium. In reality the two sides talked about different things. The issues did not become clear until Frederick W. Taylor rejected Halsey's narrow opportunistic approach and confirmed what the unionists suspected. It was to their credit that they and not the engineers first grasped the implications of systematic management.

This stage of the conflict was postponed, however, because the premium plan left the foreman's power over the workers largely intact. While the premium did eliminate some of the supervisor's discretion in wage setting, it was based, ultimately, on his judgment. One virtue of the plan that Halsey often emphasized was its modest initial impact. "The transition to it from day's work," he wrote, "is easy and natural."[102] This advantage was due to his acceptance of past performance as the standard on which the system was based. He rejected, as costly and impractical, the thorough reorganization of the foremen's and workers' activities that more extreme reformers soon urged. For Halsey time and motion study and other aspects of the Taylor system of shop management were unnecessary, even undesirable.[103]

The premium plan, like other features of systematic management, was undoubtedly more popular in the technical press than in American factories before 1910. Engineers introduced their reforms in only a small proportion of the large manufacturing plants of the day. Moreover, in numerous instances their production, accounting, and wage systems were installed and then discarded. In 1905, for example, Albert H. Morton, the new head of the Lowell Machine Shop, immediately junked the cost system that his predecessor had introduced. "There is only one way to control production," he proclaimed, "and that's to go out in the plant and watch it."[104] In 1907 Henry Ford and Charles Sorenson spent a Sunday morning emptying drawers of cards and tickets—the plant's cost system—on the floor of the factory record office. "Thus ended 'efficiency red tape' with Ford Motor Company," Sorenson recalled.[105]

Although it would be possible to count the growing numbers of engineers who made a living either as consultants or as analysts and promoters of systematic management, it is not clear that this would demonstrate more than the gradual diffusion of new ideas. In short, there is no question that some aspects of systematic management had been incorporated in the operating procedures of most large manufacturing plants by 1900. But tradition and the conservatism of shop employees were an effective bulwark against dramatic change. The factory had been changed; it was not yet transformed.

4 The Rise of Scientific Management

Scientific management, in its character and effects, is, in this aspect, merely another force emphasizing and strengthening the modern movement. In so far as this tends to eliminate economic wastes, to substitute system in place of slipshod methods of management, to improve industrial processes and methods, and to increase productivity, it, or something like it is in the direct line of progress and appears inevitable. [Robert F. Hoxie, *Scientific Management and Labor* (New York, 1918), p. 128]

Altogether it may well be the most powerful as well as the most lasting contribution America has made to Western thought since the Federalist papers. [Peter Drucker, *The Practice of Management* (New York, 1954), p. 280]

As systematic management became more influential, it also became identified with a handful of prominent, forceful advocates. By the turn of the century Horace L. Arnold and Frederick A. Halsey, for example, were acknowledged experts.[1] The most important of these individuals, however, was Frederick W. Taylor, engineer, inventor, publicist, and "father" of scientific management. Beginning in the early 1880s, Taylor combined the techniques of systematic management with a "scientific" method of rate setting and promoted his system so effectively that the other developers of systematic management were largely forgotten. Yet in the process he and his followers made scientific management appear to be something it was not—a "partial solution of the labor problem"—and generated controversy and misunderstanding.[2]

THE TAYLOR SYSTEM OF MANAGEMENT

Taylor's career as an industrial manager paralleled the rise of systematic management and was profoundly affected by it.[3] Raised in a prominent Philadelphia family, he abandoned his—or his parents'—desire for a professional career at eighteen to become an apprentice in a local metal-working plant and later a foreman and engineer at the Midvale Steel Company (1878–1890). He then became a plant manager (1890–1893), consultant (1893–1901), and publicist for scientific management (1902–1915). At the same time he had an overlapping career as inventor and technician, which began with a degree from the Stevens Institute of Technology (1883) and culminated with his election to the presidency of the American Society of Mechanical Engineers (ASME) in 1906. Taylor was thus equally familiar with the traditional approach to factory administration and with systematic management. It was not surprising that his major achievements occurred in areas that had already received attention from the advocates of systematic management.

Taylor's work at the Midvale Steel Company in the 1880s is impossible to reconstruct in detail, but the meager evidence that remains suggests a pattern somewhat different from what he and his official biographer later reported.[4] His most important innovations, it appears, were technical: he began his famous experiments with industrial belting and cutting metals and patented numerous inventions during this period. In addition, as chief engineer he standardized maintenance procedures, devised many forms (one of the remaining documents from that period is an extraordinarily detailed set of instructions for cleaning boilers),[5] and introduced his antidotes to output restriction and labor unrest, stopwatch time study and the differential piece rate, an incentive plan that rewarded the worker only if he or she met Taylor's "scientifically" determined production standard. According to Taylor's later accounts he also systematized the Midvale stores, developed the nucleus of a planning department, and began to experiment with specialized foremen.[6] He supposedly began his time studies in 1882 after an extended battle with his subordinates, but his techniques must have been exceedingly crude.[7] There was no overt labor trouble, and insofar as the workmen resented Taylor's innovations, they were more concerned about the imposition of rules and standardized procedures than about time study and the differential piece rate.[8] In any event, from his superiors' viewpoint, Taylor's activities were highly successful. By the time of his resignation in 1890 he had developed a reputation as a brilliant technician and a forceful, progressive manager.

During the following decade, as superintendent of the Manufacturing Investment Company, a paper-manufacturing concern, and as a consulting engineer for a variety of firms, Taylor refined and perfected his system of management. Yet his basic interests remained unchanged. He continued to devote much of his time to technical experimentation, which remained the key to his other activities. His inventions, most notably his discovery of "high speed" tool steel in 1899, enhanced his reputation among engineers and technicians and brought him a fortune, which in turn enabled him to devote the rest of his life to the promotion of scientific management.[9] Taylor also continued to standardize machine operations, belting, materials, and forms. Whenever possible he introduced time study and the differential piece rate. In 1895 he employed Sanford E. Thompson, a young civil engineer who had worked for the Manufacturing Investment

Company, to develop time study and apply it to the construction industry. Thompson, working independently of Taylor, became the first time study expert of the Taylor movement.[10]

But Taylor also added new features to his system of management. The most important of these was a method of accounting that aided in controlling operations and costs. Taylor took his basic ideas from a leading railroad accountant; he never maintained that his procedures were unique or original.[11] His major innovations were a series of standardized forms and procedures and a monthly balance of accounts. As a result his techniques were more elaborate than those of most contemporary writers on accounting practice and were never widely adopted.[12] Yet in the 1890s he developed a reputation as an expert in the field, and several of his consulting assignments were to introduce improved accounting procedures.[13]

Taylor's other important developments of the 1890s, a system of production planning and "functional" foremanship, also grew out of systematic management. Output restriction and low productivity, Taylor believed, were essentially the fault of the management, the inevitable consequences of vesting inordinate power in the overworked foreman.[14] Systematic management removed much of the foreman's power over production and costs; time study reduced his authority as a rate setter. By 1897 Taylor was ready to complete the process by eliminating the traditional foreman altogether. When the foremen at the Simonds Rolling Machine Company resigned en masse in 1897, he replaced them with a planning office, which directed all activities in the shop and coordinated the work of the supervisors, and with functional foremen, a group of men who each performed part of the traditional foreman's job. Henceforth a "gang boss" coordinated the movement of materials, a "speed boss" prepared the work, an "inspector" insured the quality of the product, a "repair boss" maintained the machinery, and a "disciplinarian" hired and fired.[15] Under scientific management foremen became subordinate parts of the larger system.

Other additions to scientific management appeared in the following years but were—at least from Taylor's viewpoint—relatively unimportant. In 1901, while working at the Bethlehem Steel Company, one of Taylor's assistants, H. L. Gantt, devised a new incentive wage plan, the "task and bonus" system, which he based on existing rather than "scientifically" determined times. Taylor accepted the task and bonus plan as a useful expedient: it promised to increase the worker's output and morale before the systematizing process had proceeded far enough to permit the introduction of the differential piece rate.[16] When Taylor discussed the labor features of scientific management in subsequent years, he invariably emphasized time study and the effects of functional foremanship; the specific incentive wage plan made little difference. Similarly, after 1907, when Frank B. Gilbreth joined the Taylor circle, Taylor devoted much attention in his popular writings to systematic motion study, particularly to Gilbreth's bricklaying experiments.[17] But to Gilbreth's chagrin, Taylor soon began to suggest that motion study was inherent in time study, that Gilbreth's work was merely an extension of what he, Thompson, and others had been doing since the 1880s.[18]

Taylor became even more imprecise on the nature and importance of time study in the following years. He often stated that time study determined exactly what a man could and should do, that it dispelled rule-of-thumb methods once and for all. When James Mapes Dodge, head of the Link-Belt Company and one of Taylor's closest admirers, argued that time studies were "matters of human judgment," Taylor replied rather belligerently:

> It may be true, as you say, that there are one or two elements relating to scientific management which are not based on full and exact knowledge. . . . The fact is, however, that 999 out of 1000 of the elements which under the old system of management were the owner's judgment and opinion are now matters of exact knowledge or science.[19]

On the other hand he admitted to a Congressional committee that

> the whole subject of time study is only an approximation. There is nothing positively accurate about time study from end to end. All that we hope to do through time study is to get a vastly closer approximation as to time than we ever had before. That is one reason why we have to allow this big margin of safety, as I explained to you.[20]

In 1920, when Gilbreth attacked stopwatch time study in a famous session of the Taylor Society, even Carl G. Barth, Taylor's most orthodox disciple, admitted that stopwatch techniques involved considerable guesswork.[21]

Taylor's system of management thus evolved over several decades in response to his and his followers' experiences. His procedures for belt and tool standardization, store and toolroom organization, purchasing, cost accounting, production planning, and the differential piece rate were natural extensions of ideas that appeared in the literature of systematic management and the practice of progressive managers.[22] The notion of functional foremanship carried a basic theme of the new factory system to its logical conclusion. Time study, which Taylor and his followers publicized as the "cornerstone" of the system, was the only feature that had no direct antecedent in the management movement.

Conversely, Taylor neglected or showed little interest in subjects that had received little attention from the proponents and practitioners of systematic management. Like most engineers and management reformers he

believed that an incentive wage ("scientifically" determined) would provide the answer to most if not all labor problems.[23] He was indifferent to
advanced ideas about recruiting workers. His employment office was little
more than a hiring and record-keeping bureau, and his other references to
personnel work were equally unperceptive.[24] The shop "disciplinarian,"
for example, would simply apply "the proper remedy" in the event of undesirable behavior.[25] Presumably, Taylor considered training more carefully, since he made it a "principle" of sound management in his writings.
But the result was hardly more sophisticated. In "A Piece Rate System"
(1895) he noted, apparently with pride, that at Midvale "I let them earn
all they could earn. . . . I do not care who turns out my work."[26] In later
years his training methods consisted solely of "object lessons" designed to
make the foremen and workers alike see the possibility of earning higher
wages if they would only cooperate.

Taylor was equally insensitive to a variety of labor problems. While he
often boasted that his reforms had eliminated hundreds of jobs, he scoffed
at critics who argued that scientific management would create unemployment. He became incensed when questioned about fatigue. Scientific management, he argued, only called for steady work coupled with definite rest
periods.[27] Taylor displayed a similar lack of tact, if not understanding,
when he discussed welfare programs. Like most engineers of the period he
considered welfare work a "joke."[28] In a "Piece Rate System" he argued
that "it is not the large charities . . . that are needed or appreciated by
workmen . . . so much as small acts of personal kindness and sympathy."[29]
Ultimately, Taylor's view of employer-employee relations derived from his
belief in the efficacy of the incentive wage: "No self-respecting workman
wants to be given things, every man wants to earn things."[30]

Taylor was less dogmatic on the question of labor unions. He did not
oppose unions per se; he resisted any organization that might hinder or
compromise his work.[31] He was extremely unhappy when the Link-Belt
introduced a company union.[32] In fact, there was some substance to his
assertion that he held unions in higher esteem than did most executives.
In the clothing industry, for example, where management seemed totally
irresponsible, Taylor saw a place for unions. But in general his writings
and correspondence leave no doubt that he was strongly opposed to
unionism. A good example of his thinking was a plot he proposed to David Van Alstyne, an official of the American Locomotive Company and a
Taylor enthusiast. In December 1906, Taylor advised Van Alstyne, who
was having trouble with his unionized molders, to establish a supposedly
independent foundry, hire only nonunion men, introduce Taylor methods,
underbid the union foundry, and gradually lay off the union men.[33]

Equally distorted were Taylor's claims that his techniques inspired harmony and cooperation and that his plants had never been struck, at least until the Watertown Arsenal molders walked out in August 1911. In reality, he encountered strenuous opposition, largely from managers, and his disciples confronted similar obstacles. Gantt, who was known for his appreciation of the human factor, was in constant trouble. In short, the record does not support Taylor's facile claim that the workers appreciated his efforts.

Yet in his promotional efforts Taylor always emphasized the labor features of his system. In his writings on management he stressed time study, the incentive wage, and the effects of his system on the workmen rather than the system itself. His first important paper, "A Piece Rate System," was a lightly disguised effort to attract attention to scientific management by exploiting interest in output restriction and labor unrest. "Shop Management" (1903) was essentially an elaboration of "A Piece Rate System," and *The Principles of Scientific Management* (1911) was an expanded version of a lecture that treated the system as a method of reorganizing the workers' activities.[34] To win acceptance of his methods, particularly from employers, Taylor argued that scientific management would result in higher wages, better and more skillful workers, more rapid advancements, improved personal habits, and an end to labor unrest. In the process he indelibly fixed the popular conception of scientific management as a system of labor reforms. Taylor was probably not deliberately misleading; he was, after all, the product of an environment in which men assumed that the incentive wage would solve labor problems. But he was also shrewd enough to realize that his audiences would be more interested in a "partial solution of the labor problem" than in his refinements of systematic management.

To his dismay Taylor soon learned that his promotional efforts generated opponents as well as supporters. After 1910, when scientific management became known to the public, there was growing criticism from social reformers and union leaders. Taylor's problem became apparent in 1911–1912, when a House of Representatives committee held hearings on scientific management as a result of a strike against time study at the Watertown Arsenal. The workers who testified before the committee seldom objected to the preliminary organizational and technical changes, the planning department, or functional foremanship. Instead, they protested at the use of the stopwatch and the bonus system, which they equated with the Taylor system of management.[35] The metal trades unions and the American Federation of Labor, which were already wary of incentive wage plans, echoed these sentiments and launched a concerted attack on time study and the bonus that occupied much of Taylor's attention in the years before his death in 1915.[36] Not until World War I, when Morris L. Cooke effected a reconciliation with the unions and Taylor's followers "humanized" scientific management by acknowledging the need for welfare and personnel measures, did the furor stop.[37]

IMITATORS AND INNOVATORS

In the period between Taylor's retirement (1901) and death (1915) scientific management emerged as the most widely publicized feature of the new factory system. Taylor himself became a controversial public figure, a symbol of the cause of "efficiency" and a "prophet."[38] His writings became the basis of a popular movement that soon transcended the narrow sphere of the factory.[39] The remainder of this chapter examines two aspects of these developments, the relations between Taylor and his disciples, who increasingly sought to transcend the bounds of systematic management, and the impact of scientific management in the factories where it was introduced. Both, I believe, indicate the importance of systematic to scientific management and the failure of Taylor and his associates to develop a "partial solution of the labor problem."

Taylor's promotional efforts largely determined his relations with his followers, the men who actually introduced the Taylor system. His activities generated interest in scientific management, led him to recruit new "experts," and forced him to deal with a host of outsiders who copied and modified his work. They also created problems for his orthodox disciples. His emphasis on the "principles" of scientific management and the labor implications of his system—so important in his mind to the success of his efforts—made many employers impatient with the "experts" and their insistence on the installation of systematic management before the introduction of time study or the incentive wage. Not surprisingly, the disciples, like the outsiders, began to adapt their approach to their clients' expectations, to innovate. Though they usually proved no more successful than Taylor in developing a "partial solution of the labor problem," their activities were disturbing to Taylor, whose objective throughout the period was to promote, but not to change, scientific management.

Taylor's post-1901 activities fell into two categories: he lectured at public gatherings, wrote for popular audiences, and in other ways advertised his movement to the public at large; and he attempted to persuade executives to introduce the Taylor system of management. His strategy was simple. "The best way," he wrote Barth, "is to let those who want it see that other people want you very badly, and that you don't particularly care about them. I have found that the moment you let people have an idea that you want to secure their work, then they begin to hold off."[40] Thus Taylor opposed direct solicitations but "encouraged" managers to come to him. This policy had two benefits: those who did come usually had more than a casual interest, and under these circumstances Taylor could dictate his terms to them rather than vice versa. In 1905, for example, he refused a request from the managers of the General Electric plant at Lynn, Massachusetts, for a man to help them, on the grounds that he could not supply a man without the system.[41]

In most cases Taylor invited businessmen who expressed an interest or were referred by others to visit his home. The guests stayed overnight, received a two-to-three-hour explanation of the system (the "principles") the following morning, and toured Link-Belt or the Tabor Manufacturing Company, another client, in the afternoon. Local people or less important visitors who did not qualify for the full treatment might also attend the lecture and plant tour. Potential clients who still expressed an interest— particularly after being warned of the time and expense involved—would be referred to an appropriate "expert." Taylor wrote Barth, for instance, that the Packard Motor Company "would be a splendid one for you to land."[42] The Cheney brothers, he noted to Gantt, were "about the finest set of men who have ever been here. . . . I urged them strongly to get next to you."[43]

After the client had contacted the approved "expert," Taylor ceased to be the promoter and became the protector and defender of his system. He wrote letters of encouragement to his associates when they encountered opposition. He also cautioned tact, particularly to Barth, whose abrasive manner antagonized potential clients. One of the most frequent difficulties that Taylor's followers faced was a demand for immediate results. When the client complained of the lack of progress, Taylor urged patience and insisted that the expert be given the maximum leeway to pursue his work.

To meet his converts' needs and, he hoped, to generate additional interest in scientific management, Taylor also recruited promising young men to complement Barth and Gantt. Horace K. Hathaway, who became vice-president of the Tabor Company, was his first important discovery and, after Barth, his most orthodox disciple. Morris L. Cooke met Taylor in 1906 and soon became an "approved" expert, though he subsequently devoted most of his time to the promotional campaign. Hollis Godfrey, Royal R. Keely, and C. Bertrand Thompson, former professors with backgrounds in engineering and economics, also won Taylor's favor, as did a number of able workers.[44] Starting with Godfrey, Taylor insisted that recruits serve an apprenticeship at the Tabor Company and assist Barth or Hathaway on several jobs before they embarked on an independent career. Even with this experience, however, Taylor never entirely trusted his later disciples. Cooke was the last man to win and retain Taylor's complete confidence.

As the Taylor circle grew, rivalries and disagreements were inevitable. Gantt and Cooke had several misunderstandings, and Barth seldom maintained an amicable relationship with anyone for long. In these cases Taylor played the role of peacemaker. Above all, he told Gantt, "be especially careful . . . not to say a single word that will reflect against the methods which the other [expert] is introducing."[45] But loyalty had its limits. When a conflict pitted the interests of the movement against the interests of the expert, Taylor always protected the former. One of Gantt's clients, the Joseph Bancroft & Sons Company, apparently secured his services in part to obtain information about certain devices he had developed for the Sayles Bleachery, a Bancroft competitor. Taylor was upset when he heard that Gantt had agreed to help the Bancroft Company. "This will certainly not appeal to other people if they hear about it," he wrote.[46] On another occasion when Barth supplied forms he had devised for the Tabor Company to a competitor, Taylor chided him for his behavior, explaining that he was merely trying to establish "the proper ethics between us all."[47]

While Gantt, Barth, Cooke, Hathaway, and the younger disciples occasionally created problems, they were nevertheless "competent" men. Taylor was less sure about a growing number of outside "experts" who had never worked under his tutelage and did not understand the disparity between his statements and the practice of scientific management. Taylor's concern over this group was reflected in his relationship with Harrington Emerson, an admirer who later became an antagonist and competitor. Emerson was in many respects the antithesis of Taylor—bold, romantic, malleable, the consummate opportunist. His career was an endless succession of flamboyant and usually unsuccessful efforts to achieve wealth and social position. In the two years before he heard Taylor read "Shop Management" to the ASME, Emerson had promoted underwater telegraphic cables, managed a Pennsylvania glass factory, examined coal properties in Alaska, made "some very important propositions" to the Russian government designed to "neutralize England's naval power," and contemplated an offer to become a commercial agent in the Philippines.[48] Taylor's paper raised new possibilities.[49] Soon Emerson became the leading exponent of "efficiency" in industry and the object of some of Taylor's most caustic criticism.

Although essentially the same problems interested Taylor and Emerson, the two men differed radically in their approaches and solutions. While Taylor insisted on the interrelatedness of his innovations, Emerson concentrated on the "principles of efficiency" and said relatively little about specific measures. In part this was a deliberate tactic to attract clients; in part it was a reflection of his flexibility. Emerson had no system beyond his "principles" and a line and staff organization.[50] In practice he emphasized the labor features of Taylor's system, particularly time studies and an incentive wage plan similar to Gantt's. This was an expedient strategy, since most businessmen neither wanted nor could afford the complete Taylor system. But it involved him in a variety of labor problems, most notably a strike at the American Locomotive Company's shops in 1909.[51] Taylor grew increasingly concerned. Emerson, he charged, advocated the "short cuts" and "improvements" that he warned against.[52]

The outsider who came closest to being admitted to the Taylor circle without serving an apprenticeship was Frank B. Gilbreth, a prominent contractor and builder. As a young construction worker, Gilbreth had noticed that most workers' methods were based on tradition. When he established his own construction company he provided bricklayers with better equipment and reorganized their motions, increasing their output. His success impressed Taylor, who subsequently used Gilbreth's bricklaying work as an illustration of "scientific management in action."[53]

Although Gilbreth had been acquainted with Sanford Thompson for many years, he did not meet Taylor until December 1907. Gilbreth and Taylor immediately struck up a friendship based on their common interests, and in early 1908 Taylor suggested that Gilbreth join Thompson in applying scientific management in the building trades.[54] Gilbreth and Thompson were unable to reach an agreement, but the gesture indicated that Taylor viewed Gilbreth as an acceptable, though perhaps secondary, member of his group. Gilbreth, for his part, had no reservations; he had contracted "Tayloritis."[55]

In March 1908 Gilbreth proposed that a planning department, functional foremanship, time studies, and the task and bonus system be introduced on a job he had at Gardner, Massachusetts. Taylor, Thompson, and Hathaway all concurred. But when Gilbreth tried to implement the plan he ran into trouble. The exact nature of his difficulties is not clear, but Taylor attributed them to his haste in introducing changes.[56] In any event the workers protested, and the plan was substantially modified. Gilbreth, however, was not discouraged. "I have not dismissed the Taylor system," he wrote Thompson. "I will not dismiss it, and I intend to devote the rest of my life to installing the Taylor System."[57] He continued to discuss the possibility of introducing Taylorism on all his jobs but usually with the stipulation that Gantt or Thompson be in charge of that part of the work. In Taylor's mind, however, the Gardner dispute raised serious doubts about Gilbreth's competence.

Taylor's concern for the integrity of his system was also apparent in his relationships with various organizations of actual or potential converts. Throughout his career Taylor insisted that scientific management was an outgrowth of mechanical engineering and that his followers should work through the American Society of Mechanical Engineers. He published all his major papers in the Society's *Transactions;* indeed, when the publications committee refused to publish "The Principles of Scientific Management," he distributed it privately to the members.[58] He also opposed the formation of the Society to Promote the Science of Management on the grounds that it severed the tie between engineering and management and barely concealed his contempt for the Efficiency Society, an educational organization created to advance the idea of efficiency.[59] Despite an unflagging commitment to his promotional activities, Taylor never fully accepted—or perhaps even understood—the implications of his efforts.

It was impossible, however, to insulate the Taylor system for long. For one thing, there was the growing number of self-proclaimed experts who were not personally familiar with Taylor's work or sympathetic with his efforts to retain its original character. For another, the "competent" experts found themselves under increasing pressure to increase the workers' output and "solve" the labor problem. As a result they all made modifications in the system as they confronted problems in their work. But there was a major difference between modifying details and changing the basic features. On this point Taylor was adamant.

For several years prior to 1908 Taylor and Gantt had had minor disagreements. The problem, from Taylor's viewpoint, was Gantt's flexibility, specifically his willingness to address issues that Taylor had neglected. In 1908 he wrote a paper that suggested the extent of his apostasy. Gantt had just completed a difficult assignment at the Sayles Bleachery, where he had encountered considerable resistance from the workers and had become somewhat disillusioned with Taylor's methods—or lack of methods—for dealing with the operatives.[60] His paper, called "Training Workmen in Habits of Industry and Cooperation," proposed a major innovation. To achieve greater cooperation Gantt stressed the need for formal instruction rather than "object lessons." Thus he challenged Taylor in two areas: he emphasized a point that Taylor had disregarded, and he questioned Taylor's assumption that the promise of higher wages was sufficient to elicit greater efforts. Although Gantt's approach was crude—he advocated training to inculcate obedience to orders rather than skills, a partial confirmation of the unionists' charges that Taylor's disciples sought to turn men into machines—it was an important first step toward eliminating a weakness in the Taylor system.[61]

Taylor, who advised Gantt not to publish the paper, was upset. Some months later he wrote: "It is, of course, impossible for us to agree. No men with strong individuality can possibly agree, but I think it is perfectly clear that if we expect to have weight with people outside, we must make it appear, in all cases, that we are in absolute agreement."[62] But the break was soon apparent. Taylor began to recommend Barth and Hathaway rather than Gantt when executives asked for an expert. Gantt went his own way and developed a successful consulting practice without Taylor's assistance. Their relations were never again as close as they had been.

Frank Gilbreth suffered a similar fate. After meeting Taylor in 1907,

Gilbreth became an important figure in the movement. He was a gregarious, outgoing man of enormous energies, which he devoted to the promotion of scientific management and his career as a Taylor disciple. Even after the Gardner incident Taylor encouraged Gilbreth to fill speaking engagements for him. But Gilbreth made two fatal mistakes: he began to innovate, and he developed the idea that he, too, was capable of introducing scientific management.

Gilbreth's principal innovation, "micromotion" study, was the primary source of his problems. During the summer and fall of 1911 he wrote Taylor that he was using a camera to record the motions of workers and that his films could be combined with instruction cards to teach workers new methods. Taylor, however, indicated little interest in the technique.[63] By March 1912 Gilbreth had gone one step further and coupled his motion picture technique with a timing device capable of indicating movements to the thousandth of a minute. He called this "micromotion" study to differentiate it from the "motion" studies he had undertaken in the past. Gilbreth was so excited about his discovery that he decided to "devote the rest of my life to standardizing performance of labor."[64] Yet he did not notify Taylor of his work, much less his change of career, for more than a month. In mid-April he sent Taylor a carefully worded letter describing micromotion study and suggesting its potential. Two key paragraphs made his position clear:

> I do not believe that this method will ever wholly do away with the present stop watch method, but it will have a tremendous use in teaching certain elements of processes by the exhibition of these educational films.
>
> You will see that this process not only enables me to take the time study to the thousandth of a minute, eliminating all error due to the human element or to differences in mental time reactions but that it also permits measuring the motions in three dimensions simultaneously.[65]

Taylor's reply was equally instructive. Micromotion study, he noted, "should in the future prove a most valuable method for studying movements which cannot be properly analyzed in any other way."[66] In short, he dismissed Gilbreth's contention that conventional time study permitted "error due to the human element." He also indicated that time study, obviously less accurate than micromotion study, was good enough—a curious position for a man who had made time study the "cornerstone" of his "partial solution of the labor problem."

During the next two years Gilbreth remained optimistic. He sent Taylor detailed accounts of his efforts to improve the system, including the adoption of a special slide rule for time study and the "cyclegraph" method of photographing motions.[67] He offered Taylor "ownership" of the micromotion method and established a "Frederick Winslow Taylor Hall" in

Providence, where he gave weekly lectures on scientific management. When he opened a summer school for college instructors, he assured Taylor that he was teaching "Shop Management without change or omission, from cover to cover."[68] But these gestures had little effect on Taylor. He coldly rejected Gilbreth's offer of the micromotion method and gave him little or no encouragement in his other activities. In December 1911 Dodge wrote Gilbreth that he had had a long talk with Taylor about his micromotion study and that Taylor "made no adverse criticism whatever."[69] This was small comfort, particularly after Barth told an ASME meeting that he and Merrick doubted the usefulness of photographic devices.[70]

The final break came in 1914, supposedly as a consequence of Gilbreth's failures as a self-proclaimed expert. In 1912 Gilbreth had enlisted two important clients, the New England Butt Company of Providence and the Herrmann, Aukam Company of South River, New Jersey. Hathaway and Merrick helped him in the early stages of his work at New England Butt, and Gilbreth apparently enjoyed considerable success. But the Herrmann, Aukam Company proved more difficult. According to Gilbreth, he faced an unending series of obstacles, including efforts to harass and discredit his subordinates. The climax came in March 1914 when Herrmann, the head of the company, went to Taylor for a "general kind of grouch." He told Taylor that Gilbreth was too slow, that he spent too little time at the plant for the money he received, and that he left the work to incompetents, one of whom was supposedly involved in "some very bad moral delinquencies." Although the morals charge against Gilbreth's man—Gilbreth called it a "frame up"—was a new twist, the rest of the charges were the kinds of complaints that impatient clients often made about the experts. This time, however, Taylor listened to the accusations. Herrmann, he wrote, "talked in a very reasonable and sensible way." It seems more likely that he had so little confidence in Gilbreth by this time that he would have believed almost any criticism.[71] In either case he advised Herrmann to drop Gilbreth and hire Hathaway. He explained to Gantt: " I think he [Gilbreth] is destined to make a failure of anything he undertakes in this line. He has monumental conceit and will not go down to details."[72]

Gilbreth was naturally indignant when he heard what had happened. "It sounds very much like an act of war," he wrote his wife.[73] From this point relations between the Gilbreths (Lillian M. Gilbreth soon became her husband's professional partner) and Taylor—and, after Taylor's death, the remainder of the Taylor group—deteriorated. In the following years the Gilbreths went their separate way, avoided the Taylor Society (which Frank Gilbreth had been instrumental in founding), and concentrated their attention on motion study. Soon the Gilbreth system of management differed in many details from the Taylor system.[74]

The Taylor-Gilbreth conflict was another indication of the growing awareness among Taylor's disciples of the system's principal defect—its treatment of the worker. Like Gantt, Gilbreth sensed the problem and tried, in a way consistent with the limits of systematic management, to remedy it. In the years after Taylor's death more and more of the disciples became aware of the same shortcoming and embraced new approaches, some of which transcended the bounds of systematic management. Taylor Society meetings were frequently devoted to labor issues, and men like Cooke spent much of their time trying to soften the antagonistic policies of the trade unions. By the 1920s many Taylor disciples were leading liberals, particularly on the issue of collective bargaining. Before 1920, however, scientific management had a substantial effect on the evolution of the factory but only a minor influence on the emerging "solution" to the labor problem.

SCIENTIFIC MANAGEMENT: PROMISE AND PERFORMANCE

After 1901 Taylor's followers operated on two distinct levels. They were publicists and defenders of a doctrine, a philosophy, or a set of "principles" that had wide ramifications. At the same time they were practicing consultants, advocates of the Taylor system of shop management, which they offered to executives for a fee. In the former capacity they were highly successful, but as consultants their impact was less clear. How many firms embraced Taylor's methods? To what degree?

A popular endeavor among scholars in the post-1910 period was to estimate the number of establishments that had installed Taylor or other "efficiency" methods. This was no easy task. By that time there was a large and growing group of practitioners of the new "science" and considerable rivalry. Emerson and Gilbreth, for example, refused to disclose the names of their clients after breaking with the more orthodox Taylor disciples. Equally serious was the growing reticence of businessmen to disclose their contracts with the experts, particularly after 1911, when the AFL launched its attacks on time study methods. The board of directors of the Link-Belt Company even forbade James Mapes Dodge to have any official contract with the Taylor Society on the grounds that his association would generate unfavorable publicity about the company.[75]

The estimates reflected these difficulties. Probably the most authoritative, made by a committee of the ASME in 1912, listed fifty-two industries in which one or more companies had introduced "labor saving" management. C. Bertrand Thompson, who undertook the most ambitious individual effort, claimed that there were numerous discrepancies in the committee's computation and in turn listed 212 "applications," including 4 in government agencies and 32 in Europe and Japan. Of the 169 American "industrial plants" he identified, 111 were located in the New England or Middle Atlantic states.[76] At the same time Emerson reported that his firm alone had "consulted" 200 firms, and Taylor guessed that he knew of 100 plants "in which . . . [the Taylor system] is working" and implied that there were more. Robert T. Kent, who was close to both men, estimated in 1914 that Taylor's followers had reorganized 60 plants and Emerson's, 200.[77]

Nearly all contemporary observers were careful to add that there were wide variations in the meaning of terms like "consultation" and "application." This qualification was particularly important in evaluating Emerson's work, since he was willing to do as much or as little as a particular client desired and in no case went as far as Taylor in reorganizing a firm. In C. B. Thompson's words, "the Taylor System begins where the Emerson System ends."[78]

These caveats became the principal theme of Robert Hoxie's famous book *Scientific Management and Labor,* which he prepared for the United States Commission on Industrial Relations in 1914. After examining 35 plants that had introduced some aspects of scientific management, Hoxie concluded that

> no single shop was found which could be said to represent fully and faithfully the Taylor system as presented in the treatise on "Shop Management"; no representative of the Gantt system was encountered, complete and unmixed with alien elements; no shop was discovered wherein the Emerson ideals were completely demonstrated and held full sway, and no two shops were found in which identically or even approximately the same policies and methods were established and adhered to throughout.[79]

Though Hoxie's bias is apparent in this comment, he emphasized an important point: despite much study and observation, Taylor's contemporaries were unable to reach any meaningful consensus on the extent of the application of scientific management, much less its significance for the firm or worker.

Yet the task is not as hopeless as these statements suggest. In the published and unpublished literature of scientific management there are references to at least 46 industrial firms and 2 government manufacturing plants that introduced scientific management between 1901 and 1917.[80] Of these, 29 are reasonably well documented and appear in table 4.[81] They were clients of Taylor's immediate followers with the exceptions of the

Santa Fe Railroad, Harrington Emerson's first and most important assignment, and the Ferracute Machine Works of Bridgeton, New Jersey, Frederick A. Parkhurst's most notable job. Emerson considered himself part of Taylor's entourage at the time of his Santa Fe work, and Parkhurst, one of Emerson's principal assistants, was in Taylor's estimation "a man of the Emerson school [who] does not seem to be a humbug."[82]

To determine the impact of scientific management on these firms I have evaluated the experiences of each of them in terms of the major features of the Taylor system. These were (1) preliminary technical and organizational improvements such as changes in machinery (including the introduction of high-speed tool steel in machine shops), improved belting, cost accounting, purchasing, stores, and toolroom methods—in short, Taylor's basic refinements of systematic management; (2) a planning department; (3) functional foremanship; (4) time study; and (5) an incentive wage system. The results suggest that Taylor's colleagues were generally faithful to his teachings. Although it is impossible to be certain in every instance, they typically introduced major changes in three or four of the categories. The principal exceptions were functional foremanship, which most of them apparently considered impractical, and, to a lesser extent, the incentive wage, which they advocated but often did not have an opportunity to introduce. The usual effect of their work, then, was a wide-ranging reorganization of the plant, a less thorough revision of the foreman's functions, and a modest change in the average worker's activities. To describe scientific management in these plants as an attack on traditional methods of work or a "partial solution of the labor problem," as Taylor, several of his followers, and many academic writers have done, is both inappropriate and misleading.

In every plant there was evidence of preliminary reorganization: the experts classified and standardized materials, revamped toolrooms and storerooms, adjusted machinery, and improved the layout of the shops. The only major exception to Taylor's approach was in accounting procedure, where the "experts" often made only minor changes.[83] The amount of time and resources devoted to this activity depended on the industry. A textile mill typically required less attention than a machine shop.[84] The state of the plant when the expert began was also important: most of the shops where scientific management was introduced were modern, up-to-date factories.[85] Barth, for example, found little to do except in the machine shops of the Pullman Company, and Royal R. Keely undertook the Lewis Manufacturing job because he could install "the complete system in a short period of time under favorable conditions."[86] On the other hand, Barth and Hathaway worked at the Tabor Company for four years before it became a model of scientific management operations. Sanford

Table 4. Firms introducing scientific management, 1901–1917

Firm	Principal Taylor expert	Time
Tabor Mfg., Philadelphia	Barth, Hathaway	1903–
Stokes and Smith, Philadelphia	Gantt	1902–1903?
Link-Belt Engr., Philadelphia	Barth	1903–1907
Sayles Bleachery, Saylesville, R.I.	Gantt	1904–1908
Yale & Towne, Stamford, Conn.	Barth	1905–1907
Santa Fe Railroad, Topeka, Kan.	Emerson	1904–1907
Brighton Mills, Passaic, N.J.	Gantt	1905–1908
Ferracute Machine, Bridgeton, N.J.	Parkhurst	1907–1910
H. H. Franklin, Syracuse, N.Y.	Barth	1908–1909, 1911
Canadian Pacific Railroad, Montreal	Gantt	1908–1911
Smith & Furbush Machine, Philadelphia	Barth	1908–1910
Joseph Bancroft & Sons, Wilmington, Del.	Gantt	1908–1909
Plimpton Press, Norwood, Mass.	Cooke, Hathaway, Godfrey	1908–1912
Remington Typewriter, Ilion, N.Y.	Gantt	1910–1917
Forbes Lithograph, Boston	Cooke, Barth	1910–1912
Joseph & Feiss, Cleveland	Feiss	1910–
S. L. Moore, Elizabeth, N.J.	Barth	1911–1912
Amoskeag Mills, Manchester, N.H.	Gantt	1911–1912
Cheney Brothers, So. Manchester, Conn.	Gantt	1912–1918
New England Butt, Providence, R.I.	Gilbreth	1912–1913
Lewis Mfg., Walpole, Mass.	Keely	1912–1913
Herrmann, Aukam, South River, N.J.; Lebanon, Pa.	Gilbreth, Hathaway	1912–1915
Pullman Palace Car, Chicago	Barth	1913–1919
Baird Machine, Bridgeport, Conn.	Barth, Keely	1913–1914
Eaton, Crane & Pike, Pittsfield, Mass.	C. B. Thompson	1913–1915
Eastern Mfg., Bangor, Me.	S. E. Thompson	1914–1917
Winchester Repeating Arms, Bridgeport, Conn.	Barth	1916–
Watertown Arsenal, Watertown, Mass.	Barth	1909–1913
Mare Island Shipyard, Vallejo, Calif.	Evans	1906–1911

Thompson and his associates began their work at the Eastern Manufacturing Company shortly after a new management group had narrowly averted bankruptcy.

The expert's own interests were another variable. Barth and Hathaway, the most orthodox of the Taylor disciples, devoted themselves almost exclusively to the preliminary activities, leaving other aspects of the work to assistants. Cooke apparently adopted a similar approach; Gantt supposedly became less interested in this phase of the work after 1910; and Emerson, even in 1904–1907, revealed some tendency to cut corners.[87]

In most cases there is evidence of a planning department, although the nature of its activity varied. At the Montreal shops of the Canadian Pacific

Railroad, at the Plimpton Press, and at the Mare Island Shipyard it was probably the most significant feature of the reorganization effort.[88] At the H. H. Franklin Company it coordinated the entire manufacturing process, dispatching 1,500 jobs to workers every day.[89] At Tabor, Link-Belt, and Watertown Arsenal it managed the flow of work and materials, issued instruction cards, kept records, and directed the functional foremen.[90] In most plants, however, planning departments must have had more limited responsibilities, for they received relatively little attention in accounts of the experts' work.

The experiences of the 29 factories suggest that the presence of functional supervisors was the best indication of a thorough installation of the Taylor system. There is direct evidence of them only at Tabor, Link-Belt, Plimpton Press, New England Butt, Ferracute Machine, and, in modified form, Watertown Arsenal. Gantt did not introduce them on any of his jobs listed in table 4, apparently because of a belief shared by many of the experts that the Taylor system made the foreman's job feasible for the first time. Even Barth, supposedly the most orthodox of Taylor's disciples, compromised on functional foremanship. At the Winchester Repeating Arms Company, for example, he retained the traditional system but added "general foremen," who were intermediaries between the first-level supervisors and the department superintendent, and functional "overseers," who were assistants to the general foremen.[91]

The experts' attitudes toward functional foremanship reveal much about their view of labor and personnel problems generally. Three of Taylor's functional supervisors, the "gang boss," the "speed boss," and the "disciplinarian," performed potentially important personnel functions. The "gang" and "speed" bosses were supposed to teach the workers to perform their tasks correctly (i.e., in accordance with the planning office's instructions), and the "disciplinarian" was responsible for hiring, firing, and all disciplinary problems. Yet Taylor's conceptions of their duties were exceeding crude, and his followers, by neglecting or rejecting functional foremanship altogether, showed even less prescience.[92] Gantt, who developed a reputation as a labor expert because of his emphasis on "training workmen," had little interest in vocational education or apprenticeship systems. The other Taylor disciples, at least in the period before World War I, revealed no more sophistication than Taylor on the subject of industrial education or training.

Equally grievous was their failure to develop the role of the "disciplinarian." Taylor's disciplinarian performed many of the personnel functions of the conventional foreman. Despite a similar preoccupation with the "scientific" selection of workers, promotions based on ability, and shop morale, his followers paid even less attention to the disciplinarian's potential. Like their mentor they presumably believed that time study, coupled with an incentive wage, would ensure that the right workers filled the right jobs. During World War I several of the firms in table 4 pioneered in the introduction of formal personnel management, but with one or two exceptions the experts had nothing to do with this activity.[93]

There are references to time study at virtually every firm. The only difference among the experts was over who was to make the actual studies. Barth and Hathaway relied on professional time study technicians like Merrick to do their initial work and to train men in the plant to continue it.[94] Gantt, on the other hand, developed his own experts and, because of his interest in the bonus wage, did some of the work himself. Both groups, however, employed the techniques that Taylor and Sanford Thompson had originated in the 1880s and 1890s.

Gilbreth, of course, was the notable exception. His work at the New England Butt Company was thoroughly conventional in most areas, as he assured Taylor, but also resulted in the development of a "betterment" room, "route models," and above all his "micromotion" technique of time study.[95] After the Herrmann, Aukam job Gilbreth increasingly devoted his attention to motion study and routing problems. In this limited but important sphere he became to Taylor what Taylor had been to the pioneers of systematic management, the practitioner who extended the original concept to its logical conclusion.

The experts also introduced, or intended to introduce, incentive wage plans in every firm. C. B. Thompson concluded that "where the system had been in operation three years or more, there were from 50 to 85 percent of the employees earning bonuses ranging from 10 to 60 or 70 percent."[96] The problem was that the incentive had to follow other features of scientific management. Gantt, who had a strong interest in the bonus system, was extremely reluctant to introduce the new system prematurely.[97] At Joseph Bancroft & Sons he worked intermittently for more than a year but had only 12 of 1,400 employees on the bonus when his assignment ended.[98] The other experts followed a similar course, often to the consternation of their employers. Many manufacturers, including many recruited by Taylor himself, had little patience with the experts' painstaking attention to other features of the system. Even Barth recognized this problem. At Smith & Furbush, he wrote, the employer's pressure "may compel me to stop all further repairs and badly needed improvements to machines and tools, and [adopt] the premium plan, as a temporary expedient . . . to get a little more work out of the men with the equipment as it now is."[99]

It appears, then, that scientific management as applied by Taylor's disciples had no more dramatic effect on the workers than scientific management as Taylor applied it. Insofar as it led to a rearrangement of the shop, changed routine, modified the foreman's authority, reduced delays, and increased output, it had a profound impact on the wage earner—as it did on everyone involved in the operation of the factory. The direct effects on the workers, however, were probably minimal. They were confined to employees who worked under one of the Taylor incentive wage plans, a minority of the production employees at the 29 plants. Of the workers who were paid a bonus, some—as Barth admitted and Robert Hoxie later discovered—received it prematurely. In a few cases this probably led to "speed-ups," overwork, and fatigue, as the union leaders argued.[100] In others, it promoted "soldiering" and the piecework evils that Taylor inveighed against.[101] The residual group—workers placed on the bonus plan in thoroughly systematized shops—received higher wages for more steady work. The remaining evidence suggests that this group generally favored scientific management.[102]

If the rather modest effect of scientific management on workers in these factories is surprising, its apparent failure to end the workers' traditional restrictive practices is not. Subsequent studies have documented the persistence of informal production norms and the employees' ability to defy the supervisor and the time study expert. That Taylor, his followers, and their clients believed scientific management would end "soldiering" was another indication of how little they understood the foreman's functions and the workers' outlook. If the foreman, with his combination of threats and persuasion, could not change the workers' behavior, what hope was there for an outside expert equipped with only a stopwatch and an incentive wage plan? The manufacturers who remained skeptical of Taylor's system because of its supposed dependence on time study and the incentive wage were not necessarily the hopeless reactionaries that Taylor described.

An examination of the opposition to scientific management in the 29 firms also underlines the significance of the "nonlabor" features of Taylor's system. Recent writers—following the example of Taylor's contemporaries—have generally associated resistance to scientific management with the workers. But in these plants the experts encountered more opposition from the managers than from the workers. It could come from the highest levels. At Sayles Bleachery, Joseph Bancroft & Sons, Amoskeag Manufacturing, and the Forbes Lithograph, scientific management was introduced in the course of a power struggle between younger and older executives or as a part of a larger reform program after the younger men had taken over. At Amoskeag, W. Parker Straw, son of longtime agent H. F. Straw, hired Gantt over the objections of his father and the company's treasurer. The younger Straw's activities at the time suggested considerable impatience with the conservative policies of his elders. When he entered the Army in World War I, H. F. Straw came out of retirement to act as agent. The elder Straw soon scrapped the task and bonus system, supposedly in deference to the plant's union leaders.[103]

Certainly most plant managers, particularly those at the lower levels, viewed scientific management with apprehension and skepticism. Gantt encountered serious opposition from the management at the Sayles Bleachery and Joseph Bancroft & Sons and less formidable problems at the Canadian Pacific shops; Barth antagonized his employers at the S. L. Moore Company and lost the confidence of the Yale & Towne officers; Gilbreth alienated the managers of the Herrmann, Aukam Company; C. B. Thompson complained bitterly of the opposition he encountered from supervisors at the Eaton, Crane & Pike Company; Cooke reported a similar experience at Forbes Lithograph and Sanford Thompson at Eastern Manufacturing; Evans faced substantial opposition from many superiors and foremen; and the experts who worked at the Plimpton Press and at Lewis Manufacturing Company found Kendall, Taylor's friend and admirer, a highly critical observer of their work.[104] In the majority of cases where the experts failed, the bosses' opposition was more crucial than the workers' opposition. The combined pressures of high costs, disrupted routine, and the antagonism of those who were demoted or censured obviously took their toll. The foremen, in particular, were unhappy at the erosion of their powers.

By comparison the workers were relatively docile. C. B. Thompson noted that no installation had failed because of worker opposition.[105] Where it developed it was largely unorganized and leaderless and seldom resulted in strikes. Only at Mare Island, Watertown Arsenal, and the Sayles Bleachery was it sufficient to contradict Taylor's claim that scientific management improved employer-employee relations and reduced the threat of strikes.[106] According to Taylor and his disciples, the biggest problem arose from the inability of the experts to satisfy the workers' demands for immediate task and bonus work.[107]

The experiences of the 29 factories also reinforce the conclusion that Taylor's inflexibility and contradictory attitudes toward the diffusion of his techniques, rather than substantive issues, were responsible for divisions in the Taylor group.[108] Gilbreth, Parkhurst, and Emerson, at least in these cases, were no more unorthodox than the other, supposedly more "competent" practitioners of scientific management. Gilbreth was true to Taylor's ideas, just as he insisted. Parkhurst's work at Ferracute seems equally conventional and complete, although the company hired him only after it rejected Hathaway's proposal as too expensive. He may have settled for a smaller planning office staff than Hathaway wanted, but there was apparently little difference between what Hathaway proposed to do and what Parkhurst accomplished.[109]

Even Emerson's work at the Santa Fe shops was gradually consistent with the Taylor model. He standardized equipment and operations "to better every shop condition making for improved efficiency," installed cost accounting methods, and devised an intricate "dispatching system" or planning department.[110] He also altered the old supervisory system and introduced time studies and his "individual effort" wage system. Admittedly the Santa Fe job was not typical of Emerson's two hundred pre–World War I "consultations"; it was his longest and most ambitious assignment, and Taylor gave grudging approval to his efforts.[111] It did demonstrate, however, that even the most notable "fakir" was capable of duplicating the work of the master and his followers.

If substantive issues had been paramount, Richard A. Feiss rather than Gilbreth or Emerson would have been the object of Taylor's censure. Feiss was a fervent admirer of Taylor; he was also manager of his family's clothing factory in Cleveland and thus in a position to apply scientific management to an industry noted for poor management and labor unrest. Beginning about 1910 the two men became friends, and Feiss soon began to introduce the Taylor system with Taylor's encouragement. He acted as his own expert and by 1915 had introduced or seriously considered every major feature of the Taylor system. But he also had ideas of his own, particularly in regard to the workers' role. Even before he introduced scientific management he reduced his employees' hours below the industry standard. He initiated foremen's meetings and in 1913 hired a welfare secretary who, appropriately, was interested in Taylor's methods and determined to make welfare work "scientific."[112]

Feiss's major alteration to the Taylor system was likewise an outgrowth of his interest in labor problems. With the introduction of a planning department and time study the expert typically restricted "high-priced" workers to important work; poorly paid, unskilled workers performed other tasks. In the machine shop this meant that a skilled machinist devoted his entire time to his machine, while laborers brought him tools and materials and carried away the finished product. In the Joseph & Feiss factory an analogous situation existed. Sewing machine operators usually transported their materials and finished goods to and from their machines. The prescribed solution was to hire lower-priced workers to perform these simple tasks. But Feiss balked, arguing that the machine operators would become tired and bored. As his welfare secretary noted, Feiss was probably the first of Taylor's followers to take a genuine interest in the workers as individuals and to question the effectiveness of the incentive wage.[113]

The picture that emerges from this survey is one of individual specialization within an overall pattern of conformity to Taylor's ideas. Each man had a particular interest and emphasized that aspect of his work but did not exclude other aspects of the Taylor program. Thus Barth and Hathaway stressed improvements in machine methods, Gantt the task and bonus system, and Gilbreth the movements of men and materials. As Robert Hoxie demonstrated, these variations and exceptions can be the basis of a critique of scientific management. Yet, they must be viewed in the proper context, and that context, it is clear, was one of general adherence to Taylor's ideas.

Thus the shop management movement profoundly changed the early twentieth-century manufacturing plant. The manager's duties increased in scope; the foreman's diminished. Engineers and managers began to plan, to organize, and to standardize. Aided by important technical innovations they developed a degree of control over the manufacturing process unknown even in much smaller nineteenth-century factories. Yet few of the management reformers altered the traditional methods of recruiting, training, or motivating factory workers before 1915. Almost without exception they believed that the incentive wage was the appropriate remedy for labor problems and devoted considerable attention and ingenuity to perfecting it. Compared to other developments in the personnel area, however, the incentive wage was probably the least effective and important method by which managers increased their influence over the factory labor force.

5 Recruiting the Factory Labor Force

> After about twenty years' residence in Chicago, I know but very few of what you would call native-born American mechanics. [U.S., Senate, Committee on Education and Labor, *Relations Between Labor and Capital,* vol. 1, 1883 (Washington, 1885), pp. 567–68]

> Q. What policy has your company if any, as to recruiting employees?
> A. None whatever. [U.S., Senate, Commission on Industrial Relations, *Final Report and Testimony,* 64th Cong., 2d sess., vol. 4, 1914 (Washington, 1916), p. 3488]

> For some years after the company was organized, if a foreman was short of hands he went to the gate, looked over the crowd, picked out the man he wanted, and hired him. [ARMCO, *The First Twenty Years* (Middletown, Ohio, 1922), p. 209]

While the champions of systematic and scientific management extended the manager's control over production, wage setting, and, incidentally, the workers, another group of reformers enlarged the manager's power over the factory labor force by more direct means. Their efforts paralleled the revolution in shop management and resembled it in several respects. Scattered attempts to improve the quantity and quality of the labor supply, particularly in rural areas, led to more systematic efforts to increase the number of skilled workers and reduce turnover. Employers increasingly turned to experts—professional "welfare" workers—to introduce and manage these activities. Ultimately, they revised or eliminated most of the foreman's traditional personnel functions, but their most significant accomplishment was to change the way that workers were recruited for the factory labor force.

THE INFORMAL SYSTEM OF LABOR RECRUITMENT

The pre–World War I pattern of industrial labor recruitment had two bases, the individual foreman's responsibility for maintaining an adequate labor force and the availability of millions of European workers. The foreman, burdened with other duties, had neither the time nor the inclination to develop systematic recruitment procedures. As a result he selected his subordinates from those men and women who were seeking work, a procedure that led to the employment of large numbers of immigrants and immigrants' children in American factories (See table 5.)

In most establishments the foreman recruited subordinates through personal contact or selection "from the crowds which gather in the morning and in the late afternoon around the gates of the mill."[1] Presumably, he chose an individual because he knew, or believed he knew, what the applicant could do. If the foreman erred, he discharged the employee and began again. In plants or departments where the workers performed menial tasks or exercised little discretion, the foremen often permitted an employment agent to act as recruiter. The difference, from the applicant's perspective, was negligible. At the Chicago meat-packing plants

> the employment agent would look over the group generally and pick out those who seemed to be the sturdiest and best fitted to do the unskilled work. So far as I could see there was no bargaining and discussion about wages, terms of employment, or anything of that sort. Just the employment agent would tap the one he wanted on the shoulder and say, "Come along."[2]

Henry Ford supposedly threatened to discharge any agent who exercised the slightest discretion in selecting employees.[3]

Since the informal system depended on the individual foreman's personality and outlook, it is impossible to determine what factors, other than the supervisor's knowledge of the individual's ability, affected the recruitment process. Even in instances where the managers established rules or standards, the interpretation of those guidelines remained the supervisor's prerogative. But if each foreman differed, it is likely that most of them agreed on two points: the desirability of employees of the same ethnic background and the relative fitness of other groups for various types of jobs.[4]

Both considerations contributed to the tendency of certain groups to find work in particular industries. Immigrant employers typically selected supervisors of similar background, who in turn selected workers of the same background. In the larger number of cases where the employer and the supervisors were old stock American or western European, ethnic stereotypes of eastern European immigrants were influential. The reports of the Immigration Commission contain numerous statements by employers on the "racial efficiency" of particular groups, suggesting that the stereotyped idea of what a Pole or French Canadian was capable of doing may have been a major influence in hiring and promotion decisions. There were marked discrepancies in the employers' assessments, however. Few disputed the "facts" that Italians were untrustworthy or Slovaks stupid, but there were other ethnic groups that employers had difficulty classifying. Germans and Scandinavians, for instance, appeared as quasi-

Table 5. Male employees by nationality and industry, 1907–1908

Industry	Percent of total (to nearest 1%)		
	Native born of native father	Native born of foreign father	Foreign born
Metal manufacturers			
Agricultural implements and vehicles	21	20	59
Car building and repairing	29	16	55
Foundry and machine-shop products	34	20	56
Iron and steel	29	13	58
Locomotive building	27	24	49
Sewing machine manufacture	16	26	59
Textiles			
Cotton goods	10	18	72
Silk goods	16	28	57
Woolen and worsted goods	13	20	66
Miscellaneous			
Boots and shoes	43	23	34
Cigars and tobacco	51	10	39
Clothing	4	14	83
Furniture	30	20	59
Glass	43	17	40
Leather	17	14	69
Oil refining	12	21	67
Paper and wood pulp manufacturing	42	17	41
Slaughtering and meat packing	25	13	61
Sugar refining	6	8	85

Source: Adapted from U.S. Bureau of Labor, *Report on Conditions of Employment in the Iron and Steel Industry of the United States* (Washington, 1913), 3:83.

native Americans in some accounts and as typical central Europeans in others.[5]

While many European workers obviously suffered from these biases, American-born unskilled laborers often fared no better. Southern textile manufacturers and overseers often viewed their employees with the same disdain that northerners reserved for the newest of the new "races." In the case of white workers there was some ambiguity. They were, in some accounts, honest, independent yeomen, identical in outlook with the southern employing class.[6] More often they were restless, lazy, undisciplined "white trash." But in the case of black workers there was little disagreement. They were universally lazy, childish, and unstable, incapable of concentration or of working for more than a few days at a time, despite the frequent—if inadvertent—testimony of manufacturers that black workers were equal or superior to southern whites or "new" immigrants.[7] In this if in no other case, there seems no doubt that prejudice influenced employment practices.

More important to the overall recruitment process than the foreman's procedures or prejudices were the techniques by which potential employees made themselves available for selection. Labor market studies showed that a variety of informal methods—oral or written communications among friends or relatives, rumors, plant-gate or newspaper notices, and making the "rounds"—were prevalent.[8] But there were additional factors. Large numbers of late-nineteenth-century American factory workers came from Europe, Canada, or the rural South. Did they come in response to specific job openings or economic opportunity generally?[9]

Skilled workers typically knew about specific industries and employers, as well as the state of the labor market. The typical European or American apprenticeship program, under which apprentices worked for an artisan or manufacturer for four to six years to learn the trade, introduced potential journeymen to other, more experienced men who were likely to know of openings in the trade. In some cases it provided an individual with additional advantages, such as a reputation or letters of reference. Men who had completed apprenticeships at leading English machine shops or American firms such as Brown & Sharpe and Pratt & Whitney, for example, could find work in virtually any machine shop in the United States.[10] In many cases apprenticeship also introduced young men to trade unionism, thereby offering them an even wider range of contacts and more systematic methods for regulating employment and working conditions.[11]

British factories in particular contributed an "essential cadre of mule spinners, machine makers, foundrymen" and other skilled workers to American industry.[12] British craftsmen often came to fill specific jobs or went to areas where they knew there was a demand for their skills.[13] Thus mule spinners embarked for Fall River, not Manchester, New Hampshire, or Columbia, South Carolina—textile centers where ring spinning was used almost exclusively. A downturn in the British textile, iron, or machinery industry or the introduction of a labor-saving device sent forth a flood of workers to Fall River, Paterson, Philadelphia, or Pittsburgh. The American consul reported in the 1880s that workers leaving the depressed Yorkshire woolen industry were "almost wholly of the high artisan class . . . expert wool sorters . . . machinists, foremen, managers, and supervisors . . . whom the mills here are as loth to lose as we are pleased to gain."[14] Less frequently the movement was in the other direction, as a wage reduction or prolonged strike temporarily reversed the tide. Other more fortunate workers moved back and forth with the seasons or returned to see relatives or friends.

By the 1880s employers in Fall River and Paterson began to suggest that communications between British industrial centers and their cities might be too close. They held the tie responsible for the importation and flourishing state of militant trade unionism among their mule spinners, loom fixers, carders, and weavers. Local union leaders sometimes came to the same conclusion when British unions began paying "emigration benefits" to unemployed or blacklisted members. Yet as Robert Howard, head of the mule spinners' organization, reported: "I have written hundreds of letters to secretaries of operative associations in England, and have told them that England is better than Fall River; but they have said in answer that it is no use telling the operatives; they will insist on coming to see for themselves."[15]

The unskilled worker, on the other hand, usually responded to general economic conditions. Family contacts provided up-to-date information on employment opportunities and created the "chains" common to immigration history. These ties, rather than a shared body of knowledge, work reputation, or union membership, became the prerequisites for an area or occupation.[16] Immigrant merchants, "bankers," priests, philanthropic organizations, and self-designated labor agents provided more specific information. An enterprising Bulgarian store owner, for example, personally accounted for the settlement of eight thousand Bulgarian immigrants in the mill town of Granite City, Illinois, between 1903 and 1908.[17] Immigrants who had prior industrial experience could improve their prospects by moving to areas where that experience might be helpful. Thus Polish cabinet makers settled in Grand Rapids, a furniture center, and Italian "cobblers" concentrated in Lynn and other New England shoemaking towns.[18] But they had to be more flexible than skilled job seekers. Their goal was a job, perhaps any job, that would enable them to increase their income, to make a "stake."[19] Whether East European peasants, French Canadian farmers, or Appalachian migrants, the same motives prevailed.

Based on personal relationships involving millions of individuals, the informal system of recruitment had countless forms and nuances. It posed few obstacles to the skilled worker and enabled the unskilled worker, whether European or American, to adjust to the rigors of industrial life with a minimum of regimentation and interference. From the employer's viewpoint it made the expansion of the factory labor force relatively easy. Only a word to a workman with contacts in Europe, Canada, or the local ethnic communities was necessary; the firm incurred no obligations, and the influx adjusted automatically to the swings of the business cycle. Although employers were obvious beneficiaries, workers also used the system to their advantage as they sought to reconcile "industrial time" with "family time."[20] Still, there were problems, the most important of which were the financial costs of an unstable labor force and the social costs of periodic unemployment. For both managers and workers labor turn-over was a serious—and ultimately intolerable—defect in the traditional method of matching workers and jobs.

Although it is impossible to measure the extent of worker transiency, two types of evidence suggest its dimensions. The popular fear that immigrants were "driving" native workers out of American factories resulted in numerous efforts to document ethnic succession patterns. By the 1880s there were frequent accounts of how one nationality group filled the poor-est, most distasteful jobs, arranged for their relatives and friends to follow, moved into higher-paying jobs, and perhaps saw their children or grand-children desert the factory for managerial or clerical positions. Meanwhile another group moved into the low-paying occupations and began the cycle again. Though the process often took more than one generation and no individual was assured of advancement, the rate of "ethnic turnover" in factory work was rapid.[21]

One fortunate result of this concern was the careful recording of the sequence of work groups. At the Chicago meat-packing plants, for example,

> the Americans as wage-earners have practically been driven out of the
> stock yards and are being followed by the Irish and Germans. The older
> nationalities have already disappeared from the unskilled occupations, most
> of which now are entirely manned by Slovaks, Poles and Lithuanians. The
> Poles began to appear at about the same time as the Bohemians, though not in
> as large numbers; and they have not advanced in the same proportion. The
> Slovaks and Lithuanians were first seen in 1899.[22]

At the Pennsylvania Steel Company works at Steelton, Pennsylvania, the "races" arrived in the following order:

> 1870–1880: English, Irish, German, Welsh.
> 1880–1890: German, Polish, Slovenian, Italian.
> 1890–1900: German, Polish, Slovenian, Italian, Croatian.
> Post–1900: Slovenian, Italian, Croatian, Hungarian-German, Magyar,
>   Serbian, Roumanian, Macedonian.[23]

The experiences of the Amoskeag Mills between 1912 and 1922, re-flected in table 6, provide additional perspective on ethnic turnover in the New England textile industry.[24] New nationality groups appeared regu-larly, as they did in the Chicago and Steelton plants. Yet local conditions, in particular the area's proximity to French Canada, also had a substantial impact. French Canadians were never less than one-third of all Amoskeag employees between 1912 and 1922.[25] This was natural, for Manchester was only a day's journey from Quebec, and the Canadian farmers, like other unskilled workers, gravitated to the towns and jobs that were closest to their point of departure.

Table 6. Ethnic composition of Amoskeag Mills labor force, 1912–1922

Nationality	High–low percent of the total force	Peak year
French Canadian	40–35	1920–1921
Irish	16–12	1912
United States	14–10	1922
Greek	11–5	1917
Polish	13–10	1915
German	4–3	1912
English	3–2	1919
Scotch	3–2	1917
Swedish	1	1916
Lithuanian	less than 1	1922
Portuguese	2–less than 1	1922
Syrian	less than 1	1914
Armenian	less than 1	1914
Albanian	less than 1	1917
Russian	1–less than 1	1922
Turkish	less than 1	1917–1918

Source: "Nationality of Employees," Amoskeag Manufacturing Company Papers (Baker Library, Harvard Business School), CN–1.

Only in the second decade of the twentieth century did employers discover that ethnic turnover was only one aspect of a more general pattern of resignations, layoffs, and discharges. As a few firms began to collect data on quits and discharges, the astonishing results became known. The Amoskeag Company, for example, reported that in 1912 it hired 20,000 men and women to maintain a labor force of 16,000.[26] In December of the same year 48 percent of the factory employees of the Ford Motor Company quit or were fired.[27] The records of a large steel mill for the years 1905–1910 told a similar story:[28]

	1905	1906	1907	1908	1909	1910
Employees Jan. 1	11,631	15,661	16,608	13,578	13,731	16,997
New during year	14,023	13,983	11,705	4,169	10,792	13,043

Ninety-one southern textile mills hired 57,000 new employees in 1907 but had no more than 30,000 individuals on their payrolls.[29]

After studying 105 factories and mines Sumner Slichter concluded that, on average, the sum of the "total [annual] number of terminations of employment . . . will . . . approximate the sum of the average number of men employed in the plants. In other words, the average turnover . . . will be found to approximate one hundred percent."[30] This was only an aver-

Table 7. Unemployment, by industry

| Industry | Percent working | | | |
| | 12 months | | 9 months or over | |
	Men	Women	Men	Women
Oil refining	62.7	—	79.6	—
Meat packing	54.7	64.2	80.1	86.8
Furniture	54.5	63.6	88.8	89.8
Glass	53.8	47.2	77.7	69.4
Cotton	42.9	33.2	79.1	75.3
Agricultural implements	42.6	59.8	83.0	76.6
Leather	38.6	50.9	65.2	86.8
Silk	38.3	20.9	61.7	52.2
Clothing	37.8	55.4	73.7	79.0
Woolen	37.3	33.8	67.0	64.8
Shoes	29.9	33.9	64.1	67.8
Iron and steel	20.0	56.0	44.1	71.6

Sources: U.S. Immigration Commission, *Reports* (Washington, 1911) (Oil refining, vol. 16, pt. 20, p. 803; Meat packing, vol. 13, pt. 11, pp. 87–88; Furniture, vol. 15, pt. 15, pp. 505–6; Glass, vol. 14, pt. 12, pp. 83–84; Cotton, vol. 10, pt. 3, p. 119; Agricultural implements, vol. 14, pt. 13, p. 449; Leather, vol. 12, pt. 8, p. 61; Silk, vol. 11, pt. 5, pp. 53–54; Clothing, vol. 11, pt. 6, pp. 315–16; Woolens, vol. 10, pt. 4, pp. 689–90; Iron and steel, vol. 12, pt. 9, pp. 271–72.)

age, however. In eight Detroit plants the turnover percentages for 1914, a recession year when jobs were relatively hard to find, were 315.7, 253.6, 249.3, 187.3, 161.9, 161.8, 153.6, and 101.4 percent, respectively.[31] Though the figures were often staggering, they reflected the activities of a minority of the workers. The young, the unskilled, and the newly hired accounted for most of the turnover. "Not more than one-third of the men hired by most factories remain in their employ for as long as a year."[32]

The Immigration Commission's data on unemployment are equally fragmentary but support Slichter's conclusions.[33] (See table 7.) In many industries the Commission found relatively few workers employed throughout the year. Since the overall unemployment rate was 6 percent of the labor force only in 1885, 1893–1898, 1908, and 1915, most workers must have found new positions with relative ease, only to exit again within a few months.[34] In recession years, when manufacturers laid off large numbers of employees (including foremen), there were protests and unrest; otherwise workers moved from job to job until they found a suitable position or a compatible foreman. This process may account for the disparity between the chaos and distress that students of the labor market described and the relative passivity of the workers. Undoubtedly it helps explain why employers became concerned about unemployment during World War I (after immigration had ended and they had discovered turnover) and why they led the campaign to reduce it in the 1920s.[35]

MODIFYING THE SYSTEM

Although the basis of the informal system was the manufacturer's delegation—or abnegation—of authority, there was no hard and fast rule that defined the spheres of the executive and supervisor. As a result the typical manager paid little or no attention to how or whom the foreman hired as long as trouble did not arise and the foreman did not employ undesirable workers.

The Employer's Role

The exact implications of this arrangement depended on the industry and the type of jobs that the foremen had to fill. Some manufacturers demanded that the supervisors adhere to certain guidelines. Prospective employees might have to pledge not to use intoxicants or, after 1900, submit to a physical examination.[36] When child labor laws were enforced, manufacturers often required that foremen not employ minors. Conversely, the United States Steel Company and other firms that created pension and accident insurance funds set maximum age limits to make sure they hired only "good risks."[37]

But most managers did not interfere unless the labor supply was insufficient or special conditions required uniformity in the employees selected. For example, they occasionally imported skilled European immigrants on contract, a costly and uncertain procedure that required executive attention.[38] More frequently they "stole" skilled operatives from competitors by offering wages "far higher than is intended to be permanently given."[39] When they were unable to obtain unskilled laborers, they employed labor bureaus in New York or Boston or agents in Canada to send a designated number of workers. Or they sent a foreman to a major city for the same purpose.[40]

Another exception to the standard practice was the use of labor bureaus to recruit workers for a group of firms, usually in the same city or region. Sometimes these organizations promoted migration, coordinated advertising for workmen, and prevented competition among employers within a locality. But the bureaus' primary purpose was invariably to screen out "intractable" workers—union members—before they got to the plant gate.[41] The National Metal Trades Association, for example, set up labor bureaus in many large cities after 1902 to combat the Machinists Union. Local employers agreed to hire only men who had first registered with the bureau and agreed, in effect, not to join the union.[42] Most such organizations were thus concerned with only skilled workers and considered only one or at best a few of the applicant's qualifications for the job. The actual selection remained the foreman's responsibility.

Manufacturers similarly took the initiative when they hired workers to take the places of strikers. It seems unlikely, though, that many employers understood the full implications of their actions. Because strikebreakers often came from outside the area and represented a different—and presumably "lower"—ethnic group, their use exacerbated ethnic and racial tensions and disrupted the ethnic balance of the community. In many factories French Canadians, eastern European immigrants, and African-Americans were first introduced as strikebreakers. After that the informal system usually insured their continued presence. Indeed, labor unrest and union activity were more likely to provoke sweeping changes in factory management than almost anything else.[43] It is not surprising that the years 1915–1920, a time of widespread upheaval, were also a period of rapid change in factory organization and operations.

Before that time, however, the most significant modifications in the informal system resulted not from the importation of skilled workers, from temporary shortages, or from anti-union activities but from persistent labor shortages. Though most manufacturers became involved in the recruitment process only when involvement was absolutely necessary, managers who operated plants in rural areas found that the need was almost continuous. The "one great drawback" of the rural factory was the "inelasticity of the labor volume."[44]

Glass manufacturers were among those who most often confronted this obstacle. They required large numbers of boys to aid the skilled blowers, but the location of their factories in isolated New Jersey, Pennsylvania, and midwestern towns made boys difficult to recruit. They tried a variety of expedients: they encouraged the boys to "double up," to work back-to-back shifts; imported orphans and other "boarding boys" from nearby cities; gave jobs to immigrants with sons willing and able to work as helpers (in the southern New Jersey company towns the presence of one or more boys in the plant supposedly gave the laborer's family "complete immunity as far as the company store is concerned"); and hired immigrant and black women as helpers.[45] But none of these approaches proved successful, and the "boy problem" continued to plague the glass industry.

It was the textile manufacturers, however, who most often became directly involved in recruiting programs. The Waltham or boardinghouse system of the early nineteenth century started a tradition that did not end with the arrival of large numbers of Irish, French Canadian, Italian, and Portuguese workers. Manufacturers in small towns continued to rely on native workers, and some firms in larger cities, such as the Dwight Manufacturing Company of Chicopee, sent recruiters to other New England towns as late as 1913.[46] Although the existence of a large impoverished native labor force in the Carolinas and Georgia was supposedly a major reason for the expansion of the industry in the South after 1880, southern manufacturers ultimately encountered similar shortages. In the 1880s and 1890s they attracted workers from the surrounding areas.[47] By the turn of the century, however, they had exhausted the local labor supply and found themselves in the same situation that their northern predecessors had faced sixty years before. With thousands of spindles "dead" because of the lack of operatives to tend the machinery, they embarked on a vigorous recruitment campaign.[48]

The southern mill managers employed a variety of techniques, the most common of which was to dispatch agents to rural areas to entice farm families into the mills. The recruiters distributed fliers or "dodgers" describing the advantages of factory work at fairs, circuses, and other social events and promised train fare and company housing to prospective employees.[49] At least 3,500 workers migrated from North to South Carolina in 1904–1906 as a result of these activities while others went to Virginia.[50] Even more ambitious was the plan of the South Carolina Manufacturers Association in 1906–1907 to import Belgian textile workers. Although the Association recruited nearly 500 immigrants, the experiment failed when many of the new employees became homesick and left the mills.[51]

Yet even among textile manufacturers direct recruiting on this scale was infrequent. In the South it was a product of the rapid expansion of the mills after 1900, the widespread prejudice against hiring black workers, and the practice of hiring whole families, which meant that a modest expenditure was likely to produce a large number of new employees. For most firms that operated in rural areas or small towns the company town rather than the recruitment campaign became the principal device for maintaining an adequate labor force. It was as town planners and operators that nineteenth-century managers exercised their greatest influence over the informal system and the factory labor force.

The Company Town

Whether manufacturers built factories in rural areas to gain access to raw materials, water power, or cheap land, to avoid city taxes or labor unions, or to pay lower wages, they often found that a company town was an essential part of their investment. To attract a labor force they had to build houses, schools, churches, and stores; provide water, sanitation, and, later, lighting for their employees' homes; and employ clergymen, doctors, teachers, and other public servants. A minority sought to institute a program of social reform; the majority merely bowed to necessity. In either case they soon learned that the "best operatives will not go where the tenements are bad."[52]

Late-nineteenth-century company towns—communities owned or

dominated by a single firm—reflected this pragmatic approach.[53] They dated from no particular era, social movement, or school of managerial thought. Some—like Whitinsville, Massachusetts; Millvill, New Jersey; Manchester, New Hampshire; and Johnstown, Pennsylvania— were as old as the factory system. Others were lineal descendants of earlier types of communities. The steel towns of the Birmingham district often bore a remarkable resemblance to the iron "plantations" of the eighteenth and early nineteenth centuries.[54] The textile towns of the southern piedmont likewise recalled the early days of Lowell and Lawrence. The village of the Joseph Bancroft & Sons Company, near Wilmington, Delaware, was a tangible symbol of this tie. Erected between the 1830s and the Civil War, the period of New England "paternalism," the Bancroft community remained a small, isolated, family-owned industrial site long after the best-known of the New England textile towns had evolved into cities. By 1920 "its conditions resemble[d] those of the South rather than of the New England group."[55] Finally, there were new company towns—such as Pullman, Illinois; Tacony, Pennsylvania; and Gary, Indiana—that were products of the nineteenth-century revolutions in transportation, building materials, and plant layout.

The hallmark of the company town was the clarity of the relationship between the factory and the surrounding community. In most cases the manufacturer viewed the company town as little more than an extension of the plant. The principles of utility and economy prevailed in both cases. In practice this meant that the village or at least the workers' houses were clustered around the plant to minimize travel time and tardiness. Few employees objected. At South Manchester, for example, the Cheney Company workers informally divided the company houses into "aristocratic" and "plebian" groups, depending on their distance from the plant.[56] In many company towns it was a mark of status to live in the shadow of the factory walls.

The manufacturer's businesslike approach also accounted for the drabness of most company towns. At Schoolfield, Virginia, supposedly a "model" southern village, "the monotony of row upon row of houses, essentially the same in design, materials, and color was accentuated by standard outhouses, fifty paces removed from each back door."[57] Even the idyllic New England towns seldom deviated from the standard. Yet there was at least one compensating feature. Most company towns were located in rural or suburban areas and had ample space for streets, lawns, and gardens. Residents raised vegetables or flowers. In the South, pigs, chickens, and cows were familiar sights as well. In that region, at least, farm and factory life were not mutually exclusive.

Although most manufacturers usually went no further than these elementary measures, they had to make two additional decisions that often had a greater impact on the social life of the community than the location or arrangement of housing. The first was whether to sell property or houses to the employees or to other private interests. Home ownership, or at least the prospect of home ownership, supposedly engendered thrift, sobriety, and loyalty to the firm. On the other hand, such sales inevitably weakened the company's hold on the town. In most cases the possible benefits outweighed the costs, and manufacturers initiated a policy of sales to skilled workers. The major exceptions were the southern textile manufacturers, who took their paternal responsibilities seriously, and the northern "model" town owners. The Ludlow Manufacturing Associates of Ludlow, Massachusetts, for example, at first sold company houses to employees but reversed this policy and even bought back the homes when they discovered that their workers, as private homeowners, could not be forced to maintain the company's high standards.[58]

A related problem appeared when the town expanded into areas not owned by the company. In these situations private builders and real estate speculators often usurped the manufacturer's role as town planner. In Gary, perhaps the best example, they were able to alter drastically the company's "plan" for the city despite the managers' strenuous objections.[59] The ethnic neighborhoods where unskilled immigrants often found their homes were usually the products of "private" enterprise.

The second decision manufacturers had to make was whether to enforce ethnic or racial segregation. In the southern mill towns they seldom hesitated: whites and blacks were customarily located in separate areas or districts, the former often enjoying somewhat better accommodations. In the North, particularly in larger towns, the companies often confined their building programs to substantial, well-built structures designed for skilled workers. Only the working-class elite could afford most company housing in Manchester and Johnstown.[60]

In both regions company housing was generally superior to the available "private" housing. Only in New Jersey glass towns were company houses reported to be markedly inferior to housing in neighboring non-company areas. Millville's "Grumble Alley," for example, resembled the "private" slums of other industrial towns.[61] But most managers viewed housing as a means to an end, not an end in itself. If a modest increase in housing expenditures resulted in a substantial decrease in labor turnover, the company benefitted. Most "private" owners, on the other hand, could not afford the luxury of a long-term viewpoint. They sought to recoup their investment from their rental incomes—and quickly.

In small company towns the management provided not only basic public services but schools, churches, and libraries. Often, however, there was a difference in the manner of presentation: the company supplied gas, water, and electricity for a fee, albeit a nominal one; the mill manager or owner provided schools, churches, and other public buildings as "gifts" to the operatives. Even in the larger towns where schools were tax-supported, company officials often built public auditoriums, gymnasiums, libraries, or trade schools. In many cases the owner or manager and his wife were active community leaders, serving as the honorary or real heads of the church, school, fire department, library association, hospital, and other company-sanctioned organizations. In the 1880s the general manager of the Cambria Iron Company even taught geology in the company's evening school, the Cambria Scientific Institute. His classes were unusually well attended.[62]

Company involvement in community affairs seldom was confined to the erection of buildings or the participation of high officials. Mill managers also used their influence to guide the residents' behavior in "constructive" ways. Perhaps the best example was their approach to the liquor issue. To mill officials the saloon was a source of absenteeism, crime, and domestic strife. They often used their authority to abolish the saloon and to educate the operatives to the evils of drink. Saloons were prohibited, company stores and hotels refused to sell liquor, and social events sanctioned by the management were "dry." "In nearly all the smaller mill villages . . . the operatives as a body are sober and well behaved. There is usually good order and but little drinking."[63]

In most cases manufacturers accepted the responsibilities as well as the prerogatives of their position—or so it was reported. The Whitins were "benevolent despots"; an Alabama employer was a "fatherly King" over his workers; southern mill workers expressed "little or no dissatisfaction with the system"; Disston employees had "warm and respectful opinions" of the Disston family.[64] When company town residents did complain, the issue was usually more concrete. The Pullman workers struck over high rents, not paternalism. Wage cuts, long hours, and a problem peculiar to company towns—the company store—were also common sources of grievances.

The extent of the manufacturer's power and the temptations that it created are most apparent in the company store issue. The New Jersey glass companies were particularly notorious: their policy, as tersely stated by one operative, was "trade or no work."[65] Southern manufacturers, on the other hand, used the store as a crude device for reducing labor turnover. Birmingham steel makers, for example,

> stated that negroes were preferred because their improvident habits prevented them from being able to live on cash incomes paid monthly, and thus forced them to draw their wages weekly, and even daily, in the form of commissary checks or store credits. . . . As a result, the negroes are always a little in debt to the commissaries; they are rarely the possessor of any currency, and stay in the employ of one company as long as their employers will allow them.[66]

In either case company store abuses, perhaps more than any other flaw in the operation of the company town, resulted in attacks on the manufacturers and their power. In New Jersey the glass workers' unions waged a relentless war against the company store. When they struck to abolish stores "the sympathies of the people in the localities affected were entirely with the strikers."[67] By the turn of the century most northern legislatures had already taken steps to curb or abolish the stores and prohibit payment in kind, long intervals between paydays, and other related evils.

It would misleading, however, to assume that the workers' actions ever meaningfully limited the employers' authority.[68] In the first place most manufacturers took their paternal responsibilities seriously; they did not attempt to cheat or exploit their employees, at least in a financial sense. In the second, they had good reasons for treating the workers in a reasonable, even benevolent way. The purpose of the company town, after all, was to attract and maintain an adequate labor force. Policies that led to unrest, antagonism, or turnover were, from the company's viewpoint, irrational. When coupled with a paternalistic social outlook, this fact usually dictated a policy of cooperation. But even when the manufacturer failed to anticipate an neutralize potential sources of discord, the relatively small size of the company town, the personal relations that existed between managers and workers, the employees' economic dependence on the company (most company housing leases provided for eviction in the event of discharge or a strike), and the virtual impossibility of holding a private meeting were major deterrents to concerted action.[69]

If the company town succeeded in attracting workers and the informal system became operative, traditional company town controls rarely survived if the newcomers were "un-Americanized" immigrant workers. Almost without exception manufacturers were unable or unwilling to control their foreign employees. Whatever the employers' policy, the immigrants persisted in establishing their ethnic enclaves, complete with stores, churches, and social organizations, in effect forcing the company to deal with intermediaries—storekeepers, "boarding bosses," "bankers," and priests. As a result the social organization of the town changed.[70] The managers retained their grasp on the natives and "immigrant leaders," but the foreign quarters became a community apart.[71]

Southern workers were less fortunate. Except for some of the steel towns of the Birmingham district, southern factories relied almost entirely on native workers, with newly arrived farmers filling the positions that southern and eastern European immigrants occupied in northern factories. Moreover, managers often continued their earlier policies. To outsiders they explained that controls were necessary because of the poverty, ignorance, and irresponsibility of the operative class. To buttress their case they pointed to the workers' crudities: their insistence on sending their children to work at an early age; their custom of putting the whole family in one bedroom, perhaps in one bed; their unfamiliarity with modern sanitary facilities, even privies. (Families "actually had to be 'house broken' to the use of the privy."[72]) Yet the workers' poverty and ignorance had little to do with the growth of industrial paternalism in the South. For while southern mill employees undoubtedly lacked resources and education, they were by immigrant standards relatively well off. They understood the English language and were familiar with "American ways." In short, it was because they understood English and "American ways" and were therefore understandable to their employers that they were subjected to greater restrictions.

Perhaps the best illustration of this relationship was the spread of "welfare work" at the turn of the century as mill officials realized the extent of their power and the uses to which it could be applied. By 1900, paternalism "made sense" to southern employers.[73] Building on the company town tradition, they extended and institutionalized their efforts. But when large numbers of "unassimilated" immigrants were present, employers usually introduced welfare work only for the skilled employees. In the Birmingham steel towns it was "confined entirely to the providing of school facilities, and church and lodge buildings."[74] At Johnstown "no welfare is attempted outside of medical and hospital service."[75] At Steelton, the company planned a "hotel and beer" garden for its immigrant employees but abandoned the scheme when "difficulties" arose.[76] Even at Gary the company's community programs had relatively little impact on the unskilled immigrants who constituted the majority of the labor force.[77] In this, as in other areas of community life, the "new" immigrant posed an insuperable obstacle that only time and the gradual process of "assimilation" would remove, or so most managers believed.

The New Apprenticeship

While the special problems of attracting an adequate labor force in rural areas or small towns led many manufacturers to become involved in the recruitment process, a more general problem of the late nineteenth century—the shortage of properly trained workers—produced a less dramatic but no less significant response. There were many reasons for the failure of the informal system to supply sufficient numbers of skilled wage earners. Most important were the achievements of American technology, which reduced the value of immigrant workers' skills and at the same time often rendered traditional training methods obsolete. In many industries the techniques by which apprentices acquired journeymen's skills— techniques that consisted largely of "imitating the best methods of those workmen with whom [the apprentice] comes closely into contact"—no longer sufficed in the modern factory.[78]

While contemporaries bemoaned the decline of the apprenticeship system, they often failed to distinguish between the disappearance of the system in some industries and the rise in others of conditions that made apprenticeships difficult to fulfill in the traditional manner. In industries where a technology characterized by a minute division of labor had superseded artisanal methods, the apprenticeship system had disappeared. Skilled workers were lured from other firms, and the other employees acquired their knowledge in any way they could.[79] In a few industries, such as boot and shoe making, beginners could enroll in special "schools" to learn particular machine operations.[80] More often, the foreman gave them instructions or assigned them to "learners." Or they began as laborers and gradually "picked up" higher-paying jobs along with the "rules" of the shop.[81]

In the shipbuilding, locomotive, railroad car, machine tool, steam engine, and electrical machinery industries, however, manufacturers continued to accept apprentices but found that the traditional approach no longer sufficed.[82] So much of the work had become specialized that apprentices seldom became all-around mechanics. The boy taken into the shop and handled in the traditional, unsystematic way merely became another specialist.[83] Under these conditions the system deteriorated. Verbal agreements supplanted the formal indenture. The period of "study" declined. O. M. Becker, a prominent engineer, summarized the situation in 1906:

> It would be incorrect to say that there is any such thing as an apprenticeship system in vogue in the United States. In most shops . . . a few boys are employed with a more or less distinct verbal agreement that they shall remain in the shop a specified time. They are under the foremen just as are the journeymen, and are supposed to receive some instruction from both. As a matter of fact they leave when they please, and they receive little or no instruction except where the foreman or some journeyman takes a particular interest and goes out of his way to teach the "cubs" the things they would otherwise have to pick up as best they might.[84]

A good example of the problem was the ambiguous status of the "helper" in the blacksmith and boilermaker trades.[85] In theory the helper was distinct from an apprentice; he received no instruction and had no expectation of advancement. But in reality he did the same work as the apprentice. In prosperous years, when journeymen were scarce, employers promoted helpers to journeymen status. In 1900 the Boiler Makers and Iron Ship Builders Union amended its constitution to admit helpers, in an effort to control them.[86] Yet although many helpers "picked up" the journeymen's skills and were as well trained as most apprentices, few became all-around craftsmen, and even fewer seemed qualified for supervisory roles.[87]

The manufacturers' answer was to devise new methods of training skilled workers. Two patterns emerged. Large firms, particularly in the railroad, machine tool, and electrical machinery fields, reformed the apprenticeship system to provide a steady supply of thoroughly trained employees, many of whom, it was understood, would ultimately assume managerial positions. Smaller firms and some large ones outside the machinery industry, which did not have the resources or the need for a large-scale apprenticeship program, joined reformers and educators in promoting government-subsidized industrial education. There was overlap between the two groups; some employers who adopted "new" apprenticeship programs, for example, also became leaders of the National Society to Promote Industrial Education, the lobbying organization that agitated for government assistance to industrial education. But for the most part they operated independently.

Three machinery and machine tool makers, R. H. Hoe & Company, Brown & Sharpe, and Pratt & Whitney, introduced the first of the "new" apprenticeship plans in the 1870s. These firms avoided the problems that troubled most manufacturers by conscientiously rotating their apprentices and by requiring apprentices to pursue an academic course related to their shop work. The Hoe Company established an evening night school, and Brown & Sharpe required its apprentices to study mathematics and drawing at the Rhode Island School of Design. Beyond these changes their programs were not unlike most of the "old" apprenticeship plans. They required a contract, demanded four years' service, and paid the boys a modest wage. The apprentices worked in the factory under the supervision of the regular foreman.[88]

Other firms that adopted "new" apprenticeship plans—most notably Baldwin Locomotive, General Electric, and Allis-Chalmers—made additional changes. The most important of these was the creation of special shop schools that taught mathematics and mechanical drawing.[89] The Westinghouse Air Brake Company and several railroads went a step further and contracted with the YMCA to teach the academic portion of the program.[90] Although manufacturers often disavowed any paternal interest in their apprentices, most attempted to inculcate desirable values. They emphasized the virtues of hard work, loyalty, respect for authority, patriotism, and "good" citizenship. As Samuel Vauclain, president of the Baldwin Company, explained, "apprentices offer the most fertile field for the development of a good, loyal body of men."[91]

A second major innovation, introduced by General Electric, was the apprentice supervisor, an employee who devoted some or all of his time to overseeing the activities of the apprentices. The supervisor was a response to one of the major flaws of the "old" apprenticeship: the failure of the foremen to train the apprentices in all facets of a craft. Other firms gradually established such posts, with the supervisor acting as classroom instructor and coordinator of the shop work, which was done under the foremen's aegis. Several large railroad companies, led by the New York Central and the Santa Fe, further refined this approach by designating a school instructor and a shop instructor who worked with the foremen.[92]

In 1904 Magnus W. Alexander, supervisor of apprentices at the Lynn plant of General Electric, introduced a separate training department where the boys received all their shop training during the early years of their apprenticeship. The supervisor thus assumed the role of foreman as well as coordinator or shop instructor. Alexander's principal objective was to ensure individual attention, but he had other aims as well. Since

> the attitude of many of our workmen . . . toward work is not conducive to the best interests of the boys [they] . . . should be kept under the sole influence of two or three picked instructors. These instructors endeavor to teach knowledge and skill as well as to build up the character of the boys, instilling into them honesty of purpose and a sense of their obligation to perform their work with the greatest speed and accuracy, regardless of wages or any other similar consideration.[93]

All the plans that provided for a supervisor or instructor had a common element: they compromised to some degree the authority of the plant foreman. Where the supervisor merely coordinated the boys' shop work, the degree of interference was relatively slight. Where shop instructors actually directed the work, the foreman had considerably less influence. In the New York Central plan, for example, a dual system of supervision evolved.

> The apprentices are still responsible to the foreman as formerly, but the foreman is relieved of the necessity of instructing them and is left free to run his department . . . The shop instructor . . . arranges the changes of work in conference with the foreman. He keeps fully informed of the conditions existing in the various departments of the shop; he is in close touch with the foreman and the gang bosses. . . . His position in the shop is such that his judgment is accepted by the foreman, and his recommendations followed by the shop superintendent.[94]

Under the Lynn plan, to take the opposite extreme, the foreman lost all authority over the training of skilled workers. Although foremen were often happy to be relieved of this duty, they could not have been oblivious to the precedent that was established.

After 1905 the "new" apprenticeship became a popular subject among machinery manufacturers and railroad executives. Trade associations adopted model apprentice plans, and many firms incorporated the innovations noted above. In 1913 the movement was institutionalized in the National Association of Corporation Schools. During the following years, the NACS became a vigorous proponent of the "new" apprenticeship.[95] It also symbolized the growing popular interest in industrial education, an interest that culminated in 1917 with the passage of the Smith-Hughes vocational education act.[96]

Of the many facets of the industrial education movement, the one that applied to factory work most directly was the proliferation of schools to train skilled textile workers.[97] Beginning in 1882–1883 with the Philadelphia Textile School, the effort soon spread to New England and the South. By 1900 similar institutions existed in Lowell, New Bedford, Fall River, and Lawrence and in several southern states. The Philadelphia School, which was the prototype for the others, emphasized both the artistic and mechanical aspects of textile manufacture so that a graduate would be "able to exercise intelligent supervision over any branch" of the industry.[98] The other schools also stressed textile design and chemistry as well as the various manufacturing processes.[99]

From the beginning manufacturers dominated the textile schools. The Philadelphia Textile Association, a local trade group, promoted the Philadelphia School, and the city's leading firms subscribed most of the money.[100] Massachusetts manufacturers were instrumental in obtaining state subsidies for the institutions in that state.[101] Because of this role the textile workers' unions, which included many skilled workers, at first opposed the schools, fearing they would undercut the unions and provide strikebreakers. But the specter of southern competition, one of the manufacturers' principal arguments for the schools, and the appointment of union leaders to the schools' boards quieted the opposition.[102] By World War I the textile schools had become both civic enterprises and surrogates for the "new" apprenticeship programs of the metals and machinery industries.

Direct recruitment efforts, company town practices, and the "new" apprenticeship and industrial education plans were the most notable efforts by pre-1915 manufacturers to overcome the shortcomings of the foreman's control of the factory labor force. Without exception they were tentative measures, in most cases the responses of employers who confronted specific difficulties, rather than concerted efforts to circumscribe the foreman's empire. Yet there was enough activity to indicate growing dissatisfaction with the status quo and to help focus broader attacks on the foreman's power during World War I. When combined with the welfare plans of many large companies, these efforts provided the basis for the postwar personnel management movement.

6 The Rise of Welfare Work

The machine tender who is able to raise his or her eyes from the whirring monster which requires such slavish attention to the peaceful beauties of nature, drinks in life and strength from the view. [Budgett Meakin, *Model Factories and Villages* (London, 1905), p. 204]

We make better steel and more of it by raising flowers and having them in our yards. [Eugene G. Grace in American Iron and Steel Institute, *Monthly Bulletin* (January, 1913): 5]

While manufacturers gradually reduced the foreman's power to recruit and train the factory labor force, they also added new personnel programs outside the foreman's jurisdiction that ultimately reinforced the trend toward centralized recruitment and training. No single motive accounted for the new activities. Leaders in the movement pointed to the increasing size of the factory labor force, the impersonal quality of labor-management relations, the apparent decline in company loyalty and morale, and the prevalence of labor unrest—in short, the same factors that led others to introduce safety programs, incentive wage plans, or even apprenticeship training. Their remedial efforts, known collectively by 1900 as welfare work, were based on the belief that voluntary efforts by employers to improve the lot of workers encouraged self-betterment, loyalty, and cooperation—that they inspired the employee to become a better person and a better worker.

The exact procedure for achieving these goals remained uncertain, and manufacturers and other employers showed remarkable ingenuity in interpreting their convictions. The National Civic Federation (NCF), the leading institutional proponent of welfare activities, reflected this diversity when it attempted to define the bounds of welfare work: "[It] involves special consideration for physical comfort wherever labor is performed; opportunities for recreation; educational advantages; and the providing of suitable sanitary homes . . . plans for saving and lending money, and provisions for insurance and pensions."[1]

ORIGINS

Although paternalistic or philanthropic activities were as old as the factory system, several types of measures prevalent before 1900 foreshadowed the systematic welfare work of the early twentieth century.[2] The company town, for example, was often the basis for an extensive benefit program. Relief funds for injured workers frequently played a similar role. Employers who reduced the hours of labor below the prevailing level argued that morale and productivity improved, though most of their colleagues remained skeptical. "Even manufacturers who are said to be efficient in their efforts to improve the condition of their people" frequently opposed a reduction in hours.[3]

Libraries, restaurants, club houses, and other social or recreational facilities, which appeared in increasing numbers after 1875, also anticipated institutionalized welfare work. While their introduction involved a degree of social commitment that only a minority of businessmen shared, they were seldom purely philanthropic gestures. Employers who financed libraries, for example, looked upon their expenditures as investments in a more efficient as well as a more conservative working class.[4] Yet even this rationalization was not always necessary. The Pacific Mills deducted a small weekly sum from its employees' wages to finance its large library, which for many years made a profit.[5]

Of the urban manufacturers who pioneered in this type of activity, H. J. Heinz of Pittsburgh was undoubtedly the leader. He supplied uniforms to his workers and made his factory "the cleanest place on earth." His motto, "Energy brings bread; indolence brings want," appeared in every department. The women employees had dressing rooms, washrooms, lockers, and a "roof garden" for lunch-hour strolls. By the 1890s Heinz had added a recreation room, a relief association, annual outings, and perhaps the first of the welfare secretaries, a "Mother Dunn," who hired and fired, checked on absentees, and counseled those in need. On one occasion Heinz's son told an interviewer that "heart power"—having a "really happy family that lasts"—was the company's secret of success.[6]

More frequently a rural setting and the paternalistic employer-employee relationship that often accompanied it provided the impetus for benefit programs. The Whitin family, for example, owned the town of Whitinsville and provided the customary community services—housing, schools, and churches. But the family also built a "Memorial Building" with an auditorium, a music room, a library, and meeting rooms for the city fathers to transact their presumably limited business.[7] The head of the Whital-Tatum Company of Millville, New Jersey, built a men's clubhouse complete with a gym, bathroom, club room, library, and auditorium. At the same time the company helped the local chapter of the Women's Christian Temperance Union establish a clubhouse for the mill boys, "where the ladies meet with the boys, reading, instructing, singing, and generally amusing them, so as to make their evenings pleasant and agreeable."[8] But even in these hospitable settings welfare programs seldom evolved; rather they were the product of explicit decisions by a minority of proprietors and managers, a fact that is apparent in the policies of four textile firms that introduced extensive welfare programs before 1890.

Peacedale Manufacturing of Peacedale, Rhode Island; Cheney Brothers of South Manchester, Connecticut; Ludlow Manufacturing of Ludlow, Massachusetts; and Willimantic Linen of Willimantic, Connecticut, built their plants in rural areas because of the availability of water power. Company houses and schools naturally followed. The four companies grew rapidly between 1850 and 1880; by 1880 only Peacedale had less than a thousand employees. Expansion led managers of the firms to introduce a variety of welfare activities. The ambitious Ludlow effort promised to make it "the most modern village of its class in the United States."[9] Representatives of the firms emphasized that a stable, efficient labor force was a major objective of their efforts; the Cheneys in particular insisted that they were "only conducting our business on business principles."[10]

All four firms had established libraries and numerous clubs and classes by 1880. Relief funds were not popular (assistance for the needy was still viewed as the employer's responsibility), but the Ludlow Associates built a hospital, and the Cheneys provided pensions for their elderly employees. Three of the four introduced the ten-hour day before the state required it. The crowning achievement of welfare work at South Manchester, Peacedale, and Ludlow was the erection of elaborate clubhouses: "Cheney Hall" in the 1870s, the "Hazard Memorial" in 1891, and the Ludlow clubhouse in 1905. Each company also had its own distinctive interests. Willimantic sponsored dancing classes; Peacedale introduced one of the first profit-sharing plans in the United States; the Cheneys built their homes among the workers' houses; and the Ludlow Associates established a textile school to train workers' sons for managerial jobs.[11]

Since the four firms undertook their programs for economic as well as social reasons, they did not hesitate to abandon unsuccessful measures. Thus the Peacedale managers ended profit sharing in 1909 after a strike, and the Willimantic Company abandoned its entire program except for the library in the 1890s because the workers seemed unappreciative. In 1881 Carroll Wright called the Willimantic effort one of the "grandest movements of the day," but Gertrude Beeks, a welfare secretary who visited the works twenty years later, described the company houses as "dirty and nasty."[12]

The famous "model" towns of the late nineteenth century—Saltaire, Guise, and Essen in Europe and Pullman in the United States—differed from Peacedale, South Manchester, Willimantic, and Ludlow only in degree. They were larger, better planned, and, above all, better publicized. Few visitors to Pullman were unimpressed. In 1884 the chiefs of the state bureaus of labor statistics, who presumably knew as much about industrial conditions as any group in the country, made a collective study of Pullman. Their report, printed in the individual state bureau reports the following year, cited Peacedale, South Manchester, and Willimantic. "But," the report concluded, "for comprehensive plan, for careful recognition of all the strong points, and the fullest anticipation of all weak features, for the beauty of the executed plan, for the financial and social success thereof, Pullman City . . . stands at the head."[13]

Unfortunately, the report's emphasis on "Pullman City" obscured the similarities between Pullman and the other progressive company towns. Subsequent observers also concentrated on the city, particularly its architecture and landscaping rather than the company and its welfare program, which encompassed the city and much more.[14] Indeed, Pullman's welfare program included the famous housing project; a modern, ventilated factory; an accident insurance plan and a company doctor; an excellent school system; a library; a savings and loan association; an athletic club; a company band; and men's and women's social clubs.[15]

Like other employers who introduced welfare programs, Pullman expected to profit from his investment. He wanted "to establish the place on such a basis as would exclude all baneful influences, believing that such a policy would result in the greatest measure of success . . . from a commercial point of view." That the enterprise should profit was important, he argued, from a social as well as an economic standpoint. "Capital will not invest in sentiment," he wrote. "But let it once be proved that enterprises of this kind are safe and profitable and we shall see great manufacturing corporations developing similar enterprises, and thus a new era will be introduced in the history of labor."[16]

But Pullman discovered that welfare plans were not an acceptable substitute for other, less visible activities. There were a number of labor disputes at the Pullman plant in the mid-1880s and two or three short strikes. Reports of despotic foremen, favoritism, and nepotism marred the company's reputation. The machine shops were "notoriously poorly managed," and Pullman executives advanced "their own interests . . . by methods no honorable man would resort to."[17] There are also indications of poor organization, a failure to delegate authority, and a breakdown in communications within the firm. The famous rent dispute which precipitated the 1894 strike was simply the last of a long series of problems. In the end Pullman's failure as a manger negated his success as a social innovator.

Because of the high cost of model town building and the apparent failure of the Pullman experiment, few late-nineteenth-century manufacturers adopted Pullman's approach and built "model" towns. One who did, Henry Disston, provides a useful contrast. Disston's community was an outgrowth of his decision to move from crowded downtown Philadelphia to suburban Tacony, where there was room for expansion. By the 1880s Tacony was a thriving company town; in 1887 investigators hailed it as a successful antidote to labor unrest. Disston and his sons succeeded because of an exclusive apprenticeship plan for workers' sons, low rents, and a benevolent approach to potentially disruptive issues such as layoffs.[18] N. O. Nelson, a maverick St. Louis businessman, was more flamboyantly unorthodox. In 1886 he introduced a profit-sharing plan to counter unrest and in 1890 built a new plant and the town of "Leclaire" near Edwardsville, Illinois. Nelson introduced the usual measures—schools, clubs, recreational facilities, a library, and a relief fund—although he emphasized private home ownership. He soon abandoned profit sharing for a stock distribution and purchase plan. In the 1890s he attempted to convert his business into a cooperative enterprise but retreated when some of the workers created "trouble."[19] Yet he avoided coercion, and his benevolent approach produced satisfactory results for more than thirty years.[20]

Of all the welfare plans that had appeared by the 1890s, none was better publicized or less attractive to employers than profit sharing. The reasons for this anomaly included the popularity of profit sharing in Europe and its apparent potential for reducing labor unrest. As a consequence scholars and publicists devoted numerous books and articles to the handful of American firms that literally offered "a dividend to labor."[21]

Their analyses suggest several conclusions. First, manufacturers often introduced profit-sharing plans for defensive reasons. Although successful plans usually had idealistic sponsors, the majority were designed to undermine unions or to realize other eminently practical aims.[22] Second, relatively few of the firms most closely identified with welfare work introduced profit-sharing. Even the better-known enterprises, such as the Pillsbury Mills of Minneapolis, the Ballard & Ballard Company of Louisville, and the Bourne Mills of Fall River, did not embrace other forms of welfare work before 1900. Finally, profit-sharing plans were often short-lived; of approximately fifty that appeared between 1869 and 1896, only twelve were operating at the later date.[23]

There were, of course, exceptions. The Peacedale Company and the Procter & Gamble Company of Ivorydale near Cincinnati operated profit-sharing programs for long periods. Procter & Gamble adopted its plan in 1887 in response to union agitation and a series of strikes. The company's managers wanted "to create an economically secure, steady, loyal and prospering working force."[24] But they differed from most sponsors of profit sharing by combining it with an ambitious program of welfare work, including a stock purchase plan, a pension plan for disabled employees, a savings and loan association, a short-lived cooperative store, a lunchroom for women workers, a library and reading room, and "distribution day"—an annual holiday when profit shares were announced.[25]

A common criticism of profit sharing was that its effect was diffuse, that it did not distinguish between the efficient worker and the idler. Apparently Procter & Gamble executives noted this difficulty, too, for they continually tinkered with the plan, attempting to introduce an incentive feature. In 1889 they created classes of profit sharers, reserved the right to withhold payment to "unworthy" employees, and levied fines for careless work. Finally in 1903 they dropped profit sharing in favor of the stock purchase plan; their explanation was that the new approach gave the employee a continuing interest in the firm.[26]

The abandonment of profit sharing by firms like Procter & Gamble emphasized the limits of the manufacturers' commitment to social experimentation. While giving lip service to humanitarian ends and making little effort to calculate the costs or benefits of particular plans, they ultimately justified welfare expenditures on economic grounds. And profit sharing, as one businessman explained, was "simply throwing money away."[27]

THE ADVENT OF SYSTEMATIC WELFARE WORK

Though welfare work had become prominent by 1900, two important changes after the turn of the century transformed it into a vigorous, influential movement. These were the rise of the welfare secretary—a company official who directed the firm's welfare programs—and regional and national organizations that promoted the cause of welfare work. Together they were responsible for the publicity that welfare activities received and for the increasing tendency of employers to adhere to standards based on the "best" practice. The catalysts for these developments were the social reform movements of the early twentieth century, which created a favorable intellectual climate, and, more specifically, the introduction of several ambitious welfare programs comparable in influence to the Pullman effort of the 1880s.[28]

The welfare plans of the William Filene Sons Company, the Boston department store, and the National Cash Register Company of Dayton, Ohio, both introduced in the late 1890s, had a marked impact on the development of systematic welfare work. Both foreshadowed the future course of welfare activity, notably the shift in emphasis from housing and community work to working conditions. The Filenes, moreover, introduced two important innovations. They employed, probably in 1897, the first professional "welfare secretary" to help manage their largely female labor force.[29] The following year they established the Filene Cooperative Association, the first company union, which administered the various clubs, services, and activities that the Filene Company sponsored. In addition it handled grievances, selected the welfare secretary, and under certain circumstances could overrule the management on questions of wages, hours, and working conditions. The Filene plan remained a stimulus to other employers in retailing and to many manufacturers for thirty years.[30]

In the short run, however, the NCR program had a greater impact. Equally ambitious and imaginative, it was the work of John H. Patterson, the flamboyant NCR president, whose unorthodox methods insured that virtually everything he did attracted wide attention and controversy. Although Patterson's contemporaries often regarded him and his ideas as eccentric or worse, they could not disregard him. It would have been difficult to find a prominent executive in 1900 who had not heard of Patterson or his spectacular schemes.

Patterson entered the cash register business in the early 1880s and succeeded by persuading saloon keepers that his device would encourage honesty among their employees. Production increased rapidly, and Patterson devoted much of his time to finding adequate facilities. In 1888 he moved from a rented shop in downtown Dayton to a family farm on the city's outskirts. Here he constructed a modest factory, only to find that it, too, was unsuitable for his burgeoning enterprise. Because of overcrowding—and the tyrannical activities of a few foremen—there were several strikes and even an attempt to burn the factory. In 1894 a large shipment of cash registers sent to England was returned because of faulty workmanship. On top of the other difficulties this disaster nearly bankrupted the company. Patterson decided that some dramatic action was necessary and in characteristic fashion completely reorganized his manufacturing operations and initiated a sweeping welfare program.[31]

In the following years Patterson introduced many of the latest technical and managerial innovations. He built a new factory, the "lightest, cleanest, and best ventilated [plant] in existence."[32] He also reorganized the purchasing and stores system to prevent delays and established a large tool department to ensure that the machinery was in top running order.[33] At the same time he drastically altered the managerial hierarchy, abolishing the post of superintendent and creating a unique and highly decentralized committee system. Henceforth an executive committee made up of the officers dealt with long-term problems while a factory committee consisting of department heads operated the plant.

Patterson's welfare program included suggestion boxes, prizes for the most efficient departments, and various health and sanitation measures. The company established a Relief Association, instituted strict safety rules

in the shops, and provided medical services for accident victims, baths for
the employees, a dining area and "rest rooms" for women workers, and
free cooking lessons. The women worked only eight hours and arrived
and left at different times from the men to minimize "unpleasantness and
danger."[34]

There were also traditional welfare activities, albeit with a Patterson
twist. NCR provided a library and reading room for its employees, ran a
kindergarten, organized gardening programs, and sponsored official clubs
for women workers, neighborhood boys, and mothers of employees. Patterson also established Sunday schools, choral societies, and musical
groups. He built a theater for the company's educational programs—including his frequent lectures—and the "NCR house," which served as a
club house and model worker's home. To oversee these activities he hired
a local woman, Lena Harvey, in 1897.

Before joining NCR, Harvey had been a deaconess—a religious social
worker—in the Dayton area. Patterson heard of her success in handling
unruly boys and had a long conference with her supervisor, the local Epis-
copalian minister.

> The following afternoon, who should come to Deaconess Home but
> Dr. Morgan [the minister]. "You didn't expect me, did you?" was his greeting.
> "I want to tell you that Mr. Patterson and I didn't sleep a wink last night—
> we were planning for a house at the plant, with rooms for all kinds of club
> activities. Here is the plan." He produced a sheet of foolscap paper across the
> top of which was written, "A Plan for a Settlement House at the N.C.R., Miss
> Harvey, Matron."[35]

The NCR programs operated successfully for five years, though not
without friction. Some of the executives thought Patterson was spending
too much, particularly for Harvey's work. Apparently they, like other employees, had reservations about Patterson's slogan, "It pays." Women
workers also resented the tactics used to "persuade" them to participate
in the welfare programs. Gertrude Beeks reported after a 1901 visit that
the welfare program had been "overdone."[36] In any event it was widely—
and mistakenly—believed that welfare work was responsible for a strike
and lockout that closed the plant in the summer of 1901 and led to a
reassessment of Patterson's programs.

A closer examination indicates that it was not welfare work but vestiges
of the driving system of supervision that precipitated the dispute. At the
same time he introduced welfare work, Patterson permitted local trade
unions to organize his skilled employees. Typically, he neglected to consider the views of his subordinates, including the brass foundry foreman,
a "driver" and anti-union zealot, who promptly fired the union molders
in his department. One hundred and fifty brass molders and metal polish-

ers struck in May 1901. Fearful that a union triumph would undermine discipline, Patterson first refused to reinstate the discharged men and then locked out the rest of his 2,400 employees.[37]

The six weeks' dispute that followed resulted in a costly victory for the company and important modifications in NCR policy. Patterson refused to reemploy the strikers and adopted an open-shop policy. He also eased out Miss Harvey and discontinued many of her "outside" activities, such as the neighborhood clubs. Most important was his response to the situation that produced the dispute. Since the conflict made it clear that the committee system and welfare organizations did not necessarily alter the way the plant operated, Patterson decided that an additional innovation was necessary. Soon after the lockout ended he appointed a young executive, Charles U. Carpenter, to head a new Labor Department.

The NCR Labor Department was the first modern personnel department in American industry. Before the lockout NCR had had an Employment Department, but it, like many such offices in other firms, served as little more than a hiring and record-keeping bureau.[38] Under Carpenter and his successors the Labor Department assumed a variety of other functions. It handled grievances and had the power to correct wage inequities; it shared with the foremen their power to fire—henceforth no employee could be permanently discharged without the approval of the Labor Department; it promoted sanitation and shop safety; it kept the management informed of relevant legislation and court decisions; and it conducted foremen's meetings to bring the supervisors "into sympathy with its aims and purposes."[39] Designed to curtail the powers of the foremen and increase the managers' influence over the workers, the NCR Labor Department anticipated the personnel management movement of the World War I period and after.

While Patterson was developing his program a group of charity workers in the New York area initiated the first organized effort to promote welfare work. In 1894 a number of professional social workers, led by William H. Tolman, began to meet informally to exchange ideas on social and civic problems. At Tolman's instigation, they invited several business leaders to join them and called their group the "Get-Together Club." Though their purpose was ostensibly to "promote free and open discussion by men of diverse views," the nature of the membership ensured that only conservative proposals were considered.[40] Two years later Tolman formed the League for Social Service, to advance the "Get-Together" concept. Josiah Strong, a prominent social gospel minister and journalist, became president and Tolman secretary.

Though the League promoted a wide range of social reform activities, Tolman took a special interest in welfare work. By the turn of the century his financial backers included virtually all the industrialists who had pioneered the development of welfare programs.[41] Patterson was a prominent member of the League, and Tolman visited the NCR plant on several occasions. When government officials asked Tolman to create an exhibit on "social economy" for the 1900 Paris Exhibition, he featured the activities of Patterson, Heinz, and the Filenes.[42] For the next three or four years, through innumerable speeches and articles, he promoted the cause of systematic welfare work. Gradually, the focus of the League's activities shifted to other matters, but not before it had made welfare work a familiar subject to progressive executives throughout the country.

In 1898, apparently without assistance from the League or Tolman, the Cleveland Chamber of Commerce undertook an extensive local effort to encourage welfare activities. Led by officials of the Sherwin-Williams Company, the Cleveland Hardware Company, and the Cleveland Twist Drill Company, all of whom had introduced welfare programs, the Industrial Committee of the Chamber hired a secretary, W. H. Moulton, and attempted to convince other Cleveland employers to adopt welfare plans. Moulton was highly successful: by 1901 "seventy-five of the more prominent firms are doing something," though the "something" was in many cases relatively little.[43] Tolman publicized the Cleveland effort, and employers like H. A. Sherwin of Sherwin-Williams lectured extensively on their activities. Like the League, however, the Cleveland Chamber's Industrial Committee provided little long-term leadership.[44]

The third and most important organization to promote welfare work was the Welfare Department of the National Civic Federation, the product of a series of employers' conferences sponsored by the NCF in 1904. Like most other NCF activities the real force behind the Welfare Department was NCF executive secretary Ralph W. Easley. Easley organized a meeting in January 1904 devoted to a discussion of "methods of installing and maintaining welfare work." The participants reconvened in February to formulate a plan of public education. They decided that the Welfare Department should act as a clearinghouse; it would supply information and hold conferences of employers and welfare secretaries. More than 100 employers, most of whom had experience with welfare work (three of the five officers were John W. Patterson, Edward A. Filene, and Cyrus McCormick, Jr.), agreed to provide financial support, and Gertrude Beeks, who had worked with Easley in Chicago before becoming welfare secretary at the McCormick plant, agreed to serve as secretary of the department.[45]

As its membership grew (to 250 in 1906 and 500 in 1911), the Department played an important role in disseminating information about welfare work. In addition to furnishing descriptions of the "best" practices, Beeks operated an employment service for welfare secretaries and recommended consultants to members.[46] In 1907, for example, W. M. Wood, President of the American Woolen Company and a department member, employed an expert to organize a lunchroom in his company's new mill in Lawrence, Massachusetts. The expert trained the lunchroom manager, selected the proper equipment, and generally helped the mill officials plan the operation of the facility.[47]

In addition to promoting specific activities, the League and the NCF Welfare Department sought to institutionalize and professionalize welfare work, largely through the introduction of welfare secretaries. As early as 1899 Tolman emphasized the need for an expert—"one who can devote his whole time to becoming acquainted with the employees and promoting their general welfare; one who looks after sanitary conditions, seeks to increase the general intelligence, fosters a healthful social life and strives to improve the general morale."[48] In the following years other advocates of welfare work, such as Gertrude Beeks, echoed Tolman with considerable effect. Employers with large numbers of female employees were easily convinced that a specialist was necessary to understand the problems and attitudes of women workers.

By 1906 there were more than twenty welfare secretaries, most of whom had backgrounds similar to Lena Harvey's. The women were teachers or nurses or had had experience in religious or philanthropic work. The men came from similar vocations; many had been doctors or ministers. Charles Henderson, a prominent reformer, wrote that there was "no one science or art which can be mastered in preparation for all kinds of welfare work."[49] The common denominator was an interest in improving the lives of working people in ways consistent with the employer's economic objectives.

The duties of welfare secretaries were also diverse. Some had explicit administrative responsibilities; others were merely "advisors." Secretaries trained as teachers, doctors, and nurses devoted most of their time to their respective specialties but were expected to perform other duties as well. Besides administering one or more programs, secretaries acted as troubleshooters and, in subtle ways, as disciplinarians. Depending on the firm, they took over some or most of the personnel functions that foremen traditionally performed and that personnel departments and labor unions later assumed. This was a demanding, perhaps impossible task, and the welfare secretary often led a precarious existence. The ones who had specialized duties, such as the operation of clinics or schools, and avoided controversy often held their jobs for many years, but the more outspoken and ambitious secretaries, such as Lena Harvey or Samuel S. Marquis, the head of Henry Ford's famous Sociological Department, seldom survived for long. The overt or covert opposition of superintendents or foremen, occasional charges of interference by workers, and changes in management often made the secretary's position untenable.

Fortunately, the papers of one of the earliest and most successful welfare secretaries provide a detailed picture of her impact on the supervisors and the workers. Elizabeth F. Briscoe, welfare secretary at Joseph Bancroft & Sons from 1902 until her death in 1919, began her career as a teacher in the Bancroft Company school in 1879. She became a welfare secretary when the company introduced an extensive reform program in response to the growth of its largely female labor force and of labor unrest in other communities. Bancroft installed safety equipment, lockers, dressing rooms; organized cooking and sewing classes, employee clubs, and recreational activities; and, in 1911, introduced an informal pension plan.[50]

Briscoe had several major areas of responsibility. She administered the benefit plans and clubs and became an intermediary between the management and workers, usurping the foreman's traditional role. The successful welfare secretary, she wrote,

> must first understand the feeling of the employer towards the employees. Welfare work is an expression of the friendly interest of the employer in the employee. . . . She is the exponent of [the] friendly interest of the employer in those employed.
>
> I act as the representative of the employees, and, as such, bring before the firm, or the heads of the various departments, any grievances that affect the employees individually or collectively.[51]

In addition she corresponded frequently with other welfare secretaries, visited firms with similar programs, gave lectures, and answered inquiries about Bancroft policies. In 1912 the company sent her to Europe to obtain a firsthand knowledge of welfare programs there.

Although Briscoe thus handled a wide range of labor and personnel problems, three were of particular concern to her. The first—and to her perhaps the most important—was to maintain a proper moral atmosphere in and out of the factory. This became a special challenge in 1907, when the company built a boardinghouse for single employees. Before construction began she made an extensive study of model boardinghouses. To operate it she hired Minnie C. Clark, a matron who had worked for the Ludlow Associates. The new woman arrived in June 1907, when the boardinghouse opened, but remained less than a year, apparently unable to meet Briscoe's high standards.[52] Briscoe was equally strict when the employees protested that there were too many rules and refused to live in the boardinghouse. Rejecting compromise, she opened the building to single men and older women and soon obtained enough occupants.[53]

A second challenge—one that neither Briscoe nor the Bancrofts had foreseen in 1902—was the growing role of government in factory operations. Briscoe's position was particularly difficult: as a reformer she could hardly object to factory and child labor legislation, but as a representative of the Bancrofts she could not endorse costly or "irresponsible" regulations. Her letters reflect her ambiguity. She approved a 1905 law setting minimum ages and educational requirements for minors and insisted that the foremen comply with it. But several years later she opposed legislation introduced by the local Consumers' League that would have enabled the factory inspector to stop the use of unsafe machinery. The foremen, Briscoe wrote, "act really as inspectors."[54]

Finally, she encountered many problems in interpreting the "feeling of the employer toward the employees." Often this task was distasteful. One woman, for example, learned that her husband was "unsatisfactory in every department and will not be rehired."[55] Another, whose husband had been involved in a 1907 walkout, received a similar message:

> There were a number of other strikers who went out at the same time as your husband, and if one black ball was lifted they would all have to be. At the time of the strike, Mr. John Bancroft talked to the men, and reasoned with them—gave them an opportunity to stay on at their work, but without avail. I feel very sorry for you and your little children, and hope that your husband may soon get work some place.[56]

At other times her job was more pleasant. On one occasion she paid the passage of a young employee so she could rejoin her mother in England (a girl "should not be without a mother's . . . care and guidance"); on another she arranged for an injured employee to stay with a local farmer for several weeks so he "could have the benefit of fresh air and fresh eggs and milk."[57]

Briscoe enjoyed uninterrupted success for nearly a decade. Because of her long tenure, close relations with the Bancrofts, and unquestioned loyalty to the firm, she avoided the criticism that plagued many early welfare secretaries. In 1910 she survived a contest with H. L. Gantt when the Bancrofts concluded that her methods were more likely than his to increase productivity and maintain labor-management harmony. In the same year she introduced a more thorough accident prevention program, and in 1911 she became the administrator of a formal pension plan. Yet she did not escape unscathed. In 1911 the younger executives, professional managers rather than family members, rebelled at the continued dominance of the aging Bancrofts and won control of the company's executive committee. This upheaval was unrelated to the Bancrofts' welfare policy, but it had important implications for Briscoe's position. After 1912 she reported to the committee rather than to the president, and the scant evidence that remains suggests that her influence lessened. Ironically, the very factors that had insulated her from criticism in the early years—her seniority and devotion to the Bancrofts—ultimately led to her indirect demotion.[58]

Elizabeth Briscoe was typical of the growing number of welfare secretaries. Her background and varied roles within the firm—administrator, advisor, and policymaker—were characteristic of early welfare workers. In addition, her function as coordinator of information about welfare work was one that most welfare secretaries adopted, consciously or not. By 1915 dozens of men and women like Briscoe worked in American industry combatting the "labor problem" through "assistance when needed [and] . . . friendly help and sympathy," and simultaneously bringing out "whatever . . . strength and success lies latent for better business results."[59]

THE PRACTICE OF WELFARE WORK, 1905 – 1915

By 1905 welfare work was no longer the erratic, unorganized activity it had been a decade before. There had been "so many experiments so uniformly successful" that "the practicality of sane 'welfare work' . . . is not open to legitimate question."[60] In the following decade a growing number of manufacturers were attracted to the "experiments" of the previous twenty years. Their efforts were seldom innovative; with few exceptions they remained well within the bounds established by the pioneers. Yet they extended welfare programs to thousands of workers and helped establish the patterns that shaped the personnel management movement of the war years.

The difficulty of tracing the diffusion of welfare programs under these circumstances is apparent from the problems contemporaries had in identifying the leaders. Handbooks and guides to welfare programs, which had begun to appear in the 1890s, proliferated after the turn of the century. Works by Nicholas Gilman, Edwin Shuey, Victor Olmstead, Budgett Meakin, William Tolman, and the United States Bureau of Labor Statistics described the activities of progressive firms. But there were substantial differences of opinion over what constituted a "progressive" policy.[61] Meakin, for example, listed 119 American firms in 1905; the Bureau of Labor Statistics included only 51 companies eight years later; and W. Jett Lauck and Edgar Sydenstricker maintained in 1917 that "1500 to 2000 concerns" were engaged in welfare work."[62] The problem, obviously, was that many firms adopted only a few aspects of welfare work. And since there were no objective standards for determining which of these activities were most important, each establishment was a potential candidate for the leader's mantle.[63]

By comparing lists I have identified at least 40 manufacturing firms that introduced extensive welfare programs in the decade before World War I. There were undoubtedly others and, of course, hundreds that adopted more modest programs. But the assiduousness of the handbook writers and government officials in ferreting out the leaders suggests that table 8 includes a large majority of "progressive" manufacturing firms.[64] The 40

Table 8. Firms with extensive welfare programs, 1905–1915

Textiles
Joseph Bancroft, Wilmington, DE
Pacific Mills (American Woolen Co.), Lawrence, MA
Amoskeag Mills, Manchester, NH
Talbot Mills, No. Billerica, MA
Proximity Mfg., Greensboro, NC
Pelzer Mfg., Pelzer, SC
Graniteville Mfg., Graniteville, SC
Victor Mfg., Greer, SC
Dan River Mills, Danville, VA
Eagle & Phoenix Mills, Columbus, GA
Monaghan Mills, Greenville, SC
Piedmont Mfg., Piedmont, SC

Machinery
Remington Typewriter, Ilion, NY
National Cash Register, Dayton, OH
Cleveland Twist Drill, Cleveland, OH
International Harvester, Chicago, IL
United Shoe Machinery, Beverly, MA
Weston Electric, Newark, NJ
Westinghouse Air Brake, Wilmerding, PA
General Electric, various plants
Waltham Watch, Waltham, MA
Western Electric, New York, NY, and Chicago, IL

Iron and Steel
United States Steel, various plants
American Rolling Mill, Middletown, OH
Colorado Fuel & Iron, Pueblo, CO
Cleveland Hardware, Cleveland, OH

Other
J. H. Williams (metals), Brooklyn, NY
Goodyear Tire & Rubber (rubber), Akron, OH
Firestone Tire & Rubber (rubber), Akron, OH
Procter & Gamble (soap), Cincinnati, OH
Joseph & Feiss (clothing), Cleveland, OH
Gorham Mfg. (jewelry), Providence, RI
J. B. Stetson (hats), Philadelphia, PA
Curtis Publishing (printing and publishing), Philadelphia, PA
Natural Food (food), Niagara Falls, NY
T. G. Plant (shoes), Boston, MA
Plymouth Cordage (rope), Plymouth, MA
Celluloid Co. (novelties), Newark, NJ
H. J. Heinz (food), Pittsburgh, PA
Solvay Process (chemicals), Solvay, NY

firms were concentrated in textiles, machinery, and, to a lesser degree, iron and steel. Nearly all were large, with more than 500 employees in 1905, and most employed large numbers of female workers.

While each firm acted independently, the handbooks suggest several common reasons for the introduction of welfare work.[65] In general the managers of these firms responded to the same kinds of problems that led many manufacturers to embrace systematic and scientific management. Unsettled conditions, often a result of employment growth, seemed to demand a new approach. However, the managers of these firms also shared—or professed to share—a deep concern over the inequities that had developed in American society. They bemoaned the loss of personal contacts with employees and the apparent increase in labor-management conflict. Stuart Brandes has concluded that "the most prevalent feeling among businessmen who embarked on welfare programs . . . was a vague sense that they had lost contact with their employees."[66] Finally, most were major employers of women and children, for whom they felt a special sense of responsibility.[67] Contemporary critics emphasized the degrading character of factory work, the noise, dirt, and monotony, the physical frailty of the female operative, and the dangers of immorality when young women were exposed constantly to strange, rough men.[68] The "responsible" employer could not be indifferent.

Of the 40 firms, those that employed large numbers of women became more deeply committed to welfare work at an earlier date. Even Patterson's schemes, the most comprehensive of all, were heavily weighted toward the women who constituted one-sixth of the NCR labor force. By contrast the steel and rubber manufacturers, who employed few women workers, apparently reacted to special circumstances. Gary and George Perkins, the principal instigators of welfare work at U.S. Steel, wanted to promote a "good trust" image as well as retain their skilled employees and forestall unionization.[69] Colorado Fuel and Iron introduced welfare work at Pueblo incidentally as part of an elaborate community service program for its isolated mining camps.[70] Goodyear and Firestone began welfare work during a period of rapid expansion, largely because the Akron community could not meet the workers' needs for housing and recreation.[71]

Once the manufacturer decided that some action was necessary, the next step was to ascertain what measures would be effective. By 1905 there were numerous descriptions of successful programs in many fields; Beeks and the NCF Welfare Department, moreover, were ready with advice, literature, and names of qualified secretaries. For a modest investment of time and money any executive could familiarize himself with the latest information. But it seems likely that the availability of information and counsel did more to spur interest in welfare work than to advance any particular plan. In any event the meager evidence suggests that many manufacturers went to the NCF and other agencies with specific proposals already in mind.

The single most important determinant of the type of program a manufacturer introduced was the location of the plant.[72] If it was in a rural area some possibilities were foreclosed and others enhanced. Clubhouses, recreation centers, athletic programs, and adult education courses naturally followed assistance to schools and churches.[73] Yet isolated mills seldom introduced pension or insurance plans, apparently because of the custom of providing informally for the sick and the aged. Contrary to the usual pattern, paternalism could deter the adoption of welfare work.

If the factory was located in a city, the pattern was often reversed. Libraries, social clubs, recreational activities, and evening or weekend activities held little promise; the employees had access to other diversions and often lived too far from the plant to return after work. NCR, Heinz, Curtis Publishing, and Stetson solved this problem by organizing lunchhour activities or by allowing their employees to quit early on special days. U.S. Steel did not make such concessions, and as a result the Pittsburgh area was known for its unused libraries and clubhouses.[74] On the other hand, cafeterias, "rest rooms," medical departments, and insurance and savings plans were of special value to urban workers. Such programs offered workers a degree of protection against the unhealthy conditions in which they frequently lived.

A second basic consideration was the composition of the labor force. Manufacturers who employed large numbers of women usually emphasized measures to make the factory more habitable. Lunchrooms, "rest rooms," landscaping, and related activities conveyed the idea of a home away from home. At the same time classes in domestic economy, social clubs, outings, and dances (women only) assured the worker that she need not sacrifice her femininity when she entered the predominantly male world of the factory. But because the female operative was (or was assumed to be) a secondary wage earner and probably a transient, she was not offered a pension, a savings program, or an insurance plan. Conversely, in the minority of cases where most workers were men, manufacturers shunned comfort and domesticity and emphasized financial security and recreation. The steel mills and tire factories were cheerless places, but their employees had generous savings and insurance plans and athletic programs of every description.[75]

Needless to say, multiplant corporations attempted to tailor their programs to particular factories. The Westinghouse Electric plant located in downtown Pittsburgh introduced an elaborate industrial education program for its employees, but little else. The Westinghouse Air Brake Company in suburban Wilmerding built a company town complete with YMCA, library, kindergarten, and hospital.[76] The General Electric Company also operated different plans at its Schenectady, Lynn, and Harrison, New Jersey, works.[77] The United States Steel program was so decentralized that it is virtually impossible to discover what was actually done by the various subsidiaries and plants. It seems clear, though, that until the formation of the corporation's Safety, Relief, Sanitation, and Welfare Bureau in 1908, Gary, Perkins, and other Big Steel executives exercised only nominal control over the factory officials.[78]

In contrast to this diversity there was relative unanimity on the proper way to administer a welfare program. With few exceptions manufacturers agreed that they should control and direct the benefit programs. Even in the case of mutual benefit plans, largely or wholly financed by employees, they often interceded to ensure that only responsible employees were elected to positions of trust. M. W. Alexander of General Electric explained how he intervened without appearing to intervene:

> I take pains to see that the Secretary of the different divisions is the proper man; for instance, when it comes time to elect the Secretary, I call in one of the men and say, "I hear that Smith is going to be elected Secretary of your division." He will say, "Is that so? I hadn't heard of that." I will say, "Yes, and I think he is a good man." Then he will go out and say to some one else, "Say, Smith would be a good man for Secretary of our Association." In that way it happens that I influence the men to put good men in office.[79]

Managers like Alexander must have been shocked at the assertion of William Redfield of the J. H. Williams Company, a welfare advocate and later Secretary of Commerce, that welfare plans should not be imposed on workers.[80]

There were several reasons for retaining control. First, employers introduced welfare work for specific purposes and logically sought to ensure that their objectives were realized. The fact that they viewed welfare appropriations as investments dictated a businesslike approach to their utilization. Second, they feared that agitators and trade unionists would capture the clubs and insurance societies. And finally, they often introduced welfare work to aid people who were considered incapable of intelligent decision making. Women workers in particular were thought to be at the mercy of their environment. To suggest that they could help themselves was to question the need for welfare work. During World War I, as this view changed, "industrial democracy" plans, emphasizing worker participation, superseded welfare work. The employment of women in men's jobs and the campaign to "Americanize" immigrants, to transform them into first-class citizens, were the first steps toward the company unions of the 1920s.

Manufacturers who administered welfare programs found that they created new and often onerous administrative burdens for themselves and their chief associates. Some employers did not consider this a problem; after all, welfare work was supposed to restore personal relationships.[81] But most had neither the time nor the inclination to assume the additional responsibility. Their answer was to hire a welfare secretary, such as Lena Harvey or Elizabeth Briscoe, who would direct the day-to-day operation of the welfare plans. At least half of the leading firms had a high-level staff employee whose functions were similar to Briscoe's.[82] Others employed teachers, nurses, safety directors, or other functionaries who shared the duties. Textile mills most often employed a person with the title "welfare secretary."

In a few cases the welfare secretary had evolved into a personnel manager by 1915. But in most instances he or she remained a social worker who was only occasionally involved in discussions of wages, hours, recruitment, discipline, and other issues that directly affected production. The welfare secretary's threat to the foreman was usually less obvious and was with few exceptions confined to two areas. The secretary shared responsibility for maintaining morale (listening to grievances, handling personal problems, and in theory acting as a conduit between the management and the workers) and effectively prevented any accretion in the foreman's power. These modest achievements seldom satisfied the secretaries, however, and they gradually extended their activities into labor recruitment, training, and discipline. The NCR experience in this, as in many other aspects of early personnel management, was instructive. Lena Harvey was an archetypal welfare secretary, but modern personnel work was not introduced until after her departure. Clarence J. Hicks, an apparently ineffective welfare secretary, became one of the best-known personnel managers of the 1920s and 1930s. He understandably hailed the shift from "somewhat paternalistic" to "sound" programs.[83]

Perhaps because the welfare secretary rarely posed a direct threat to the foreman's personnel functions, there are few records of the supervisors' reactions to welfare work or the secretaries. In a few cases production managers protested that welfare activities interfered with their work or that the secretaries spent too much money.[84] But there is no way of knowing if these men articulated the foremen's views or if they merely voiced the typical engineer's distaste for "coddling" employees.

The workers likewise left little record of their feelings about welfare work. The handbooks often noted improvements in morale that occurred after the introduction of lunchrooms, rest rooms, or insurance plans, but they were hardly unbiased. Some employees doubtless resented welfare work or considered it demeaning. Manufacturers often acknowledged that it did not automatically ensure against strikes or labor agitation and that welfare plans could provoke opposition if carried too far.[85] C. L. Close, director of U.S. Steel's Safety, Relief, Sanitation, and Welfare Bureau, recalled the case of a teacher at one of the plants of the National Tube Company who sent an employee's child home with instructions to wash her face and hands.

> Next day she returned, but her hands and face indicated that she had paid no more attention to them than had her mother. The young woman said, "Jenny, did you tell your mother what I told you?" "Yes, Madam." "What did she say?" With some reluctance Jenny answered, "She said you could go to hell." [86]

While these examples hardly constitute a basis for generalization, most workers apparently accepted the programs without great enthusiasm or significant objection. They were prepared to trade cooperation for tangible gains. [87] As a consequence both proponents and critics of welfare programs were able to find abundant evidence to support their contentions. In the last analysis, welfare work probably had a greater impact on the evolution of business administration than on the worker's attitude toward the supervisor or the firm.

Thus, through a process that bore striking resemblances to the steps by which the managers increased their control over production, the employer extended his control over the factory worker. The manager perceived a problem (whether it was an inadequate supply of skilled workers, labor unrest, or a growing gap between the management and the worker), adopted various ad hoc solutions, employed specialists to deal with the problem, and slowly increased the specialists' responsibility at the expense of the foremen. The apprentice supervisors and welfare workers (they were occasionally the same) in turn standardized and systematized their functions as their authority increased. The process seldom occurred exactly in this way, of course, and welfare secretaries still occupied precarious positions in the factory of 1915. But a seed had been planted that, under wartime conditions, would grow into the personnel management movement of the postwar period.

7 The New Factory System and the Worker

"Rest yourself," he said, "we work hard when de big bosses come." [Charles R. Walker, *Steel: The Diary of a Furnace Worker* (New York, 1922), 48.]

"It was no use for a puddler to come into a mill . . . without his tickets, password and grip, and the first thing he would do was to inquire for the mill committee. . . . Oh, that the good old times were here today in the puddle department. . . . What a pity that things are not as they were. . . ." ["One of the Boys," in *National Labor Tribune* 27 (March 9, 1899)]

"Isn't there some way we could work things out so that it would be good for both parties?" [Sidney Hillman, ca. 1912, quoted in Mathew Josephson, *Sidney Hillman, Statesman of American Labor* (Garden City, 1952), 66.]

As the factory labor force grew and the proportion of employees who worked in large plants increased relative to the total, the workers' options also changed. In aggressively managed plants, management systems supplemented or superceded the foreman's traditional authority, creating a more structured environment. At the same time large firms provided attractive financial incentives for compliant employees. Workers could take advantage of improved working conditions, higher wages, and welfare plans or they could seek opportunities in smaller plants or other industries that offered greater autonomy. The haphazard data on employee turnover suggests that both choices were popular. But there was another option. If workers responded collectively, through a union, they could influence the operation of the factory and win even better wages and working conditions. Yet before they achieved any tangible gains or even a formal voice, they had to overcome major obstacles. Finding a basis for collective action was difficult, given the variety of occupations and skills in the factory and the varying ethnic backgrounds of the workers. Overcoming the employer's hostility to a formal workers' voice was even more challenging. Workers thus faced a dilemma: they had more to gain by organizing than most wage earners because of the productivity of the factory, but forming and sustaining a union was more difficult than in most industries because of the nature of the enterprise and the employer's power. As factories grew in size and complexity, the workers' dilemma became painfully evident.

A COLLECTIVE TRADITION, 1880 – 1895

Mechanization, loss of autonomy, intrusive supervision, and the conflicts inherent in the employment relationship created an often contentious environment in nineteenth-century factories. Aggrieved workers had two choices, exit and voice.[1] They could leave in search of a more accommodating employer, or they could stay and express their dissatisfaction. Their voice could be informal or formal. The informal voice, like the informal system of worker recruitment, had numerous forms and nuances, most of which attracted little attention. They included casual negotiations with supervisors; explicit or implicit limits on output, noted in chapter 3; understandings about what was and was not appropriate behavior; and the like.[2] Although generalizations are hazardous, three seem warranted: informal group activity was ubiquitous; employers viewed it as a cost of production, permissible as long as it did not impose excessive burdens; and factory workers had fewer opportunities to influence the character of their work and their relations with supervisors than miners, construction workers, manufactory employees, and others who were less dependent on machinery. When social scientists discovered the informal workplace organization in the 1920s, they focused almost exclusively on factory operations, presumably because the collective behavior of other industrial employees was already well known and taken for granted.[3]

Factory workers were vastly more influential when they organized formally and made explicit demands on their employers. Formal organizations were hard to create because of the range of occupations and skills in the typical factory and the employer's hostility to a formal voice. Yet in industries such as shoemaking and printing workers successfully organized and bargained with employers.[4] Like other unions, factory workers' organizations were based on the workers' labor market power. They defended members against encroachments by outsiders, blunted the effects of technological change, restrained greedy employers, and provided a mechanism for expressing the workers' social and political interests. The attractiveness of these services grew as market pressures increased and ethnic competition intensified. Although most evidence of worker militancy is anecdotal and local, it is likely that factory worker activism peaked in the 1880s and early 1890s, when factory workers' organizations became active in a variety of industries and received more publicity than ever before.

The strike data that the commissioner of labor collected from 1881 to 1905 is the best single source on the turmoil that accompanied the growth of the industrial labor force. Table 9, based on that information, compares the experiences of various groups. It lists the number of strikes, the percentage "ordered" by union leaders (versus spontaneous or "wildcat"

Table 9. Strikes, 1881–1894

Industry	Strikes	Percent ordered	Percent failed[a]	Strikers	Percent female[b]	Relative incidence
Construction	8,565	94	45	372,869	<1	.026
Mining	2,769	59	58	934,048	0	.198
Transportation	2,104	61	59	301,365	<1	.024
Manufacturing	15,533	75	45	980,608	18	.016
Clothing, tobacco	6,347	91	34	274,608	29	.049
Textiles	795	28	63	95,429	47	.015
Metals	2,379	68	47	230,706	<1	.043
Glass, pottery	344	58	57	35,992	11	.040
Boots, shoes	807	78	57	43,038	30	.023

Sources: Third Annual report of the Commissioner of Labor, 1887, Strikes and Lockouts (Washington, 1888), table 6, pp. 782–829; *Tenth Annual Report of the Commissioner of Labor, 1894, Strikes and Lockouts,* vol. 2 (Washington, 1896), table 6, pp. 1500–57.

[a] 1887–1894 only. "Percent failed" is the percent of establishments involved in the strike at which the strike failed.

[b] 1887–1894 only.

strikes), the proportion of establishments where the strikes failed, the aggregate number of strikers between 1881 and 1894, the percentage of the strikers who were female, and the average number of strikers per year compared to the number of employees in that industry, a measure of the intensity of strike activity.

Table 9 indicates that strikes were frequent, positively correlated with union organizing and bargaining, most likely to be successful if union-ordered, and uniformly risky undertakings for workers, regardless of industry. Mining was by far the most turbulent industry. It employed only 6 percent of all workers in industry and transportation, but it accounted for as many strikers as manufacturing, which employed nearly 60 percent of all industrial workers. In the 1880s and 1890s, miners were thirteen times more likely to be strikers than factory workers. In the manufacturing category, clothing and tobacco accounted for more than one-third of all strikes and strikers. Metals, embracing the iron and steel, foundry, and machinery industries, were also turbulent, while shoe making was comparatively peaceful. Union activism in clothing and tobacco contributed to the contentious atmosphere; in shoe making, it was a force for stability. Most surprising, perhaps, was the large number of female strikers. Indeed, women workers were only marginally less likely to be strikers than men.[5] The women's behavior, like the miners', emphasized the role of environmental influences. Variations between industries reflected the character of the work more than the characteristics of the workers.

The data provides some support for the common observation that workers producing for local markets were more likely to organize and bargain (and strike) because of the employer's isolation and vulnerability.

Construction workers were obvious examples. But local market production does not explain the militancy of clothing and cigar makers, shoe workers, and many metal workers or the high failure rate of building trades strikes. Manufacturers producing for local markets could be as determined as their employees. When they worked together they were often as successful in thwarting organization as the largest firms.

More compelling is the association between strikers, union activity, and workers who retained a high degree of workplace autonomy. Miners and construction workers were obvious examples. Railroad and streetcar employees also worked independently, though they were subject to rigid schedules. In manufacturing, clothing and tobacco (primarily cigar) workers, clustered in artisan shops and manufactories, stand out. Like miners and construction workers, they set their own pace, worked with minimal supervision, and operated independently of their co-workers. Their relations with their employers resembled the relations between an outside contractor and a business; issues of price (the piece rate) and time (the hours of labor) were paramount, and disputes arose when either side proposed changes in the status quo. New York, the center of artisan production, was also the strike center in both industries.[6]

The other manufacturing industries were characterized by factory production and a high degree of mechanization. Many strikes were the results of bargaining impasses between employers and high-skill groups such as lasters, weavers, glass blowers, and potters. Others involved unorganized workers (or workers who organized after striking) and less clearly defined goals. A rate reduction, change in the length of the work day, or "speed up" in the pace of work was often the precipitating event. Factory workers easily disrupted production but had great difficulty sustaining strikes that depended on cooperation between employees from different departments or with different occupations. Clashing interests and perspectives and the low pay of the less skilled made prolonged strikes as unlikely as industrial unionism. The textile industry provides many examples of these distinctions. Skilled workers' strikes in Paterson and Philadelphia resembled carpenters' or bricklayers' strikes, whereas more general uprisings at Fall River resembled strikes in unorganized coal mines.[7]

These patterns temporarily merged in the mid-1880s with the dramatic rise and fall of the Knights of Labor, a "hurricane" that swept through the labor force.[8] The Knights' inclusive appeal, simultaneous identification with traditional values and labor radicalism, and broad reformist agenda accounted for their remarkable popularity. Organizational deficiencies and poor leadership explained their precipitous decline. Yet for a few years the Knights served as a magnet for discontent, embracing hard-headed craft unionists, socialists of varying perspectives, skilled and unskilled workers, and a surprising number of individuals (such as farmers

Table 10. Knights of Labor local assemblies, distribution by industry (percent of total)

Industry	Pennsylvania	Massachusetts	Illinois
Service	3	8	10
Construction	3	6	4
Transportation	2	4	2
Mining	43	<1	23
Mixed	19	23	35
Manufacturing	30	58	25
Clothing	2	2	4
Tobacco	2	2	1
Boots, shoes	2	24	<1
Iron, steel	5	<1	2
Textiles	4	7	<1
N =	1297	434	568

Source: Jonathan Garlock, *Guide to the Local Assemblies of the Knights of Labor* (Westport, 1982).

and homemakers) who never before considered themselves potential union members or even workers.[9] Even in their major role, as a union, the Knights were different. They often included different occupations within a single local or "assembly," which became a "mixed assembly." In Pennsylvania, Massachusetts, and Illinois, which accounted for one-fifth of all local assemblies, between 19 and 35 percent of the assemblies were "mixed." Though mixed assemblies were not effective bargaining organizations, they could be highly influential. In the late 1880s, for example, the Knights elected dozens of mayors and other local officials, mostly in midwestern towns. In Milwaukee, Cincinnati, and Chicago, among others, they posed a brief but formidable challenge to the two-party system.[10]

To what extent did the Knights attract factory workers? Table 10 summarizes the pattern of organization in Pennsylvania, Massachusetts, and Illinois. It excludes assemblies that had no occupational designation (approximately 20 percent of the total) and assumes that mixed assemblies included relatively few factory workers and even fewer employees from the largest plants. With these qualifications, the data suggests that the Knights made only limited inroads among factory workers except in the shoe industry. At least three-quarters of the local assemblies in Pennsylvania and Illinois consisted of nonmanufacturing employees or manufacturing employees who worked in artisan shops or manufactories. Less than 10 percent of the assemblies consisted of employees of textile, iron and steel, and other large plants.

The comparatively low level of factory organization presumably reflected obstacles to organization more than indifference or hostility to the labor movement. Case studies of factory workers report the same enthusiasm and sense of expectation that animated other workers. The most compelling example was the New England shoe industry, which had a long history of organization in manufactories and factories. In the 1870s the Knights of St. Crispin embraced both types of establishments and became the largest American union. Many local assemblies of the Knights of Labor were simply reconstituted Crispin lodges.[11] The workers' behavior reflected various influences, though two stand out: the prevalence of native-born workers and English-speaking immigrants and the predominance of small, primitive factories.

Both characteristics of the industry encouraged the workers to develop a formal voice. The relative homogeneity of the labor force removed one of the most significant barriers to organization. The Crispins had vigorously fought the advent of "green hands," or inexperienced factory workers, but the Knights (and their successors) discovered that the green hands were highly organizable. The women were as assertive as the men.[12] Comparatively small (typically less than two hundred employees), simple factories and labor-intensive production processes also reduced the employer's power vis-à-vis the workers. In Lynn, the industry center, manufacturers rented space in large multistory buildings and leased machinery. Most companies operated sporadically, with long seasonal shutdowns. Over the course of a career, the typical shoe worker was likely to have many employers. The most ambitious and fortunate workers became employers themselves. In this setting, there was little advantage in creating a specialized environment, a distinctive management, or a loyal labor force. Manufacturers relied on skilled and experienced employees to fill their orders. Workers in turn depended on their unions to serve as employment agencies, police agreements with employers, and provide benefits during layoffs. Though strikes and lockouts were common, unions played important roles in the operation of the industry. Most employers recognized those contributions, however reluctantly.[13]

Other factory workers organized with similar enthusiasm but less success. In Saginaw, Michigan, lumber workers conducted one of the Knights' most ambitious and disruptive strikes in 1885.[14] The most memorable incidents of the eight-hour campaign of 1886 were outgrowths of strikes at the McCormick works in Chicago and the North Chicago Rolling Mills plant in Milwaukee, among the largest manufacturing establishments in their respective communities. Detroit factory workers were also leaders of the strike movement.[15] Most impressive was the behavior of low-skill textile workers, especially in the southern piedmont. In 1885 and 1886 more than twenty textile assemblies appeared in Georgia and the Carolinas. The most substantial organizations were in Columbus, Atlanta, and Augusta, Georgia. Augusta Local 5030, with more than 2000 members, was "the South's most militant local."[16] Its long, bitter, and ultimately disastrous strike against the city's manufacturers in the summer and fall of 1886 symbolized the workers' willingness to organize and the formidable problems that they and other factory workers faced.

The Knights' ideology and popularity temporarily obscured other contemporary developments that would make the voice option even more difficult and costly. The influx of immigrants from eastern and southern Europe raised cultural barriers between skilled and unskilled workers and sharpened distinctions between jobs. One example was typical: At the Laughlin and Junction steel company, skilled employees seceded from the Knights local assembly in 1887 and affiliated with the Amalgamated Association of Iron and Steel Workers because of the assembly's industrial structure. A battle between the two organizations led to the defeat and collapse of the local assembly, leaving two-thirds of the employees without a formal voice. The Knights had failed to recognize "the desire for status distinctions between the skilled and less-skilled employees."[17]

At the same time, the transformation of iron and steel production emphasized the vulnerability of many skilled worker unions to technological innovation. The advent of mass production in the steel industry created new jobs and skills and tilted the workplace balance in favor of managers, engineers, and technical staff workers. Companies that built new steel plants refused to deal with the Amalgamated Association. By 1890 the union was confined to smaller, specialist iron works and a few steel mills that had started as iron plants.[18] The best known of these was Carnegie's Homestead Works, near Pittsburgh. The union's strength at Homestead reflected its aggressive leadership, close relations with groups that represented the unskilled, and ability to take advantage of the close-knit, isolated Homestead community.[19] The company's extraordinary efforts to destroy the union, culminating in the famous 1892 lockout, were testimony to that strength. In the following years other steel companies followed Carnegie's lead, and the Amalgamated Association declined rapidly. In mass production plants skilled blue-collar workers played a smaller part in the production process, a point often emphasized in contemporary accounts and historical works.[20] But an important corollary has received less attention. The workers' informal voice may have become less influential in the new plants, but their disruptive potential—their ability to immobilize large amounts of capital—grew as production became more mechanized and the manufacturer's investment increased. As the potential costs of strikes and other disruptive acts rose, employer resistance to union activity grew accordingly.

Regardless of their potential, unions faced severe difficulties after 1893. The depression of the mid-1890s, unprecedented in its severity, led to widespread layoffs and wage reductions. Many weak or vulnerable organizations, including many of the remaining Knights assemblies, simply disappeared.[21] Even when they survived, unions were unable to influence the deflationary spiral. Their failure to win prior recognition of layoff procedures and seniority rights—or in most cases even to raise these issues—left their members unprotected. By 1897 the labor movement had fewer than 450,000 members, about 40 percent of whom were in manufacturing. In this setting the workers' formal voice was reduced to a whisper.

SKILLED WORKERS STRUGGLES, 1895 – 1915

Skilled workers had dominated the unions of the 1880s and would spearhead the turn-of-the-century recovery of union influence. Their role was an indication of their market power and importance to their employers. In retrospect, the issue was not whether they would opt for a formal voice as the economy revived but what lessons they had learned from the experiences of the 1890s. Several possibilities existed. In the 1890s the United Mine Workers emerged as the largest and most powerful American union. Defeated in a series of violent conflicts in 1894, it won a new round of strikes three years later. By the turn of the century it had organized almost all eastern and midwestern bituminous miners and was poised for a decisive confrontation with the anthracite employers. An industrial union, the UMW enlisted workers of all skill levels, nationalities, and races. Transcending ethnic parochialism was the key to success in a competitive, labor-intensive industry.[22] Another major lesson of the 1890s was the importance of leadership and management to workplace and labor market power. The formidable unions of the 1880s had proven to be surprisingly fragile, largely because of organizational deficiencies. Their failings accelerated a trend toward more systematic, businesslike operations. Union executives centralized power, expanded staffs, raised dues, emphasized fixed-term contracts and union security, and began to standardize wages and working conditions. Led by the construction workers' organizations, particularly the Carpenters, they created formidable organizations.[23]

While acknowledging the miners' achievements, skilled factory workers generally opted to follow the building trades example. If the spread of mass production provided a foundation for industrial unionism, the arrival of ever-larger numbers of new immigrants and the growing association between skill and ethnicity reemphasized the diversity of the factory labor force. As the potential benefits of union membership rose, organization along narrow occupational lines and the explicit or implicit omission of most low-skill employees became the path of least resistance. In some cases, such as textiles and shoes, high-skill groups amalgamated but made little effort to enlist low-skill workers. Their limited approach left the Brewery Workers, with 10,000 members in 1897 and 30,000 in 1904,

Table 11. Union membership in manufacturing, 1897–1915 (thousands)

Industry	1897	1904	1915	Percent gain, 1897–1915
Clothing	14.6	77.9	173.7	1190
Metals	50.1	213.3	224.2	448
Lumber	5.5	51.6	21.1	383
Printing	37.9	92.2	115.6	305
Textiles	8.1	14.8	22.4	276
Tobacco, food	45.5	135.6	119.0	262
Glass, clay	23.3	48.6	53.1	228
All manufacturing	200.2	677.1	781.9	390
Percent of all union members	40	33	30	
Percent of all manufacturing workers	4	12	11	

Source: Leo Wolman, *Ebb and Flow in Trade Unionism* (New York, 1936), pp. 174–92.

as the preeminent example of industrial unionism in manufacturing. At the same time, these organizations adopted many of the internal reforms that the building trades and other nonmanufacturing groups were implementing.

The revival of the economy in the late 1890s temporarily obscured the unions' limitations. Thousands of former members rejoined, and many new workers became union members. Table 11 summarizes this development. Membership in manufacturing tripled between 1897 and 1904 and embraced more than one in ten manufacturing workers by 1904. The major beneficiaries were the established organizations of the 1890s. (The decline in the lumber category resulted from the disappearance of the Amalgamated Woodworkers into the Carpenters' burgeoning multicraft empire.)[24] Yet the membership data indicate more than a healthier economy and better-led unions. Despite many obstacles, the boom atmosphere and the workers' militancy began to overshadow skill and ethnic distinctions, creating the possibility of UMW-type organizations. New or revived industrial unions, including the Brewery Workers, Rubber Workers, Garment Workers, and Wood Workers, had enlisted more than 150,000 members by 1904.[25]

Within the AFL there were also signs of change. The amalgamated and industrial unions were increasingly critical of the practice of chartering narrow craft groups. They argued that jurisdictions should be broad enough to permit unions to dominate industries and enforce multiemployer agreements. In 1911 they succeeded in changing the direction of Federation policy. By 1915 only 28 of 133 unions were pure craft unions. Most of the others, including the most important unions of factory workers, were craft-industrial organizations that enlisted skilled workers and less skilled but strategically placed co-workers.[26] Craft-industrial unions recognized the growing interdependence of industrial tasks, especially in manufacturing, but continued to disregard the less skilled. In the few large plants that organized under craft-industrial auspices, unions formed a series of locals based on occupation; an umbrella organization then coordinated the activities of the semiautonomous locals.[27]

For a few years it was possible to argue that a new generation of realistic leaders had created a formula that maximized the likelihood of an effective and durable workers' voice. The revival of collective bargaining in industries where it had existed in the 1880s—in foundries, glass works, potteries, machine shops, and northern textile plants—together with the growth of union membership in other industries suggested that many employers recognized the potency of the new unionism as well. Perhaps the best example was the pottery industry, which depended on a cadre of highly skilled workers, virtually all British immigrants. During the depression of the 1890s the Knights of Labor, dominant in the Trenton shops, had collapsed and the National Brotherhood of Operative Potters, dominant in East Liverpool, had become inactive. With the economic revival, the NBOP expanded to include skilled and strategic workers in both centers. The skilled potters were as hostile to the unskilled as in the past, and the NBOP remained a craft-industrial union until the 1930s. Employers, however, were impressed with the possibility of stabilizing labor costs. The agreement they signed with the NBOP in 1900 marked the beginning of an era of stable, routine collective bargaining that lasted for nearly two decades. Government investigators cited the industry as a model for all employers and workers.[28]

Pottery, however, was exceptional. Other national collective bargaining agreements were less satisfactory and durable. Disputes between the Molders and the National Founders' Association and between the Machinists and the National Metal Trades Association were among the most bitter struggles of the early twentieth century. By 1904 the agreements were dead, metal trades employers were committed to the open shop, and labor market competition had revived.[29]

The new unions of the turn-of-the-century period faced even greater difficulties. The Amalgamated Rubber Workers lost a series of strikes in New Jersey and Massachusetts and disbanded. The Butcher Workmen lost a major strike against the Chicago meat packers in 1904; henceforth it was confined to small packing plants and retail shops. The Boot and Shoe Workers and United Textile Workers confronted a deteriorating industrial relations environment that greatly magnified their internal divisions. The Amalgamated Association retained its foothold in the iron mills but made no progress in the steel mills, now the dominant sector of the industry.[30]

These setbacks emphasized the difficulty of organizing in the face of determined employer opposition. Besides the problems that always made organization in manufacturing risky, the rise of big business added another formidable challenge. The turn-of-the-century merger movement created more than a hundred giant, multiplant manufacturing companies that had greater resources than the largest nineteenth-century firms and were willing to spend freely for welfare programs and other personnel measures that were implicitly or explicitly anti-union.[31] U.S. Steel and International Harvester exemplified this development. With a few unimportant exceptions, large factories would remain off-limits until the World War I production boom.

Small and medium-sized manufacturing firms, with fewer resources, opted for more systematic union avoidance tactics. The formal open-shop movement had its origins in a Dayton, Ohio, employers coalition that grew out of the 1901 NCR strike and in the Chicago Employers Association, formed in 1902. In 1903 the National Association of Manufacturers embraced the open shop and subsequently provided most of the leadership for the burgeoning movement. After 1903 a Citizens Industrial Association coordinated the activities of local groups.[32] Open-shop organizations were soon active in most industries. Their principal purpose was to organize traditional anti-union tactics, strikebreaking and spying in particular. In many cases they did little else. However, in cities with histories of militant unionism, large concentrations of manufacturers, or active National Metal Trades Association affiliates, more ambitious and sophisticated open-shop organizations appeared. These organizations typically set up labor bureaus, which kept records on past and present workers and screened prospective employees. The Employers Association of Detroit, for example, had files on 16,000 workers by 1904, on 180,000 by 1912.[33] Union members were intimidated and often blacklisted. Yet the labor bureaus also sought to win the workers' allegiance by providing valuable services. Philadelphia's Metal Manufacturers' Association, one of the most durable and successful open-shop organizations, offered "one-stop job shopping for skilled metal tradesmen."[34] It persuaded many workers it provided a superior, more cost-efficient service, undermining the unions' function as employment agencies.

The dramatic eclipse of the Detroit labor movement illustrated the potential of the new union avoidance tactics. The fastest growing auto makers, such as Ford and General Motors, refused to deal with unions and discharged potential troublemakers. Worker exits, not unions, were their most pressing labor problems. The smaller companies, more closely tied to Detroit's preautomobile past, were more vulnerable and more vigorous in attacking the resurgent labor movement. They created the Employers Association and took the lead in undermining the Detroit Federation of Labor. By 1912, they had virtually obliterated the local labor movement outside the building trades. A year later, Studebaker executives easily replaced workers who struck against poor working conditions in the city's only significant prewar strike.[35]

Manufacturers in Detroit and elsewhere increasingly interpreted their success in avoiding organized labor as evidence of organizational and moral superiority. They had devised arrangements for themselves and their employees that made unions obsolete. Frederick W. Taylor summarized this view when he told audiences that unions were appropriate for backward industries but could play no responsible role in systematically managed factories.[36]

Union officials responded by attacking the most visible symbols of the new factory system. The National Civic Federation, formed in 1900 as a bridge between management and organized labor, increasingly became a target. Though most labor leaders identified with the NCF were not from unions of factory workers, NCF policies were closely identified with manufacturing. The premier example was welfare work. To union leaders the simultaneous growth of welfare work and open-shop activism were not unrelated. Had they known the full extent of the financial relationships between the union officials and the employers who served on the NCF board of directors, their suspicions undoubtedly would have grown.[37] The union attack on scientific management, which escalated after the Watertown Arsenal strike of 1911, was likewise a reflection of union defensiveness as well as the real or imagined perils of time study and incentive wage plans.[38]

Though these reactions often created favorable publicity for the labor movement, they apparently had little or no effect on union membership, the spread of the new factory system, or the behavior of factory workers.[39] The membership of the factory workers organizations (with the exceptions discussed below) changed little between 1904 and 1915. Most employees, including most skilled and strategic employees, avoided unions and relied on informal methods to improve conditions. A buoyant economy made the exit option attractive when these methods did not succeed. For the least competitive factory workers, however, these were unappealing options. As individuals they had little influence on the shop floor. As low-skill employees, often with minimal fluency in English, they were unlikely to find better positions. Only an effective voice was likely to bring immediate improvements.

TOWARD INDUSTRIAL UNIONISM

Between 1909 and 1914 the limits of the unions' and employers' policies of the turn-of-the-century recovery period became more apparent. A series of spontaneous strikes involving low-skill factory workers challenged the old and new management, the skill and ethnicity-based social hierarchy in industry, and the organizing philosophy and policies of the AFL. The rebellion of 1909–1914 was not specifically a reaction to the spread of scientific management, welfare work, or other features of the emerging twentieth-century factory system; indeed, most of the strikes occurred in primitive textile and clothing plants and were protests against low wages, harsh working conditions, authoritarian supervisors, and other traditional evils. But they were a source of concern that few employers could disregard. Workers in a handful of modern plants struck with the same determination as employees of sweatshops and decrepit textile mills. Moreover, several of the strikes—unlike virtually all unskilled worker strikes since the 1870s—produced lasting unions. The new or reinvigorated organizations of the clothing industry, the principal beneficiaries of the strike wave, promised to have an effect similar to the UMW. Would they have a similar impact on other manufacturing industries?

The year 1909 was a turning point in the labor history of the American factory. In that year two large and largely spontaneous strikes underlined the workers' potential and anticipated the upheavals of the war years. The managerial methods of the Pressed Steel Car Company of McKees Rocks, Pennsylvania, and the New York City women's "shirtwaist" industry were highly dissimilar. In both cases, however, low-skill, low-wage employees, mostly of new immigrant heritage, dominated the labor force. Once the conflicts began, they overshadowed the skilled employees, recruited outside allies, sustained the strikes for many weeks, and won significant concessions. The subsequent histories of the two groups were as dissimilar as their prestrike histories. Yet for a few months they demonstrated that industrial workers could create an effective formal voice.

The Pressed Steel car plant was a prominent example of a situation that Taylor and his disciples often attacked. The managers had selectively introduced systematic management but made no effort to integrate the new systems or to eradicate old managerial methods. Thus up-to-date assembly methods, including, by some accounts, an assembly line, coexisted with the foreman's empire and ad hoc personnel methods.[40] To low-skill workers the combination was unfair and contradictory. On the one hand, they were expected to work faster and more precisely; on the other, they were subject to the petty tyrannies of traditional supervisors. Low wages reinforced a determination to exit to better jobs as soon as possible. But wage cuts in June and July 1909 encouraged several hundred workers to call for immediate improvements. The strike soon spread to the rest of the plant and idled more than 3000 employees. As the conflict escalated, tensions between skilled and unskilled employees, between natives and new immigrants, made unity difficult. When the skilled leaders seemed too conciliatory, the less skilled invited the Industrial Workers of the World (IWW) to take charge of the strike. The Wobblies' presence raised the level of conflict—twelve men were killed in an August 22 clash with police—and pressured the management to bargain. A September 8 agreement included promises of wage increases and fairer treatment. Though the agreement was short-lived, and the union soon collapsed, McKees Rocks became a symbol of what immigrant workers could accomplish if they acted with determination and persistence.[41]

The McKees Rocks conflict also marked the emergence of the IWW as a significant force in American manufacturing. Formed in 1905 by the leaders of the Western Federation of Miners and various socialist politicians, the IWW was a response to the parochialism of the labor movement and the ferocity of the open-shop campaign. The IWW was also implicitly hostile to contemporary socialism. Particularly offensive were the efforts of supposedly radical politicians to mimic Republicans and Democrats, create machinelike organizations, and reap the spoils of party or municipal office. Wobblies shared a "common alienation from reformist American socialists" and a desire for a "non-political revolution."[42]

If the Wobblies were certain about who and what they did not like, they had only the most general notions of how to promote revolution or what it might achieve. Like syndicalists in Europe and elsewhere, they viewed strikes as potentially revolutionary acts and achieved their greatest influence as strike leaders. Their identification with the poor and downtrodden also enabled them to transcend divisions between new immigrant groups, demonstrating that new immigrants were no more difficult to organize than western European or old stock American workers. Though they had less success bridging the gap between old and new immigrants, their Achilles heel was an outgrowth of their antiestablishment perspective. Hostility to the AFL and its policies meant hostility to the new, more centralized union structure, formal contracts, elaborate grievance procedures, and other impedimenta of contemporary collective bargaining. Wobblies were highly successful in creating strike organizations, less successful at resolving strikes to the workers' advantage, and markedly unsuccessful in converting strike organizations into viable unions. In retrospect it is easy to contrast the dynamism of industry, based on superior organization, with the ineffectual efforts of the IWW. But such a contrast overlooks the Wobblies' other services.[43] Unsuccessful as unionists, they dramatized the limits of contemporary factory reform and the plight of many industrial workers.

Before 1909, the IWW was only sporadically involved in eastern industry. It helped mobilize textile workers in Skowhegan, Maine, electrical workers in Schenectady, New York, and steel workers in Bridgeport, Connecticut, in 1906–1907, but the only substantial Wobbly unions were in Paterson, New Jersey, and New Bedford, Massachusetts. The Wobblies' flamboyance and uncompromising hostility to employers won the admiration of many aggrieved industrial workers. But as itinerate organizers, distrustful of bureaucracy, collective bargaining, and formal agreements, they were ill equipped to represent industrial workers or confront industrial managers. McKees Rocks temporarily obscured these deficiencies and created an image of militancy and success.

For the next four years, the IWW was involved in nearly a dozen additional strikes against eastern and midwestern manufacturing firms, including conflicts at New Castle and Butler, Pennsylvania (1909), East Hammond, Indiana (1910), New York City (1910), Lawrence, Massachusetts (1911–1912), Little Falls, New York (1912), Paterson, New Jersey, (1913), Akron, Ohio (1913), and Detroit, Michigan (1913). The Wobbly strikes were among the largest and most famous of the time. The number of strikers at Lawrence, Paterson, and Akron, the three largest strikes, exceeded the membership of every AFL metal trades union and of the United Textile Workers. In some instances the strikes were the results of union activity. The IWW had been active in Paterson, for example, since 1907; and in Lawrence since 1910. In other cases IWW leaders responded to calls for help from local strike leaders. In either case, IWW agitators helped organize the strikers, conducted public meetings, and advised the strikers' negotiating committees. The strikers' demands invariably reflected the Wobbly prejudice against contracts and long-term obligations. Wobbly organizations cut across ethnic lines, but they had no more success bringing together the skilled and unskilled than they had had at McKees Rocks. Friction between skilled and unskilled workers contributed to the failure of most of the strikes. Poor internal organization was another common defect. Worst of all, perhaps, the Wobbly presence enabled employers to rally public opinion and make strikebreaking a community enterprise.[44]

Though most Wobbly strikes were against old-fashioned firms, there were exceptions. At the American Sheet and Tin Plate plant in New Castle and the Studebaker plant in Detroit the old and new management existed side by side. The Firestone Tire & Rubber factory and the other Akron plants were among the most advanced anywhere. Did the Wobblies recognize these distinctions? The available evidence suggests that they did not. Their critiques of employer policies during the Paterson and Akron strikes, which occurred at the same time, were essentially interchangeable.[45]

Two months after the McKees Rocks settlement, Local 25 of the International Ladies Garment Workers Union, a small AFL union with jurisdiction over the highly competitive women's clothing industry, called a strike of New York shirtwaist makers that began the transformation of industrial relations in the clothing industry. Women's clothing was made in small plants that bore little resemblance to the typical nineteenth-century factory, much less the new plants of the early twentieth century. Even in the largest and most substantial plants, the sewing machine was the principal machine, and investment and energy use per employee were low compared to the average factory.[46] Employers were often former workers. They had limited resources and depended on their skilled workers during the "rush" seasons when most production occurred.

The workers were also different. A large percentage—62 percent in 1900, 59 percent in 1910—were women, among the highest proportion for any industry.[47] Most workers were eastern European immigrants; in New York and other big city markets Jews and Italians held most jobs. They chose the clothing industry because their other options were even more unappealing. A large minority also had prior experience in clothing manufacture. Unlike most new immigrants they were familiar with industrial work and with the ideas of European industrial workers. From their perspective, the issue was not whether to act collectively but whether collective action would be effective in a given setting. Finally, in contrast to most industrial workers they were highly successful in recruiting outside supporters. Their most reliable ally was the Women's Trade Union League, an organization of middle- and upper-class reformers that sought to improve the lot of women wage earners through AFL membership.[48] Unlike most male factory workers, who faced a hostile community, the clothing workers commanded broad sympathy and support.

Though less successful than the McKees Rocks strike, the "uprising of the twenty thousand" of 1909 had a remarkable impact. It too "illustrated that the most unlikely candidates for unionization could be united for organized economic action."[49] Other clothing workers soon grasped this lesson. For the next two years the industry was in continuous turmoil as larger and larger walkouts halted production and spurred organization. The ILGWU grew from 1800 members in 1909 to 65,300 in 1915 and became one of the fastest-growing American unions. Its popularity reflected not only the workers' militancy but also their success in translating that militancy into immediate concessions and a collective bargaining structure that promised additional gains. The heart of the ILGWU approach was an elaborate grievance system with final appeals to impartial boards and arbitrators. Under the Protocol of Peace (1910), the most famous of the settlements, full-time representatives of the employers and the union worked to reconcile the myriad conflicts that beset the fragmented New York industry.[49]

The upheavals of 1909 awakened workers in the men's clothing industry as well. In Chicago a spontaneous strike of low-skill employees at Hart, Schaffner and Marx in September 1910 quickly tied up the nation's largest clothing plant and spread to other Chicago companies; by early November as many as 40,000 workers were on strike. The leaders of the

Garment Workers local negotiated an agreement with Hart, Schaffner and Marx in January 1911 that had many features of the Protocol of Peace, including an arbitration plan. The company appointed a university professor, Earl Dean Howard, as its labor manager, and the union selected one of the strike leaders, Sidney Hillman, to represent the workers. Together with J. E. Williams, who became Impartial Chairman in 1912, they would make the Hart, Schaffner and Marx arrangement one of the most noted collective bargaining achievements of the era. Hillman emphasized the need for a strong union to enforce the agreement and ensure that the workers fulfilled their obligations. By 1914 he, Howard, and Williams had demonstrated that labor peace, rising productivity, and improved working conditions were possible and compatible, even in an industry noted for conflict, primitive production methods, and sweatshop conditions.[50] Hillman moved to New York to take charge of the faltering Protocol arbitration system but soon shifted his attention to a growing revolt against the national leaders of the Garment Workers. In 1914 he became president of the new Amalgamated Clothing Workers, an independent union that soon became one of the most successful industrial unions in manufacturing.[51] Under his leadership, the Amalgamated was highly centralized and committed to collective bargaining based on the Hart, Schaffner and Marx model, a cooperative but aggressive approach to employers, and scientific management.

Thus the unrest of the early 1910s produced two new but markedly different approaches to industrial unionism: the Wobbly approach, based on hostility to employers, continuous confrontation, and minimal structure and planning, and the clothing workers' approach, based on an elaborately organized union and complex, detailed collective bargaining agreements that made the union an economic force in the industry. Both approaches had antecedents in earlier years. The surprising thing was their limited influence in the 1910s. Preoccupied with the anti-AFL sentiments of the Wobblies and the Hillman group, most union leaders made little effort to redefine their organizing strategies. One modest initiative, a UTW effort to enlist strikers at the Fulton Bag and Cotton Company of Atlanta, failed after a promising start.[52] Only a dramatic change in the economic environment, a result of the industrial boom that accompanied World War I, would force them to reconsider the potential of a formal workers voice in manufacturing and especially in large-scale manufacturing.

8 The Impact of Progressive Government

If the employer becomes satisfied by experience that his profits increase in proportion as his employees are protected against accidents and the destruction of their health, he will, in accordance with an immutable law that governs the conduct of mankind, be more careful as to their welfare, and not begrudge the expenditure of a few dollars for the purpose of securing their comfort and safety. [Chief State Inspector of Workshops and Factories, *Fourth Annual Report,* Ohio, 1887, p. 3]

"Hello, Kiddo. What's the matter, been fired?" "Oh, no, the boss sent us home because the factory inspector is coming around today." [New York, Factory Investigating Commission, *Preliminary Report,* 1912, vol. 3 (Albany, 1912), p. 1281]

In addition to the internal developments described in previous chapters, a major exogenous force—state labor legislation— helped define the twentieth century factory system. Regulatory statutes were a response to the growing size and complexity of the factory. But they also reflected other factors—an increasing public awareness of the "plight" of the industrial worker and the growing power of organized labor, for example—that were only indirectly related to the operation of the plant. As a consequence many manufacturers at first viewed the laws as burdensome and undesirable. But they soon realized that the statutes often complemented their voluntary efforts to modernize the factory and penalized employers who had refused to adopt new methods or violated community values regarding the employment of dependent workers. By World War I most managers had accommodated themselves to the growing role of the state in factory operations.

THE EBB AND FLOW OF FACTORY LEGISLATION

The labor reform movement of the pre–World War I period encompassed a wide range of protective measures, many of which had only limited relevance to the large manufacturing plant. Most of the legislation, in fact, applied to railroads, mines, department stores, bakeries, and

136

"sweatshops" and therefore had no direct impact on the factory. But two broad categories of laws did apply. The first group included measures related to the physical environment of the factory, principally sanitation and safety regulations. The second consisted of laws restricting the labor of women and children—laws based in part on preconceived ideas about the role of women and children in society. To enforce both types of legislation lawmakers relied on a variety of administrative bodies, the most important of which was the state factory inspection department.

Every legislature followed a separate course, but the less progressive states tended to follow the lead of the more progressive and in time narrowed the gap between them. This was due to the gradual diffusion of ideas and the growth of regional and national reform groups. As a consequence most industrial states had similar kinds of laws by 1920. The differences in their impact resulted from variations in the details of the specific laws and in the state enforcement efforts.

The regulation of factory working conditions illustrates these processes. The movement started in Massachusetts in 1877, when the legislature passed a general factory act modeled after British statutes. This law covered fire escapes, factory ventilation, dangerous machinery, and elevators and created an inspection force to enforce it. In the next decade and a half every major northern industrial state followed the example of Massachusetts. Ohio passed a factory act in 1884, Wisconsin in 1885, New Jersey in 1885 and 1887, Connecticut in 1887, Pennsylvania in 1889, New York in 1890 and 1892, Michigan in 1893, and Rhode Island in 1894.[1]

By the turn of the century all the northern industrial states except Illinois had arrived at approximately the same position. Every state required factories to be clean and properly ventilated, every state had some provision for guarding machinery, elevators, and hoist openings, every state except Rhode Island and Connecticut required the reporting of serious accidents, all but Rhode Island and Pennsylvania demanded exhaust fans for dusty work. Less common were requirements for belt shifters (to stop belt-driven machinery in emergencies), guards for hot liquids, railings on stairways, and doors that opened outward.[2] There were, nevertheless, substantial differences between the provisions of similar laws. The "field of danger in factory work . . . [was] differently measured" in states with identical problems.[3]

In Illinois the legislature created a factory inspection department in 1893 but was extremely slow to enact regulatory legislation. One measure, a fire escape law passed in 1893, was repealed six years later when it was discovered that the senator who sponsored the law also owned the patent on the required equipment.[4] In 1907 the chief factory inspector wrote that "while Illinois ranks third as an industrial state, it ranks absolutely last on the record it has made in securing appropriate legal measures to protect properly its working classes."[5]

By that time, however, a reform coalition embracing the governor, factory inspectors, and labor and reform groups had formed to work for legislation. The reformers promoted a bill drafted by Charles R. Henderson of the University of Chicago, which embodied many standard safety and sanitation measures. It failed, but the legislators appointed an Industrial Commission to investigate factory conditions and report to the next session. After a year of study the commission recommended detailed provisions for machine guarding, ventilation, and sanitation. Its report became the basis of the 1909 Health, Safety, and Comfort Act. "By this new law Illinois, which had been practically without factory legislation, took its place in the front rank of the states making provision for the health and safety of employees."[6]

A similar pattern emerged when reformers and legislators became interested in the plight of industrial accident victims. The unwillingness of many employers to assist injured workers, the difficulty of winning negligence suits (due to a large measure to the employers' common law defenses—"assumption" of risk, "contributory" negligence, and the "fellow servant" rule), and the new European state insurance systems all helped make workmen's compensation legislation a major political issue after the turn of the century. The passage of employers' liability acts, which deprived employers of one or more of their common law defenses, was also an important ingredient in the political movement for accident compensation.[7]

The northern industrial states were leaders in enacting workmen's compensation legislation. The critical factors were the presence of active reform groups and a general awareness of the extent of the problem. Between 1910 and 1913 Massachusetts, Rhode Island, Connecticut, New York, New Jersey, Ohio, Wisconsin, Michigan, and Illinois passed compensation acts. Only Pennsylvania and Indiana among the major northern industrial states lagged behind.[8] Yet the laws passed by the northern legislatures were remarkably dissimilar. Though a "single fundamental principle underlies the entire group," a government report explained, ". . . its expression and application present great diversity of details in the different states."[9]

Owing to the Ives decision (1911) of the New York Supreme Court, which declared a compulsory compensation law unconstitutional, only three important industrial states—New York, Ohio, and Illinois—established compulsory systems before 1920.[10] In the other states the laws were "elective": each employer could refuse to insure but in the event of legal action was deprived of one or more common-law defenses against the injured employee. Though the employer thus faced the risk of a substantial court award, "a large proportion" of employers in the elective states did not insure.[11] In addition every industrial state except Ohio permitted private companies—either stock or mutual—to operate in the compensation field, and every state except Massachusetts allowed employees to self-insure.[12]

In other respects the laws were similar. Injured workers typically received compensation for their medical expenses and one-half to two-thirds of their lost wages, but only after a waiting period and only for a limited number of weeks in cases of partial or temporary disability. Higher or indefinite payments were made in instances of death or permanent disability.[13] In most of the major industrial states a commission administered the law. In New Jersey and Rhode Island, however, courts settled disputes over the operation of the act.

Other labor laws that in theory applied to all factory workers were of relatively little consequence. In the 1870s northern lawmakers began to legislate against long intervals between paydays and payment in script or store orders. These laws were usually designed to benefit miners, but they also aided glass and iron and steel workers. Two other types of legislation with greater potential significance in reality amounted to little. State boards of arbitration and public employment offices, designed to reconcile disputes and reduce unemployment, were created in virtually every major state before 1900. But only in Massachusetts, where shoe manufacturers and shoe workers' unions had a long tradition of arbitrating disputes, did the arbitration board work effectively, and state employment offices had virtually no impact on factory employment practices before World War I.[14] In the first case the stakes were usually so high that neither side dared rely on the state; in the second the informal system of recruitment was sufficiently effective to discourage interest in the state service.

While laws regulating the labor of women and children also varied between states, legislators showed greater willingness to reduce interstate differentials. This was largely because regulations pertaining to women and children were more comprehensible to the average citizen (and legislator) and had strong moral overtones. Conversely, since they were more difficult to enforce—a machine guard, once purchased, was usually installed—the exact provisions were often less important than the extent of the enforcement effort.

Before the Civil War many states in the Northeast enacted laws establishing minimum ages and maximum hours for industrial employment and requiring school attendance for a designated period each year. But these restrictions, which depended on local officials for their enforcement, were often disregarded. A Connecticut town official explained that "the village would be too hot to hold" him if he attempted to enforce the law.[15]

In Massachusetts the Bureau of Statistics of Labor reported that the child labor law "neither is, nor can be, enforced."[16] In the 1870s and 1880s, however, several northern states, led by Massachusetts, enacted more stringent child labor regulations and created state factory inspection bureaus. In New York, New Jersey, and Pennsylvania, for example, the legislatures established inspection departments at the same time they passed stricter laws. By 1910 every northern industrial state had followed these precedents, and fourteen had become the uniform age for factory employment.

The southern textile states were slower to act. By 1906 Virginia, the Carolinas, Georgia, and Alabama had enacted laws that set a minimum work age of twelve but failed to provide factory inspection.[17] The early education laws had demonstrated that reliance on local authorities or the "thousand eyed police, public opinion," was not sufficient to insure compliance. The failure of the southern states to create inspection departments (Alabama was the first to do so in 1907; South Carolina followed in 1909) automatically limited the effectiveness of minimum-age laws in those states. In addition, most northern states required that each working child (usually between fourteen and sixteen years of age) have proof that he or she complied with the age and education requirements of the law. The southern states, on the other hand, frequently exempted special groups of children below the minimum age and relied on the parents' statements of the child's age.[18]

The effort to establish a maximum workday and workweek followed a similar pattern. In many states the laws that set age limits for children also specified the maximum number of hours per day and week that eligible children could work. By 1900 ten hours per day and sixty hours per week was the uniform standard in the North; by 1916 Massachusetts, New Jersey, New York, Ohio, and Illinois had adopted the eight-hour day for children.[19] Although there were exceptions, the legislatures often extended these restrictions to adult women as well. Massachusetts enacted the first significant hours law in 1874, when it limited women to ten hours per day. This law, which did not become fully effective until 1879, had far-ranging consequences. It created the ten-hour shift in the Massachusetts textile industry, since manufacturers could not operate with male employees alone. It was also an important breakthrough for labor reformers, who began to agitate for ten-hour legislation in other states.[20] By 1900 the ten-hour day and the sixty-hour week were the legal maximums for women in every northern industrial state except Pennsylvania, Michigan, Illinois, and Ohio.[21] In the following years most states retained the ten-hour day but reduced the maximum workweek. By 1912 Massachusetts, New York, Michigan, and Ohio had adopted the fifty-four-hour week for women. In 1919 Massachusetts adopted the forty-eight-hour week.[22]

Although there were substantial delays, a decline in women's hours generally followed a decline in men's hours. When the process was reversed, trouble followed. In New Jersey, for example, the legislature passed a fifty-five-hour law in 1892, a major innovation at a time when Massachusetts retained the sixty-hour week. But the law proved to be almost wholly ineffective, partly because it was poorly drafted and partly because the public would not accept so "radical" a measure.[23] It was superseded by a sixty-hour law in 1912. In Illinois the legislature passed an eight-hour day, forty-eight-hour-week law for women in 1893, only to find that the manufacturers' opposition to the law was so intense that it was virtually impossible to enforce. Indeed, the eight-hour law prompted the formation of the Illinois Manufacturers' Association, a militant employers' organization that fought labor reform for decades.[24] In the meantime the state supreme court declared the law unconstitutional.

Many northern legislatures also passed measures to protect women and children on the job. The prohibition of night work for children was common, though not in states like New Jersey and Pennsylvania, where young "helpers" in glass factories worked through the night. When the New Jersey legislature passed a law in 1910 prohibiting night work for children under fifteen, its supporters considered it "a most satisfying achievement."[25]

Far more popular were laws to protect the health and morals of female factory workers. Many states prohibited women and children from cleaning machinery while it was in operation. A few also prevented women from performing certain types of factory jobs. In New York, for example, the legislature forbade women from working as core makers or metal polishers unless special precautions were taken to guard their health. By 1900 all the northern industrial states except laggard Illinois required separate toilet facilities for women. In the following years special "rest" and "changing rooms" also became mandatory in many states. But the most popular—and apparently least enforced—labor law was the requirement that employers provide seats for women workers. Only Illinois and North Carolina had failed to enact such a law by the turn of the century.[26]

THE EFFICACY OF FACTORY LEGISLATION

Although the overall pattern of factory legislation is clear, the meaning of these laws for the individual manager and worker is more difficult to assess. The miscellaneous observations of employers and workers that appear in government reports, hearings, and other documents are often self-serving and therefore suspect; moreover, there is no way of determining whether the small minority who appeared in print was representative of the larger, anonymous group.[27] I have therefore relied on two surrogate measures to ascertain the impact of government on the evolving factory. The first, developed in this section, is the types of political alignments that appeared during the debates over legislation. The possibility that loopholes often negated the apparent intent of the statutes and the likelihood, emphasized in recent studies of progressive legislation, that some regulatory laws were passed for the benefit of managers rather than workers make it imperative to look beyond lists of laws to evaluate their potential effects.[28] The second and ultimately more important measure, the effectiveness of the state enforcement effort, is discussed in the following section. In both cases I have concentrated on sanitation and accident prevention, workmen's compensation, minimum ages for children, and maximum hours for women and children—the four major types of legislation—in the major manufacturing states.

In general, support for and opposition to legislation came from groups that have been traditionally assigned these roles. Labor unions and reform groups—the National Child Labor Committee, the Consumers Leagues, and the American Association for Labor Legislation are probably the best known examples—invariably initiated the regulatory bills. In most states, as in Illinois, "labor laws have been enacted as a result of persistent demands by organized labor."[29] Employer groups, with equal frequency, provided the principal opposition. By the turn of the century state manufacturers' organizations, trade associations, and ad hoc political groups formed to agitate for or against a particular bill were active in all the leading industrial states. Although the evidence is not conclusive, it appears that many of these organizations were formed for the specific purpose of opposing organized labor and resisting labor legislation. In any event they were often dominated by conservative employers to whom regulatory laws were anathema. "Individual employers," Josephine Goldmark wrote, were often "humane and enlightened, but their official organizations and representatives have won a sinister distinction in opposing labor legislation."[30]

Manufacturers rarely opposed factory acts to improve sanitation and prevent accidents. The promise of increased productivity, reduced turnover, and higher morale, in addition to purely humanitarian considerations, more than offset the immediate financial outlays that were necessary to guard machinery, install separate toilets, or expand the janitorial staff. In the few instances where manufacturers did oppose the acts, they based their positions on principle—government "interference" and "snooping"—or on narrow financial grounds.[31] The attacks on state fire prevention standards, for example, were usually led by "sweatshop" proprietors and seldom succeeded. On the other hand, spectacular instances of the violation of such laws, like the famous Triangle Company fire in New York City in 1911, outraged public opinion and resulted in new, more stringent regulations.

The position of most managers of large plants was reflected in the fire prevention work of insurance companies and in the private accident prevention campaigns of the early twentieth century. As we have seen, insurance companies were responsible for major changes in mill construction in the late nineteenth century, changes that were inconsistent with the spirit of the factory laws and the profit motive. The same was true for voluntary accident prevention. The steel manufacturers, who took the lead in the movement to reduce accidents, always noted that their work could be justified on either humanitarian or economic grounds.[32]

But it was workmen's compensation that provided the classic case of regulatory legislation designed to "meet the needs of the private business groups as much as those of injured workers."[33] In addition to providing benefits—usually modest—to injured workers, the compensation laws also promised to reduce costly litigation that occurred under the employers' liability laws, to foreclose the possibility of high jury awards to workers, and to end the rancor that accompanied court suits. Moreover, by allowing employers to form mutual insurance companies and to self-insure, the laws encouraged accident prevention work. The potential benefits to both the employers and employees under such a system were so obvious, in fact, that the compensation laws were later used as a model for other reform efforts. In the campaign for unemployment insurance, for example, the workmen's compensation laws were the basis for most of the bills drafted before the Depression of the 1930s.[34]

There is no doubt that many manufacturers supported compensation legislation and that many of them did so for wholly practical, selfish reasons. The National Association of Manufacturers, many state and local employers' groups, and even the Illinois Manufacturers' Association endorsed compensation laws. The United States Steel Company actively lobbied for legislation in Pennsylvania and Illinois, where it was a major employer. A recent account argues that after 1909 the National Civic Federation "was at the center of agitation for the workmen's compensation bills."[35]

But the fact that employers' groups helped draft legislation and agitated for its passage does not prove that their influence was dominant or that the laws were designed for their benefit. Case studies of various states show, on the contrary, that the same reform and labor groups that promoted most legislation—presumably for the benefit of the employee—also led the compensation campaign.[36] The one exception was the state AFL federations, which refused to endorse the compensation approach until 1909 or 1910. But that position reflected the unions' commitment to the older campaign to liberalize the employers' liability laws, not their opposition to accident compensation per se. If any single group played a decisive role it was the American Association for Labor Legislation, not the National Civic Federation.

A close examination of the state campaigns reveals that the attitudes of most businessmen and business groups were accurately summarized by a Pennsylvania labor leader:

> It is a common thing for employers to say, "We are in favor of a compensation law if it is the right sort," but I find . . . that they differ as to what is the right sort of a compensation law. No matter how a measure is drawn up, there will be some group of employees opposing it because it does not suit their views.[37]

Many business leaders, especially big business leaders, did support legislation, provided, of course, that the legislation was consistent with their objective of reducing or at least stabilizing accident costs. But many other manufacturers opposed the compensation bills, either because they disliked the specific features of a proposed measure or more likely because they did not believe that the promised financial benefits of workmen's compensation would actually materialize. A major weakness of the state systems before World War I was the large number of employers in the elective states who chose not to participate and took their chances with the weakened employers' liability laws, precisely the obstacles they were supposedly trying to eliminate.

Judging by the political alignments that appeared during legislative campaigns, then, neither accident prevention and sanitation laws nor accident compensation laws promised clearly predictable results. Because employers supported and opposed legislation for practical, economic reasons, it seems apparent that the potential impact of such laws depended on other factors. Thus a manufacturer who had a modern factory and who was undertaking an accident prevention campaign on his own initiative could reasonably anticipate fewer additional costs and inconveniences than a manufacturer who occupied an older structure and who had done little to reduce accidents. Indeed, it is conceivable that the first employer might support legislation as a method of forcing backward rivals to meet his standards. In the other major areas of legislative activity, however, this ambiguity did not exist. Despite the reformers' arguments that minimum-age and maximum-hours legislation would improve the quality of the factory labor force, manufacturers believed that such legislation would adversely affect industries that employed large numbers of women and children. In most cases this conclusion dictated a second: that the laws were therefore undesirable.

Middle-class reform and philanthropic groups, especially women's organizations, typically initiated campaigns for child labor legislation. In New York the Children's Aid Society and the Society for the Prevention of Cruelty to Children worked toward this goal in the 1880s; in Pennsylvania the Working Women's Association, the New Century Guild, the Women's Christian Temperance Union, and the State Federation of Women's Clubs agitated for regulations in the 1890s; in New Jersey the Children's Protective Alliance represented the interests of many charitable groups; in Illinois the Cook County Child Saving League and the State Federation of Women's Clubs were among the leaders at the turn of the century.[38] In 1901 Edgar Gardner Murphy, a Birmingham minister, formed the Alabama Child Labor Committee, which became a prototype for other state committees and the National Child Labor Committee (NCLC), founded in 1904. After 1904 the NCLC through its officers and its state committees, initiated, led, or coordinated the attack on child labor in state legislators and Congress.[39] These organizations usually had the support of organized labor, although union leaders were often suspected of giving mere lip service to a cause that did not immediately affect their constituents.

The reformers' opponents were invariably the manufacturers and their organizations. It was no coincidence that the National Civic Federation favored private welfare work over legislation to combat the child labor problem in the southern textile states. In the 1880s and 1890s many business organizations in the North opposed restrictions on child labor, but by 1900, as technological change reduced the demand for child workers and public opinion became aroused, manufacturers' groups that had a direct interest in child labor usually took the lead.[40] In New Jersey, Pennsylvania, and Indiana, glassmakers were vocal opponents of minimum-age and night work regulations. In the Carolinas, Georgia, Virginia, and Alabama cotton textile interests adamantly opposed meaningful legislation.[41] Glass manufacturers feared that age and night work restrictions would prevent them from operating the night shift; southern mill owners believed that they would lose their advantage over New England industry. To these manufacturers—whatever their theoretical position—regulatory legislation threatened to have a serious practical impact.

The employer's standard response in such situations was to oppose legislation when that course seemed expedient or to offer alternatives, compromises, and amendments when it did not. Thus textile manufacturers in North Carolina, who had formerly opposed all restrictions on child labor, "voluntarily" set minimum-age and hour limits in 1901, when lawmakers threatened to enact a strong bill. As a consequence the legislature passed a "very mild" child labor law with no enforcement provisions.[42] The result of this type of activity was a series of symbolic but largely meaningless victories for reformers in southern states.[43] The legislatures passed laws, and the manufacturers continued to operate in their customary manner.

The willingness of southern manufacturers to accept legislation that was "mutually satisfactory" reflects the difficulty of ascertaining the meaning of the laws that were enacted. Laws that were "mutually satisfactory" were apt to be laws that had little effect, except perhaps to placate public opinion. Yet on paper they were often similar to acts that did promote changes in factory operations. The difference was frequently the enforcement mechanism. Only a large corps of qualified inspectors could ensure more than minimal compliance. In the last analysis it was the inspectors rather than the legislators who determined the impact of progressive legislation.

THE EFFICACY OF FACTORY INSPECTION

Factory inspection began in Massachusetts in 1877 and in other northern manufacturing states in the decade 1885–1895. From that time the agencies grew rapidly in size (in number of employees, appropriations, etc.) and in function.[44] Though legislatures often assigned the enforcement of one or more types of laws to other agencies—for example, state or municipal health departments or fire inspection bureaus—the total volume of regulatory legislation increased so rapidly that inspectors faced ever-widening responsibilities. By the turn of the century they typically enforced laws regulating working conditions (ventilation, heating, and lighting), safety (machine and elevator guards, fire escapes, exhaust fans, and protection from molten metals), female workers (maximum hours, lunch periods, seats, and separate toilets), and child labor (minimum age, certificates, and hours). In addition they often were responsible for bakeries, mercantile establishments, sweatshops, mines, schoolhouses, and theaters.[45]

Their success in performing these duties was a subject of frequent debate. Reformers and labor leaders often chided the inspectors for a lack of initiative and commitment. John Fitch, for example, concluded from a study of accidents in Pittsburgh steel mills that Pennsylvania had no regulations or inspectors worthy of the name.[46] The inspectors, on the other hand, pointed to reductions in accident rates, fire losses, child labor, and unsanitary working conditions as evidence of their diligence. An early historian of Rhode Island labor legislation tried to explain these contradictory claims: "The inspectors seem not to have been very strenuous in their inspections and the manufacturers were not troubled with prosecutions. Still, there was a substantial gain. Perhaps the inspectors were weak on prosecution but strong in persuasion."[47]

The single most important determinant of the inspectors' zeal was the level of public support for restrictive legislation and its enforcement. In states and communities where trade unions or social reform groups evaluated the inspectors' performance, they were necessarily more aggressive.[48] As a Fall River manufacturer noted:

> In large centers where there is an active and aggressive labor organization attention has to be paid to these laws by the State officials. If they do not, they hear from them, and properly so. But we know well enough that in certain sections of the State these laws are very loosely enforced.[49]

The first Alabama inspector complained that it was impossible for him to perform his task because of public indifference to the law.[50]

Yet public concern was difficult to sustain for lengthy periods, even in the most hospitable settings. As a result the reformers who occasionally became the heads of factory inspection departments—Florence Kelley in Illinois (1893–1896) and P. Tecumseh Sherman in New York (1905–1907) were the best examples—had short, frustrating careers, and inspectors increasingly found themselves in the cross fire between employers who opposed their activities and reformers who demanded ever more stringent measures.

Even where there was wide public support the complexity of the statutes was a major obstacle to enforcement. In part this was because the problems they attacked were complex. But it was also a result of the compromises that had been incorporated in the legislation. Reformers often suspected that the regulations were intentionally complicated to create the illusion rather than the substance of regulation. After reviewing the state maximum-hours laws, Josephine Goldmark concluded that innumerable loopholes and exceptions created "a genuinely impossible task. . . . The difficulties of inspection become almost insuperable."[51] A recent student of child labor legislation in New York is even more explicit: the laws, he writes, "probably were not intended to be enforced."[52]

Further aggravating the situation was the role of the courts, which were usually charged with levying penalties against violators. In small towns, particularly in company-dominated communities, the inspector had virtually no chance of obtaining convictions against the major employer. In other areas the judges were often sympathetic to the objectives of the law but hesitant to levy more than the minimum penalty. First offenders customarily received no more than a reprimand. In New York many cases "are dismissed with a warning or . . . [a fine] and the fine later suspended."[53] Many inspectors concluded that prosecutions were a waste of time.

Still, there were marked variations in the effectiveness of the state bureaus that cannot be attributed solely to the complexity of the statutes or the role of the courts. If public opinion established a minimum acceptable level of enforcement and the law created a theoretical maximum, the quality of the inspection force determined at what point the law was actually enforced.

The best illustration was the situation in New England. The Massachusetts inspection department was generally acknowledged to be the most active and efficient in the United States.[54] Those of Maine, Connecticut, and Rhode Island were among the least effective. In Maine, the most extreme case, the department was apparently moribund from the beginning; the single inspector did not attempt to prosecute a violator for more than twenty-five years.[55] In Connecticut the inspection department at least a viable organization, yet federal investigators discovered in 1909 that there had been no prosecutions for five years.[56] And in Rhode Island a writer who accompanied the inspectors on their rounds concluded that their "inquiries into the conditions of the mills visited appeared to be no means thorough, in fact they seemed rather perfunctory."[57] When this record is combined with that of the southern industrial states, it is not difficult to understand why Massachusetts textile manufacturers often complained that they bore an unfair burden.

The most common complaint of reformers was that the inspection departments were understaffed, necessitating various short cuts in enforcing the law. Even in Massachusetts "the inspector visits the larger factories first and if it is necessary to omit any the smaller shops are not visited."[58] The usual procedure was to concentrate on the most likely offenders, especially firms that employed large numbers of children. Inspectors reinspected plants only if the employer had a bad reputation or if there were specific complaints. One of the most zealous chief inspectors conceded that one visit a year was "about all you can give."[59] In many cases, however, this was not the inspectors' only compromise. They made hasty plant tours, judged children by their size or appearance, and disregarded unpopular laws. In New Jersey, where orphans under fifteen were not subject to the school attendance requirement, the inspectors helped needy children circumvent the law.

> When the law first went into effect, the difficulties in the way of immediate compliance led the inspectors to grant permits under this provision to large numbers of children. From this extension of discretion it was easy, in time, to grant permits to children actually under age because of family poverty. . . . By the end of the period it had come to be a frequent practice of most inspectors, especially during vacation periods. Many children, whom the law intended to keep from the factories, were thus admitted under cover of administrative approval.[60]

Many inspectors were political appointees who lacked the knowledge and zeal to enforce the laws effectively. Only Massachusetts, New York, and Wisconsin required civil service examinations for prospective inspectors before 1910; in other states trade union officials, war veterans, or politicians typically received appointments. To many the position was a sinecure, a reward for past services. The historian of Pennsylvania labor legislation attributed the "spasmodic" enforcement of the laws in that state to the deficiencies of the chief inspector. "The present incumbent of the office," he wrote, "is a perfectly legitimate product of spoils politics."[61]

The most thorough investigation of a state inspection department in the prewar period occurred when the New York legislature appointed a Factory Investigating Committee to study the causes of the famous Triangle fire of 1911. The results confirmed the reformers' charges. The New York department, supposedly one of the best in the nation, was hopelessly inefficient, its inspectors lazy and inept. An exchange between the committee members and Charles M. Cassells, the Troy inspector, was indicative of the testimony:

> Q. And then you take the employer, or somebody he details, and you go through the factory? A. As a guide.
> Q. You never go through alone, do you? A. No.
> Q. Then you go through the factory with the employer, and you expect the employees to tell you of any condition that they might want to complain of. Is that right? A. I do not know how to answer that question. I never looked at it that way.[62]

While reformers often bemoaned the inspectors' incompetence, they seldom considered a second problem, the tendency of inspectors to adopt the manager's point of view. Lacking the reformers' enthusiasm and subject to constant political pressures, the inspectors naturally sought to avoid trouble. The easiest way to do this was to reach a tacit understanding with the employer—to enforce the law but to do so in an acceptable way. As a result manufacturers who had bitterly fought the enactment of regulatory measures soon showed signs of a remarkable transformation. In Massachusetts they reacted to the inspectors' orders with a "cheerful spirit of compliance."[63] In New Jersey "manufacturers now receive the inspectors with courtesy and a ready willingness to comply with every request." In Connecticut an inspector "was greeted cordially and invited to make an inspection of the premises." In Pennsylvania the "orders from the department are readily complied with."[64] For their part the inspectors emphasized that their role was largely educational, that they had no intention of harassing the employer or prosecuting for "technical" violations, and that they would "require only what is practicable."[65]

Although the cumulative effect of the vagaries of public opinion, the complexities of the law, and the deficiencies of the inspection force created a significant disparity between the letter of the law and the way it was applied, the impact of regulatory legislation in most states was substantial. This was due in part to the persuasive powers of the inspectors, in part to the threat of prosecution. But equally important was the fact that the law made it possible to attack the "extreme cases," the minority of employers who remained oblivious to demands for change. These manufacturers refused to comply with the inspectors' orders or pretended to cooperate until they found ways to circumvent the law. In most cases they were small businessmen; the sweatshop operators of the clothing industry were perhaps the best examples. But a few large manufacturers were also guilty of serious abuses. Unlike the majority of employers who accommodated themselves to the law at minimal cost, these firms became the focal point of the enforcement effort.

The experiences of the Harmony Mills Company of Cohoes, New York, and the Illinois Glass Company of Alton, Illinois, emphasize the inspectors' effectiveness in confronting "extreme cases." Harmony Mills, the largest employer of child labor in New York, became a prime target of the state inspection department. In 1886 inspectors found that 1,200 of the 3,200 employees were under sixteen and discharged over 200. They reinspected the plant frequently because of its notorious reputation and their belief that the management was recalcitrant.[66] Despite obstructionist tactics by local authorities the inspectors eventually prevailed. By 1897 only 181 of 3,000 Harmony employees were under sixteen.[67] Eight years later, after an extensive personal inspection, one observer was "convinced that there can be no general violation of the factory law by the employment of young children in the city of Cohoes and that a remarkable change in this respect has taken place through the influence of factory law."[68]

Virtually the same situation existed at Alton, where the Illinois Glass Company employed over 500 boys (out of 1,800 workers) in 1895. The managers at first refused to comply with the law, arguing that they could not operate without child labor. But the persistence of inspectors and the negative publicity that the inspectors generated had a telling effect. By December 1896 Illinois Glass employed fewer than 200 boys.[69]

These examples were in marked contrast to the situation in the southern industrial states, where factory inspection was nonexistent before 1915. Though southern manufacturers invariably gave lip service to minimum-age laws, they could not resist the temptation to exploit a cheap labor source. A North Carolina firm "kept within the pale of the law by keeping the names of helpers off the pay rolls and ignoring their presence in the factory. Some of the helpers worked regularly full time; others worked only before and after school hours and on Saturday."[70] A South Carolina mill superintendent

> explained the deserted appearance of the spinning room by the statement that owing to the perfect atmospheric conditions which were maintained and the excellent machinery each spinner tended from 14 to 18 sides. He had just added, "We haven't got a lot of babies in our spinning room as they have in some mills," when a tiny little girl, apparently not over 6 years old, was seen trying to reach the frames. It was found later that she was a sister of the adult spinner who was in charge of the hidden children, and sisterly discipline had failed to keep her out of sight.[71]

Yet even where there was little or no enforcement effort, the labor laws appear to have had a restraining influence on many manufacturers. There was always the possibility that flagrant defiance of the law would generate demands for improved inspection methods and higher penalties. Where children were employed there was also the inconvenience of periodic inquiries and the maintenance of employment certificates (fraudulent or not) that could be eliminated if the employer set a sixteen-year minimum age limit. Manufacturers knew that many "respectable" citizens condemned child labor and the mistreatment of women even if only immigrant or "poor white" workers were involved. Many employers, the Census Bureau noted, were "disinclined" to report the number of children they employed "even if [they were] within the law in this particular."[72] The result was a gradual reduction in the number of underage children and an improvement in working conditions for many women. Even in the South, where the child labor laws were "flagrantly violated," the laws "had no little effect in reducing the number of children under 12 years of age."[73]

Reinforcing these tendencies were other developments that made voluntary compliance easier and in many cases economically rational. Mechanization increased the value of mature, responsible operators. New methods of plant organization and construction, electric power, and labor-saving machines had a similar impact. Steel and concrete construction reduced fire risks, the elimination of shafting and belting ended one of the most important sources of industrial accidents, and machinery reduced or eliminated the demand for child labor, particularly in the glass and textile industries.[74] The rise of systematic management, particularly cost accounting, made it less difficult for reformers and factory inspectors to convince employers that low wages and long hours did not lessen labor costs. Halsey, Towne, Taylor, and many proponents of welfare work insisted that in mechanized industries, well-paid workers were the least costly workers and that long hours did not ensure high production. Their arguments were, indirectly at least, also arguments against child labor and excessive hours, and they apparently had an effect. Melvin Copeland reported in 1912 that among cotton textile manufacturers "the conviction is gaining ground . . . that the employment of young children is not profitable."[75] A more recent study of the canning industry concludes that economic factors had a "stronger effect on the extent of child labor . . . than legal restrictions."[76]

The best example of the convergence of public policy and private interest was the spread of the safety movement. Large firms in the steel and machinery industries that had initiated accident prevention work before the passage of compensation acts on the premise that injuries were a form of unnecessary waste, redoubled their efforts after the laws went into effect. They hired private safety experts, introduced safety education programs, and spent large sums on special equipment. In addition they enlarged infirmaries, hired more doctors and nurses, and began to require medical examinations.[77] In 1920 U.S. Steel had 25 hospitals, 286 emergency stations, 167 full-time physicians and surgeons, 107 part-time physicians, 189 nurses, 68 visiting nurses, 101 safety inspectors, 16,801 employees who had received first aid training, and 25,948 employees who had served on safety committees.[78]

Although factory inspectors had cooperated with employers in reducing accidents since the 1880s, there was no formal recognition of the possibilities of a joint program until 1912, when the Wisconsin Industrial Commission hired a full-time safety expert, Charles W. Price of International Harvester, to work with the state's employers.[79] Price began an aggressive campaign to "sell" safety, first to manufacturers and then to foremen and workers. Drawing on the experiences of U.S. Steel, International Harvester, and other large corporations, he soon developed a standard technique. He would persuade the superintendent of a plant to head a safety committee consisting of "high grade men." The committee would invite foremen to a quiet banquet to discuss organized safety work. "Price felt that the banquet meetings convinced superintendents and foremen that safety had become company policy, thereby infusing the work force with a new spirit."[80]

Price's methods were successful in Wisconsin, and other states soon adopted his approach. Beginning in 1913, for example, the Pennsylvania Commission of Labor and Industries held conferences of employers to promote safety work. In addition to encouraging individual manufacturers to establish plant committees and educational programs, the commission sponsored rallies, traveling exhibits of safety devices, and state conferences of industrial physicians and welfare workers.[81] The alliance of industry and government in the safety field was institutionalized in the National Safety Council, whose membership of private and public organizations increased from 40 in 1912 to 3,300 in 1917.[82]

Though this cooperative approach was unique to the safety movement, it does illustrate a trend that was apparent to a greater or lesser degree in all areas of labor legislation before World War I. The employers' vested interests in law and order and greater efficiency together with the revolution in building techniques and managerial practices were important aids to the factory inspector. They helped offset the often insuperable problems of enforcing the law and contributed to the improvement in shop conditions and the decline of child care. Above all, they help explain how a largely ineffective system of law enforcement contributed to a decline in the traditional evils of the factory system.

9 World War I

The employment department in this view becomes the vestibule not alone to the factory, but to a better life. [Boyd Fisher, "Employment Managers Conference," *Bulletin* 227 (1916): 34]

The manager should, on greeting the candidate, look at him attentively and earnestly and during the first part of the interview, study his face carefully. [Katherine Huey, "Problems Arising and Methods Used in Interviewing and Selecting Employees," *Annals of the American Academy of Political and Social Science* 65 (May 1916): 213]

As originally expounded and recommended, employee representation was not thought of as an agency for collective bargaining but as a fair and practical means of giving workers a contact with their management. [Clarence J. Hicks, *My Life in Industrial Relations* (New York, 1941), p. 87]

The war boom of 1915–1920 affected American industry in numerous ways. The number of wage earners in manufacturing increased from 6,500,000 in 1914 to 8,400,000 in 1919—a 29 percent rise in a half decade. Factories doubled or tripled in size, and new plants, as large as any that had existed in 1915, appeared overnight in places like Carneys Point, New Jersey, and Nitro, West Virginia. Money wages increased dramatically, by approximately 11 percent in 1916 alone, but real wages barely advanced, because of the spiraling cost of living.[1] The strikes of 1909–1914 introduced a broader and more dramatic upheaval that attracted unprecedented attention to labor-management relations in industry. The federal government became involved in the operation of the factory to a degree that few factory inspectors ever dreamed of. Manufacturers, in turn, responded to these changes by refining, adapting, and introducing the managerial innovations of the previous decades. In many respects World War I was the climax to the trends of the preceding forty years.

Despite the general climate of change that accompanied the war, the European holocaust directly affected a relatively small number of industries before the United States entered the conflict. Of the nearly 2,000,000 new factory workers recruited during the war, more than 1,500,000 were employed in a few major industry groups.[2] Steel, machinery, ship building, industrial chemicals and rayon, explosives, automobiles, petroleum refining, rubber, and meat packing absorbed the bulk of the new workers.[3]

Even in these industries the effects of the war varied widely. The Remington Arms Company built a huge, modern structure in Bridgeport to manufacture rifles, and Ford began work on its remarkable River Rouge plant in 1918. When the federal government began its Nitro gunpowder works in 1917, it solicited plans from DuPont, Hercules, and several other private explosives makers. Supposedly the ordnance officials "were putting all such information in a melting pot and were going to build a better plant than any."[4] But most plants constructed during the war were jerry-built: the scarcity of construction workers, inflated costs of building materials, pressure for increased output, and uncertain future of the war business discouraged careful planning and a long-term perspective.

Under these circumstances working conditions deteriorated in many factories. Accident rates rose precipitously, and fire losses were far above the prewar level.[5] Employers reported that "adverse labor conditions . . . severely hindered" the safety movement.[6] In the explosives industry:

> Men were found working in buildings half finished. Fumes were heavy, because exhausts had not yet been installed. One factory . . . operated for 17 months with practically no exhausts to carry off very dangerous fumes, with no medical care for the men, and without any provision for personal cleanliness.[7]

Night work became common for men and women, and the twelve-hour shift was prevalent in many boom towns. A prewar movement to end the seven-day week in the steel industry collapsed in the rush to increase production. Though government and union pressure ultimately reduced the worst abuses and, indeed, inaugurated a countermovement to lower working hours and improve shop conditions, the war on the whole reversed the long-term trend toward improvements in the physical setting of the factory.

Equally serious were the problems the worker encountered after leaving the plant. In Detroit, Akron, Bridgeport, Gary, and other centers of the war business, there was a marked decline in the quality of working-class housing and city services. At Bridgeport, for example,

> land values and rents have jumped. There is a shortage of homes. Company owned, multi-family dwellings are going up. Dormitories are being built to house 4,000 unattached girls. Recreation facilities are swamped. Law-breaking and drunkenness are on the increase. Traffic problems are suddenly acute, and the school authorities don't know what to do with the children.[8]

Few builders were willing to invest large sums in a boom that might evaporate with the first sign of peace, and most firms that built factories in urban areas put up houses only for skilled or supervisory workers.

Where they did provide housing for unskilled workers, the results were seldom impressive. The Chester [Pennsylvania] Shipbuilding Company housed "140 or more of its employees in a garage, and seventy-eight more in an old building where every room is crowded with double-decked beds."[9] Abysmal living conditions in the steel mill district of Youngstown, Ohio, sparked a 1916 riot and fire that destroyed hundreds of homes.

Even when factories were built in rural areas, as in the case of most of the explosives plants, housing was often neglected. The massive DuPont works at Carneys Point, Hopewell, Virginia, and Nashville, Tennessee, were better planned than many plants but still left much to be desired. There were never enough dwellings for all the workers, and those that were available were drafty, poorly built structures designed to last only "for the duration." "Davisville," at Hopewell, soon became "Shacktown."[10] At Nitro "the cots . . . are very narrow, hardly sufficient for a man to turn around on. . . . The windows must be kept open at night and . . . there is not sufficient cover to keep warm. . . . The toilet and bath facilities are not at all desirable." Above all, however, the food was "bad in quality and high in price." "Even negroes were embittered against the Grub."[11] Other settlements and "camps" declined to the point that the workers moved out, preferring to trust their luck to outside speculators who threw up "hotels" and rooming houses around the plant. At Carneys Point many Italian workers deserted their rent-free quarters, complaining that living conditions were intolerable.[12]

In other respects, however, the war boom accelerated the trends of the prewar years. Scientific management, for example, became more popular and acceptable as Taylor's disciples adopted a broader view of the worker's role in the factory. Even more far-reaching developments occurred in the labor and personnel area. The pressures that led manufacturers to construct temporary factories, compromise on safety and sanitation, and disregard social problems also encouraged them to take a renewed interest in the recruitment, training, supervision, and organization of the factory labor force. By 1916 most of them would have agreed that the "greatest business problem today is the human problem of labor and the wise handling of men."[13]

RECRUITING THE WARTIME LABOR FORCE

The most serious threat posed by the war was the possibility that the informal system of labor recruitment would break down. The outbreak of hostilities stopped the flow of European peasants into American factories at the same time that it created a vast new market for American goods. The result was a severe labor shortage, particularly in steel, automobile, and meat-packing plants, which were both major employers of unskilled immigrants and producers of war materials or related commodities. A representative of the steel manufacturers observed that "each month . . . makes the situation as to our foreign-born labor supply just so much more critical, as for many years we had been accustomed to a regular influx," and Judge Gary of U.S. Steel reportedly discussed the possibility of importing Asian laborers.[14] In Pennsylvania employers overlooked physical disabilities and hired men they had formerly considered unfit.[15] In Fall River the population declined despite the boom in textiles because many immigrant workers left to take higher-paying jobs in munitions factories.[16]

The severity of the crisis is apparent from the remedial measures that were undertaken. Private employers, acting on the assumption that the informal system had ceased to operate, turned to traditional methods they had used in emergencies. Dispatching recruiters to neighboring towns or to the South, they attempted to lure workers from other occupations or firms with promises of higher wages. Under the circumstances these efforts were counterproductive: wages and turnover increased while the labor shortage persisted. As an alternative, labor reformers advocated an expanded public employment office system. Their ideas attracted widespread interest and resulted in improved state organizations. The establishment of the United States Employment Service (USES) in January 1918 was striking evidence of the impact of the war on industrial management.

The Employment Service, however, faced enormous obstacles. There was no meaningful tradition of government activity in this area; the private and state offices that existed before World War I had seldom recruited factory workers and were in many cases "simply . . . loafing places for the bums and hoboes of the community."[17] To compound this problem the Service itself was organized in a haphazard manner and never wholly escaped the administrative chaos that attended its birth.[18] Equally serious was the mediocre quality of most officials. Federal investigators reported from Nitro, West Virginia:

> An improper recruiting plan and the lack of correct publicity are permitting men who do not have a true understanding of the conditions, to be transported greater distances, to be disappointed on arrival. Men have been brought from New York City, Chicago, and New Orleans and are at present being shipped from Oklahoma and Arizona.[19]

Finally, employers in many cities were convinced that the USES was union-dominated, a belief based largely on the activities of the Seattle office, which recruited workers for unionized shipyards. By 1920 at least thirty-seven employers' associations had passed resolutions opposing the USES. By that time the agency's fate had been settled; in 1919 Congress first reduced its budget and then virtually abolished the Service.[20]

A second major deviation from the prewar recruiting pattern involved, ironically, the foreign-born. Since the turn of the century a growing number of Americans had become concerned over the threat to "American institutions" that the informal methods posed. Their apprehensions were expressed in the formation of organizations designed to promote the assimilation of immigrants. Manufacturers apparently took little interest in this movement until the Wobbly-led strikes at Lawrence and Paterson magnified the specter of labor radicalism.[21] The growing labor shortage after 1914 deepened this concern and led thousands of employers to participate in a campaign to "Americanize" the immigrant.

The specific Americanization programs that employers introduced— such as language training and vocational education—were invariably part of the broader effort to secure and retain an adequate labor supply. As early as 1907 Peter Roberts, the industrial secretary of the YMCA, had started a language and citizenship program for factory workers. Although Roberts was principally interested in promoting assimilation, he "knew how to adjust his program to the needs of corporations."[22] As a consequence his language courses, which many large companies adopted, emphasized "useful" words and phrases and, at least as taught by his followers, attempted to instill good work habits and loyalty to the firm. International Harvester officials, for example, wanted the immigrants to become "good" Americans at the same time they learned to "think and talk intelligently about all the important operations in the works."[23]

The Ford Motor Company, which developed the most ambitious "industrial Americanization" program, initiated mandatory English language classes for its foreign employees in 1914 as part of a far-reaching effort to reduce labor turnover and increase the efficiency of the work force. The company required immigrant workers to attend classes for six to eight months and discharged those who refused or who did not make a sincere effort to learn the language. In July 1915 the first class of 115 workers graduated. A huge parade, including more than 6,000 Ford employees, and an Americanization Day program highlighted the occasion.[24] This demonstration so impressed local proponents of Americanization that they convinced the Detroit Board of Commerce to promote Ford's methods in other local factories. What had started as a pragmatic effort to reduce training and production costs became the basis of a broad patriotic and nationalistic endeavor.[25]

In the following years many other firms had similar experiences. At U.S. Steel Americanization became part of the safety and welfare program; at Goodyear language study was the first step in an increasingly ambitious industrial education program that led to the creation of "Goodyear University" in 1920.[26] Spurred by the U.S. Chamber of Commerce and several government agencies, most large manufacturers became involved in some aspect of the campaign before the end of the war. By 1920 the era of the unnoticed immigrant worker and the isolated ethnic neighborhood was only a memory.

Still, most new factory workers continued to be recruited in the traditional way. Women, for example, had long been employed in the textile, boot and shoe, and clothing industries but generally not in metals and machinery. After 1915 the high wages offered by the machinery and munitions makers and the growing respectability of factory employment drew an increasing number to those industries. A study of 131 metal trades plants employing 49,000 women workers in 1918 concluded that most of the women came "from other industries, or from department stores, offices, restaurants, laundries, and domestic service."[27] Executives of the Remington Arms Company boasted that they employed many former school teachers and nurses.[28]

Employers seldom adopted special programs to obtain women workers. In some cities where the labor market was particularly tight, propaganda campaigns and, after 1917, patriotic appeals attracted women.[29] But in most cases workers recruited their friends or relatives. A large proportion of women employees came from families where one or more male members had factory jobs, often in the same plant.[30] Most employers simply had to "pass the word." In 1920, as in 1900 and 1880, social and familial ties and competitive wage rates were the principal means of attracting unskilled workers.

Occasionally the manufacturer played a more active role in the recruitment process, but one designed primarily to create the "right" atmosphere in the plant and assuage public opinion rather than to attract workers directly. There remained a strong popular prejudice against factory work, a belief that it was brutal and demoralizing and that it encouraged sexual immorality. The employers' self-appointed goal was to eliminate this stigma and make manufacturing respectable, even for "American" women. In most metal trades plants welfare work was introduced with the first women workers. The Detroit Executives Club, with the assistance of various women's organizations, drew up a list of "standard" working conditions for auto plants that employed women.[31] The Wagner Electric Manufacturing Company of St. Louis required female employees to wear uniforms designed to preserve their "modesty" and the "respect of the men with whom they work." To "cater" to their "innate delicacy" all the machines on which they worked were painted white. Finally, Wagner managers "openly" advocated marriages between workers, "and to that end hire no girls or young men that we do not think desirable."[32]

Methods of preparing women for their new occupations also reflected the employers' conception of the proper role of women in society. Since women were likely to be confused and frightened "when they first stood before a big machine tool, the like of which they had never seen before," many large firms established "vestibule" schools to familiarize new employees with factory operations.[33] Similar to those set up to train apprentices, the schools enjoyed a brief vogue. Yet they proved to be too expensive for all but the largest firms, and most women, like most male workers who preceded them, received their training on the job.[34]

The experiences of southern migrants, the other major group of new workers, also demonstrate the persistence of the informal system. Women who took factory jobs after 1915 usually became machine operators, but many unskilled positions, including thousands of common labor jobs, remained. To fill these openings manufacturers relied increasingly on southerners, white and black, who left their homes and agricultural occupations in much the same way that eastern European peasants had abandoned their native countries in previous decades. A million individuals, evenly divided by race, left the South between 1915 and 1920. Whites gravitated to small midwestern cities such as Akron, Ohio, in the throes of the automobile boom. Black migrants went to large cities in the East and Midwest. By mid-1918 more than 4,000 African-Americans worked in Detroit factories; 4,000 labored at the Midvale Steel Company in Philadelphia, 3,500 at the Newport News Shipbuilding and Dry Dock works, and 4,000 at the Carnegie Steel plants in Pittsburgh.[35] Of these only a handful escaped unskilled labor. "The jobs into which the blacks went were usually those which native Americans or Americanized foreign-born white labor did not want."[36]

The role of the employer in this movement was largely passive. In 1916 the Pennsylvania and Erie railroads provided free transportation to thousands of black Floridians and Georgians who agreed to work in the North. Steel companies also sent "labor agents" to Alabama and Mississippi to solicit workers. But these were exceptional measures. Despite the concern of southern state and local officials over the activities of northern agents, "the number at work in the South appears to have been greatly exaggerated."[37] Pennsylvania employers, for example, "will not risk paying transportation, as they have found that those who have previously come north, have not been stable in employment."[38] Nor was it necessary for them to recruit directly. The knowledge that good-paying jobs were available was sufficient to entice many recruits.

In any event the volume of migration increased rapidly. Even before 1915 low agricultural prices, the spread of the boll weevil, floods, increased living costs, lynchings, and repressive police tactics had created a widespread desire for change.[39] Once the exodus began, letters from migrants, northern literature, and the reports of those who returned—the "living example of the prosperity of the North"—accelerated the process.

> The talk in the barber shops and grocery stores where men were wont to assemble soon began to take the form of reasons for leaving. There it was the custom to review all the instances of mistreatment and injustice which fell to the lot of the negro in the South. It was here also that letters from the North were read and fresh news on the exodus were first given out.[40]

Soon it was "just naturally fashionable" to go North, and more and more African Americans "contracted the northern fever."[41]

For most southern migrants as for most European immigrants the routes that posed the fewest problems were the ones that were usually selected. African Americans from southeastern states usually settled in the Northeast because of north-south rail connections. Black Belt migrants, on the other hand, usually went to Chicago, Detroit, or other midwestern centers. Black enclaves also formed in many towns along the rail routes, as migrants ran out of funds or deserted "free" trains for fear of having to repay the cost of their transportation.[42]

Once a group had established itself in a northern city, the flow of migrants to that area continued automatically.

> Each member of the vanguard controlled a small group of friends at home, if only the members of his immediate family. Letters sent back, representing that section of the North and giving directions concerning the route best known, easily influenced the next groups to join their friends rather than explore new fields. In fact . . . the most congested points in the North when the migration reached its height, were those favorite cities to which the first group had gone.[43]

A contemporary observer discovered three stages in the migration process. First came the "less responsible characters, younger men for the most part, who readily respond to the promises of high wages and free transportation." Next came the "industrious, thrifty, unskilled workers. . . . The men usually go first to earn money and look over the ground. Their families soon follow." Finally there followed the "skilled artisans and business and professional men" who accompanied the "rank and file on whom they largely depend for patronage."[44]

If black workers were recruited in the same manner as immigrants, the treatment they received on the job was also remarkably similar. Several steel and machinery firms in Pittsburgh employed black welfare workers to handle complaints, and the Newport News Shipbuilding and Dry Dock Company and American Rolling Mills Company developed extensive welfare and recreation programs.[45] In general, however, little was done. Since black workers were available and obviously "Americanized," there was no compelling reason to interfere with the traditional, informal methods of the past.

THE EMERGENCE OF PERSONNEL MANAGEMENT

Far more important were the changes in the recruitment process that occurred once the prospective employee entered the plant. Overnight the employment department and employment manager became standard features of the progressive factory, superseding the old-time foreman, the welfare secretary, and, to a lesser degree, the efficiency engineer.[46] Many activities of the new departments and managers had been introduced before 1915. But the idea that personnel relations constituted a distinct, important, and identifiable function was comparatively novel and can only be explained in terms of the labor market turmoil that developed after 1915.

Although the modern personnel department dated from the NCR strike of 1901, few employers imitated the eccentric Patterson in the following decade. Firms in meat packing and steel, for example, continued to operate employment bureaus to select unskilled or skilled labor, respectively, but it is unlikely that any of these offices performed the functions of the NCR Labor Department or the post-1915 employment departments.[47] In 1911, when officers of the Vocation Bureau of Boston invited fifty men responsible for "the hiring of employees in the large shops and stores in the city and vicinity" to establish the first "Employment Managers' Association," they reflected their own hopes rather than the state of personnel work in Boston.[48]

Meanwhile, progressive firms were introducing many of the new activities that personnel offices would later perform. The new apprenticeship became popular after 1910; welfare and "efficiency" work also became widespread, and labor legislation—spurred by the rising tempo of political reform—became more stringent and enforceable. Yet each series of innovations remained separate and distinct, both in the eyes of their promoters and in those of the employers who adopted them. A few firms that initiated extensive welfare programs also introduced scientific management, but they were a small minority before World War I.[49] In 1912 L. P. Alford noted in a famous report on the "Art of Industrial Management" that the "most important change" of the previous decade had been the development of "an attitude of questioning, of research, of careful investigation . . . of seeking for exact knowledge and then shaping action on discovered facts."[50] Although there was abundant evidence of this trend, the "discovered facts" had not yet dictated a comprehensive approach to the human problems of industry.

This was apparent in the most ambitious and widely publicized prewar effort to reduce labor turnover—the 1913–1914 reform program of the Ford Motor Company. By that time the Highland Park plant was one of the best organized, most modern factories in the country. The foremen had virtually no voice in the acquisition of materials, in scheduling and routing, and in determining the pace of work. But in all matters relating to the largely immigrant labor force they remained supreme. Two signs of their authority were a plethora of wage rates and an astronomical turnover rate. Fifty-two thousand men were hired to fill thirteen thousand jobs in 1913. Of those who left, the foremen discharged at least eight thousand.[51]

The Ford reform plan was introduced between mid-1913 and the spring of 1914 and accompanied the technological and organizational innovations that made Ford famous. Despite the wide publicity given the five-dollar day, the most famous part of it, the exact provisions of the plan remain unclear. What is certain is that a large number of men were responsible for it and that there was little central coordination. Apparently John R. Lee, the new head of the employment office, first suggested the need for change. Henry Ford was receptive and sent Lee on a "tour of inspection" to observe other plants. Lee's itinerary is unknown, but judging from his conclusions it was probably confined to auto plants and other factories in the Detroit area. "He returned convinced that not a single plant had met the situation wisely, and that the Ford Company would have to devise its own policies. It did not occur to him or Ford that trained experts in labor relations might be helpful."[52] In any event it seems clear that the Ford plan was a pragmatic response to existing problems rather than an effort to copy or emulate the best practice of the day.

The Ford program consisted of three important measures. The first, introduced in late 1913, stripped the foremen of much of their remaining authority. It established seven classes of workers, each with specific ranges of wage rates; it eliminated the foremen's power to discharge—at least without appeal and review; and it gave the employment department, heretofore a typical hiring office, increased responsibility.[53] In the future departments heads would requisition new workers, and the employment department would determine which applicants were suitable. When a foreman discharged a worker,

> the man may then protest his discharge to the head of the employment
> department, who passes on the case and may either make the discharge final,
> or decide that the man may be a worthy servant. In the latter case, he files the
> man's name as an applicant for Ford service, and if possible places the man at
> once in another department.[54]

The other two reforms were the five-dollar day and the "Sociological Department." The former, unlike customary incentive wage plans, was designed to attract and retain a hard-working but docile labor force: managers relied on machine-paced work and "driving" supervisors to achieve production goals. The Sociological Department was likewise an unusual and perhaps ominous development. Its principal responsibility was to insure, through investigations of the workers' homes and family life, that they shared their employer's middle-class values and warranted the five-dollar day. Inadvertently, the department also popularized the idea of home visiting in urban ethnic neighborhoods, a practice that was subsequently adopted by other firms to combat congested and unsanitary living conditions, one of the principal sources of turnover during the war period.[55] In later years Samuel M. Marquis, Lee's successor as head of the Sociological Department, noted that Ford had no welfare plan beyond the home visits, that there were "no cafeterias, no recreation places, no entertainment, nothing."[56] His statements underlined the idiosyncratic character of the Ford reforms and the type of response that unacceptable levels of turnover could evoke during the war period.

Ford executives, however, were not the only managers who discovered the costs of turnover in 1914. Businessmen had long been aware of the costs of skilled workers exits, but before this there were no systematic studies of turnover and no definite knowledge of its expense to the firm. In 1913 M. W. Alexander attempted to remedy this omission by studying turnover in twelve metals and machinery plants and estimating the actual money cost of labor force fluctuations. His study, first published in 1914, and others that followed attracted considerable attention because of the apparent magnitude of the problem they revealed.[57] As a result employers became aware of turnover and initiated a widespread movement to reform recruitment practices. As Paul H. Douglas noted in 1919, the "chief argument" for the creation of employment departments and hence for the revision of employment practices generally "was the possibility of reducing the turnover of labor."[58]

Under these circumstances it was natural that hiring and firing procedures received the closest attention. The methods that had prevailed since the origins of the factory system suddenly were inadequate and wasteful. Meyer Bloomfield summarized the new view when he wrote that "in no other phase of management is there so much unintelligence, recklessness of cost, and lack of imagination."[59] As a consequence the early literature of personnel management emphasized selection and interview techniques, employment office operations, "follow-up" procedures, curbs on the foremen's power to discharge, and other activities that had been tried at pioneering firms like NCR and Ford. Together these measures constituted the principal functions of the new employment departments and the most significant challenges to the traditional methods of recruiting employees.

The emphasis on turnover and hiring was also reflected in the new techniques that appeared during the war. One of these, psychological testing, antedated World War I but had seldom been used in industry.[60] Walter Dill Scott, a pioneer industrial psychologist, had developed intelligence tests for industrial workers by 1916. Scott's clients—which included Cheney Brothers and Joseph & Feiss—provided the experience he needed to improve his methods and sell an extensive testing program to the Army in 1917. By the end of 1918 his Committee on Classification and Personnel had tested over three million men.[61] Psychological testing became popular among employers in the postwar years. Together with his associates from the Committee on Classification, Scott formed a consulting firm—the Scott Company—that served over forty corporate clients between 1919 and 1923.[62]

Another innovation, less dramatic but closely related, was "job analysis," or the standardization and classification of occupations and pay rates. This was an extension of Taylor's time study techniques that made little headway until employment managers usurped the foreman's role as labor recruiter.[63] To hire employees for a large factory required more technical knowledge than the typical employment manager possessed; thus written job specifications became necessary. At the Westinghouse Electric and Manufacturing Company a special committee established standard occupations throughout the plant, analyzed "all the jobs in each occupation," classified the jobs in accordance "with their relative value to the industry," established general wage categories, and determined what method of wage payment was appropriate for each type of job.[64] The Labor Department's Bureau of Labor Statistics prepared "the most complete set of job analyses" for the federal Employment Service.[65] In the postwar years job analysis became a standard feature of personnel practice in large firms.

A third major innovation logically derived from the new concern over turnover and selection procedures. Once employers acknowledged that foremen had too many duties to perform and that hiring and firing were jobs for experts, they often reconsidered other traditional personnel functions as well. But instead of following Taylor's logic and creating specialist—or functional—foremen to handle various types of labor problems, they adopted the opposite course. Within their more circumscribed realm, foremen were encouraged to be broader, to become personnel experts as well as production supervisors. Bloomfield contrasted the "new" foreman who was urged "to think of [his] duties in a professional way" with the "old" foreman who "is a producing engine merely."[66] There were new attempts to identify the qualities of a successful foreman, but these seldom went beyond the superficial generalities—the need for tact, sincerity, loyalty, initiative, trade education, and executive ability, for example—that would apply to any managerial position.[67] More important was the development of a "new foremanship" based on systematic training. Foremanship training first took the form of informal discussion sessions, but in many plants such meetings soon became "part of a plan for deliberate training."[68] By the 1920s foremen training was an accepted feature of advanced personnel programs.

Even the "new foremanship," however, could not obscure the fact that personnel management, like the managerial reforms that preceded it, developed largely at the expense of the foreman's traditional role. The supervisor's haphazard approach to hiring and firing led to the creation of a new group of factory experts, just as his haphazard approach to costs, materials, wages, and production schedules had earlier generated other groups of experts. The real thrust of the events of 1915–1920 was most explicitly demonstrated at Goodyear, where a "Flying Squadron" of select workers under the control of the factory manager was created to handle specific problems anywhere in the plant. Understandably "the foremen did not like the idea of men coming to them but really working for someone else."[69] The leader of the "Flying Squadron" subsequently became the first head of the Goodyear employment department.[70]

Despite its emphasis on selection and dismissal procedures, the wartime attack on turnover was by no means confined to these areas. Experts on employment management listed scores of additional activities, from paying "adequate" wages to visiting workers' homes.[71] The ones they mentioned most frequently were welfare programs. A study of 431 establishments (approximately half of which were factories) by the Bureau of Labor Statistics in 1916–1917 revealed a growing interest in medical facilities, lunchrooms, "rest" rooms, savings plans, libraries, social clubs, and "family work."[72] A handful of companies also introduced stock purchase, pension, or group insurance plans—the "new" welfare measures of the 1920s.

The Bureau's statistics also indicate an important distinction between the manufacturers and other firms. Most factories had first aid or hospital facilities, washrooms, lockers, and drinking fountains.[73] Many also introduced "entertainment" and "family work"—the latter a product of the rise of "home visiting" in both northern immigrant neighborhoods and southern mill towns.[74] But they lagged behind stores, utilities, and railroads in other activities, including the "new" welfare plans. Only U.S. Steel and a few metal-working plants, for example, had pension programs. Apparently a growing number of manufacturers were becoming skeptical of the value of additional welfare measures for factory workers. In the postwar years welfare plans were increasingly designed for white-collar workers. Even in 1916, 317 firms provided salaried workers with paid vacations, but only 16 provided vacations for all employees.[75]

The organization that administered these activities and that inevitably provided much of the impetus for new programs was the employment department. Although there was no necessary sequential relationship between the adoption of personnel methods and the introduction of a specialized administrative entity, most firms centralized personnel work in a distinct department. The process differed from firm to firm.

> One began with the mere keeping of employees' records so that some satisfactory data might be available concerning each employee. [In another] . . . the management realized that its policies with respect to the treatment of employees were not being adhered to by its executives, and for that reason these functions were later given over to the employment manager.[76]

In some firms the welfare department became the employment department; in others the employment office was upgraded into a personnel department.

While most managers agreed that these departments should be involved in the selection, training, and discharge of employees and should administer the firm's benefit programs, there was no consensus on the exact jurisdiction of the employment department. "In no area of management," wrote Clarence J. Hicks, "is the character and personality of the controlling executive or group more clearly reflected than in policies dealing with labor relations."[77]

Equally diverse in training and experience were the men who headed the new employment departments. John R. Lee had been a production superintendent, Samuel Marquis a minister, and Hicks a YMCA worker. Lawyers, teachers, doctors, nurses, and clergymen also became employment managers. The only obvious tie was with welfare work. "The line from the social and welfare secretaries to the employment manager is a direct one."[78] By 1917, however, this situation was changing. Employment management had no figure comparable in stature to Taylor, but men like Meyer Bloomfield and Roy W. Kelly of the Boston Vocation Bureau, Boyd Fisher of the Detroit Executives Club, and Ordway Tead and Robert Bruere of the Bureau of Industrial Research played major roles in making personnel management a distinctive occupation.[79] By 1920 they had made substantial progress in defining the employment manager's qualifications and in creating the inevitable trappings of a profession.

A major step in this process was the introduction of employment managers' training programs in 1917–1918. To reduce turnover and labor unrest various government agencies, notably the Ordnance Department and the Emergency Fleet Corporation, urged the use of employment managers in munitions factories, shipyards, and other war plants. Since there were only a handful of men who had experience in personnel management, the government sponsored six-week cram courses at a dozen universities. At the University of Rochester, where the first classes were held, the program included lectures on employment office practice, labor economics, and industrial management; visits to local factories; readings; and discussions. "We have been bringing the factory into the classroom," wrote the head of the Rochester project.[80] By the time of the Armistice more than 360 graduates of these courses were working as employment managers.[81]

More important for the movement as a whole, perhaps, was the development of local and national organizations of employment managers. After the creation of the Boston Employment Managers' Association, similar bodies appeared in other major cities.[82] The first step toward a national organization came in 1914, when a group of employment managers met in Minneapolis. They met regularly in the following years and formed a National Association of Employment Managers in 1918. More than two thousand persons attended the Association's 1919 convention and more than five thousand the 1920 meeting. The organization lost much of its membership during the recession of 1920–1922 and merged with the National Association of Corporation (Schools) Training in 1922 to form the National Personnel Association, the leading institutional sponsor of personnel management in the 1920s.[83]

The practical effects of this activity are difficult to assess. Though several hundred firms introduced employment departments between 1915 and the beginning of the postwar recession, only a minority embraced more than a handful of the most widely discussed programs. Paul Douglas estimated in 1919 that only fifty firms were doing "well-rounded and thorough work."[84] Yet this small leadership cadre had a profound effect on the factory and on the wider personnel movement of the 1920s.

The activities of seven companies that were acknowledged leaders— Cheney Brothers, Curtis Publishing, Plimpton Press, Joseph & Feiss, Eastern Manufacturing, American Rolling Mill Company, and Dennison Manufacturing—suggest several conclusions about the maximum effect of personnel management before 1920.[85] First, a firm's previous commitment to welfare work was an accurate predictor of wartime activity. At Cheney Brothers, Joseph & Feiss, Curtis Publishing, and American Rolling Mill, employment departments evolved out of earlier welfare programs and reflected this origin. Employment managers at these companies were welfare secretaries who also assumed responsibility for hiring, training, and firing.[86] In fact, only Cheney Brothers and Curtis Publishing appear to have made any distinctions between welfare work and employment management. Plimpton Press and Dennison Manufacturing first established employment departments as hiring offices, gradually expanded their functions to include welfare activities, and finally made them formal personnel departments. Eastern Manufacturing, on the other hand, had only introduced scientific management before the war. Indeed, the company's wartime personnel program was a reflection of the growing flexibility of Taylor's disciples. Keppele Hall, the engineer who guided the Eastern reorganization, explained:

> A big factor is . . . the human relationship. It is one thing we are emphasizing more and more at the plant of the Eastern Manufacturing Company. . . . It makes the men feel the responsibility more. We have meetings with the men every Saturday night. We are endeavoring, moreover, to make every employee feel that he or she is getting absolutely a square deal. . . . We have organized a "Service Department" which is essentially an employees' department.[87]

The change may have been too rapid for the workers, who initially opposed the employment manager's activities.[88] Her experience underlines the important role that welfare work played in facilitating the introduction of personnel management.

Second, whatever the method of introducing personnel management, the employment manager assumed many of the foreman's former powers. In all seven firms they were responsible for selecting new employees, and in every one except American Rolling Mill and Eastern Manufacturing they had some authority over discharges. While most of them were also involved in job analysis and training activities, they did not actually set wage rates.[89] In general, then, employment managers at these companies usurped the foreman's traditional prerogatives of selection, training, and dismissal. In addition they indirectly affected the manager-worker relationship by administering the firm's welfare programs.

Third, the employment manager, once established, had a major influence on the type of activities that the company introduced. After hiring an employment manager, Joseph & Feiss initiated a program of home visits, Dennison introduced a foremen's training course, and American Rolling Mills created one of the most advanced welfare programs for black workers. Thus employment managers were more than heads of departments: they were also representatives of a point of view that had never been consistently articulated in the past.

The experiences of other, less adventurous firms reveal the same tendencies. Roy W. Kelley, who made an intensive study of employment practices at thirty-seven New England companies in 1916, found that the introduction of employment departments eliminated much of the foremen's authority and introduced a more systematic approach to recruitment. Firms with employment managers also exercised greater care in selecting employees, provided more opportunities for advancement, and attempted to eliminate causes of turnover.[90] While the effectiveness of these efforts diminished as the efficacy of the employment department declined, the overall effect was sufficient to mark the beginning of systematic employment management as a milestone in the development of the twentieth-century factory system.

THE ADVENT OF FACTORY "ORGANIZATION"

The labor upheavals of the immediate prewar years had created new interest in organization and two approaches to industrial unionism. By 1914 the clothing workers had demonstrated that a unified and committed factory labor force was no more difficult to organize than a craft group and that an industrial union could match the best craft-industrial organization. During the war years this demonstration would have a profound effect. Yet an alternate approach won even greater attention and support. The alternate was not the IWW, which, after a last flurry of activity, was mortally wounded by the attacks of the Wilson Administration.[91] The second type of wartime organization was the "works council," "employee representation" plan, or, more directly, company union, which encompassed all workers in a plant and was designed to achieve the employer's as well as the employees' objectives. This feature was the key to its success. Because of it, the initial phase in the "organization" of the factory labor force mostly occurred under management auspices.[92]

The origins of company unionism are obscure. Apparently the practice of delegating authority to the foreman delayed its appearance until the turn of the century. In any case, the first important organization was the Filene Cooperative Association, introduced by the innovative Filene brothers in 1898. The Filenes' association gradually took control of the company's extensive personnel program, achieving extraordinary influence, but it had little immediate impact on other firms.[93]

Another early plan, the "factory committee" of the Nerst Lamp Works in Pittsburgh, was more influential. Devised by H. F. J. Porter in 1903–1904 to administer a suggestion system he modeled after the one Patterson had introduced at NCR, the Nerst organization quickly expanded into a full-scale "industrial democracy" plan.[94] The committee consisted of representatives of the management, workers, and foremen, with the plant superintendent acting as chairman. Its function was to evaluate the employees' suggestions. The foremen were instructed to "encourage their employees to think for themselves . . . and if there seemed to be a lagging of the supply from a department at any time, its foreman was promptly called to account and urged to stimulate his employees to further initiative."[95] Perhaps because of this mandate the committee soon expanded and acquired new functions. It formed numerous subordinate organizations, including a musical and dramatic association, Literary Club, Camera and Sketch Club, Athletic Club, and Mutual Aid Association.[96] In addition the factory committee "considered the taking on and laying off of all employees and succeeded in stabilizing the working organization."[97] For its part the management introduced the premium plan, hired a nurse and visiting doctor, and instituted fire drills.

Porter developed his ideas in the following years. In 1907 he introduced a similar amalgam of personnel and welfare work at the Nelson Valve Company of Philadelphia.[98] In 1908 he described his plan as a "democratic system of government very similar to that which exists in our states or at the national capital."[99] The workers' committee functioned like the House of Representatives, the management committee like the Senate. Both had to agree on "legislation," which the company president could "veto."[100] Porter's approach won a few adherents before the war. Its most important convert was another reformer, John Leitch, who introduced "industrial democracy" at the Packard Piano Company of Fort Wayne, Indiana, in 1912 and became the leading exponent of the "congressional" type of company union during and after World War I.

A third important prewar experiment took place at the Colorado Fuel and Iron Company in 1913–1914 as a consequence of the famous "Ludlow massacre." The deaths of women and children shocked and embarrassed John D. Rockefeller, Jr., the company's principal stockholder, who then hired MacKenzie King, a Canadian labor expert, to devise a solution that would prevent a recurrence of the disaster. The "Rockefeller Plan," as King's solution was known, was introduced in the company's coal mines in 1914 and in its steel mill at Pueblo, Colorado, in 1916. It provided for the election of employee representatives, meetings between them and the plant managers, and joint committees on grievances, safety, recreation, and sanitation. The committees could recommend but not initiate changes, and the management reserved the right to act on personnel matters without consulting the employee representatives.[101] An assistant to the company president administered the program.

The operation of the plan resulted in several major improvements. The company installed safety devices and modern sanitary facilities. The foremen lost their right to discharge, and even disciplinary actions could be appealed. "The superintendents do not like it," explained one worker, "because it takes too much authority from them."[102] Yet the representatives had little influence on other policies. One of the workers' chief demands was an end to the twelve-hour day, but the company refused to make any concessions until 1918, when other steel firms reduced the work day or paid overtime for more than eight hours' work. Company policy in these areas continued to reflect industry trends, not the deliberations of the committees.[103] In any event the Rockefeller Plan was no more influential than the Filene or Porter-Leitch programs in the prewar period. A handful of firms adopted works councils, but compared to scientific management or welfare work the company union movement was of little consequence.

The emergence of worker organizations during World War I was due, in part, to the same problems that led employers to introduce employment departments and extend their welfare programs. The impact of war business, both on the firm and the economy, produced numerous dislocations. Employers who could not resist the opportunities of the moment nevertheless worried about the possible loss of the "old spirit," that—at least in their minds—had animated their relations with their employees. Or they wondered "whether there was a limit to the size a plant could grow and still be efficient." [104] Equally challenging was the expanded role of government. Public expenditures created and sustained the industrial boom, but with the dollars came formal and informal restrictions, most notably in the transportation, communications, and energy industries. In manufacturing, the overriding public policy goal of sustained high levels of output dictated an aggressive approach to any action, such as a strike, that might curtail production.

Industrial workers, on the other hand, were often new to the factory and uncommitted to a particular firm or city. Even when they did not move from job to job, their situation was highly unstable. Inflation led to frequent wage increases but little or no increase in purchasing power. The working day (with frequent overtime) was long, and shop conditions often deteriorated.[105] There were more work stoppages in 1916 than in any previous year, and 1917 set another record. Nearly three-quarters of these strikes resulted from disputes over wages and hours.[106] One way to bring order to a seemingly chaotic environment, to convert problems into opportunities, was to organize.

The outpouring of nationalistic and idealistic sentiment that accompanied American involvement in the conflict also influenced worker behavior. Though patriotic appeals were often used to combat the IWW and other antiwar groups, they provided a powerful stimulus to conventional organization. To many workers and employers it seemed illogical to fight for democracy in Europe when it did not exist in American industry. This type of reasoning, coupled with the Americanization campaign, brought a marked change in the viewpoint of many immigrants. As David Brody has written, "the [war] experience recast many of the immigrants' basic assumptions. By the end of the war they felt themselves *of* as well as *in* America. The change fulfilled the prime precondition for the unionization of the Hunky workmen." [107]

In this setting the enlarged role of government in labor relations proved decisive. At one level the Wilson Administration's inclusion of the AFL in the war effort, symbolized by Samuel Gompers' presence on the Council of National Defense, the President's chief advisory group, gave the orthodox labor movement a new status, an aura of respectability it had not enjoyed before. On another level the government provided a setting favorable to union activity. This was due both to the close relationship between the Wilson administration and the labor movement and to the exigencies of the war effort. Many of the men who occupied high positions in the agencies that dealt with labor issues were advocates of independent union-ism.[108] Felix Frankfurter of the War Labor Politics Board, for example, employed various devices to convince—or coerce—U.S. Steel to accept unionization. The USES office in Seattle was a major factor in the organization of the city's shipyard workers.[109] But even if the Administration had not been allied with the AFL, the demand for increased production dictated a policy of labor harmony and cooperation. The dramatic increase in the number of strikes in 1916–1917 emphasized the importance of this policy. Thus, when packinghouse workers threatened to strike in 1917, the President's Mediation Commission worked out a compromise that provided for the arbitration of all disputes and encouraged the unions to undertake an extensive organizing campaign.[110] In other industries a similar pattern emerged.

But in some situations government agencies played an even more active role. Both the Shipbuilding Labor Adjustment Board, created in August 1917 to handle shipyard disputes, and the National War Labor Board (NWLB), established in March 1918 to deal with conflicts in other war industries, eventually insisted on some form of worker organization and collective bargaining. The Shipbuilding Board was at first inconsistent; it required shop committees in some awards but not in others. But after October 1918 the Board demanded committees in all shipyards where managers were already bargaining with independent labor unions.[111] From the beginning, the NWLB attempted to chart a middle course. It guaranteed workers the right to organize and bargain collectively, but it did not permit unions to demand recognition. The result was the widespread adoption of shop committees or workers' councils in firms covered by NWLB awards.[112] In some cases independent labor unions "captured" these committees; in most, however, they remained company unions backed by the authority of the government.

Yet direct or indirect restrictions on anti-union activities had a greater immediate impact than the awards of the Shipbuilding Board or the NWLB. The lure of business and profits and the government's emphasis on uninterrupted production, labor harmony, and teamwork temporarily hamstrung antilabor employers. Most of those with a stake in the war business relaxed their traditional policies as long as formal union recognition was not an issue. Accordingly, the unions most directly affected by the war boom experienced the greatest gains. The metal trades organizations expanded dramatically; the Machinists alone increased their membership from 112,000 to 1917 to 330,000 in 1920. The Amalgamated Association, virtually moribund before World War I, had 31,000 members in 1920.[113] Even employees of aggressively managed corporations such as General Electric began to form coalitions of locals to increase their bargaining power. Union leaders who had the time or energy to think about the future generally emphasized political action. Apparently few of them thought seriously about the special challenges of factory organizations or the successes of the International Ladies Garment Workers and the Amalgamated Clothing Workers. In most organized plants, union leaders devoted their attention to placating factious ethnic groups and formulating wage and hours demands—the keys, they believed, to retaining the workers' support. Grievances were dealt with on an ad hoc basis. Collective bargaining was equated with contract negotiations.

A promising exception appeared in the northern textile centers, where a decade of rivalry between the United Textile Workers, the IWW, and various local and craft organizations had left most employees unrepresented and disheartened. In 1918 Sidney Hillman and his colleagues created a new independent union, the Amalgamated Textile Workers of America, as an antidote to the industry's endemic factionalism. For officers, they turned to a group of social gospel minister-turned-militants, headed by A. J. Muste. Muste and his colleagues were successful at first, winning several strikes and recruiting more than 40,000 members. But as the environment for organizing deteriorated, their fortunes plummeted. The ATWA never became a force inside the plants and in 1920 succumbed to the postwar recession, leaving the industry with pockets of organization but little or no prospect of a larger or more effective union presence.[114]

The decline in government spending and regulation spelled disaster for many other unions. The termination of government contracts for ships, armaments, vehicles, food, and clothing, coupled with the deflationary policies of the Federal Reserve, resulted in massive layoffs that undermined the workers' organizations. By 1923 the Machinists had only 97,000 members; a nascent auto workers' union had vanished. At the same time the end of government-sponsored collective bargaining removed another prop of the wartime union movement. The open-shop campaign and the strikes of the postwar period, notably in steel in 1919 and meat packing in 1921, suggested the bleak future of trade unionism in the manufacturing sector without government assistance.

These developments, so disastrous for the labor movement, had the opposite effect on company unions. The turmoil of the war period created a more receptive attitude among employers to the idea of organization. The demands of the NWLB and other government bodies exposed hundreds of managers to the operations of shop committees. And while there was much opposition to "imposed" plans, the results, from the employer's viewpoint, were often surprisingly good. In Bridgeport, where an NWLB award led to the introduction of shop committees in thirty-five firms and where most manufacturers remained bitterly opposed to unionism in any form, the general manager of the Remington Arms Company praised the operation of his shop organization.[115] A representative of the Bridgeport Brass Company was even more explicit:

> About 100 meetings of committees have been held . . . at 25 percent of which hours and wages have been discussed, and in no case has the conclusion reached been other than unanimous and entirely satisfactory to the employees and the management. . . . In order to get the greatest benefit out of these committees, the safety and sanitation work, as well as the work of the sick benefit association with the insurance features, have been turned over to them. Joint committees are also handling recreational and athletic activities in all plants of the company. . . . Many feel that agitators may gain control of the committees and organize them as union representatives, but I am convinced that this danger is not to be feared as long as the management has the confidence of the employees.[116]

The war experience thus suggested to many employers that the ideas of Porter, Leitch, and Rockefeller were consistent with the goals of systematic management, personnel administration, and the open shop.

This realization was a major factor in the spread of company unionism during the postwar period. Despite the fact that many NWLB plans did not outlive the board, the total number of "works councils" increased from approximately 225 in 1918 to at least 725 in 1922.[117] Most firms modeled their organizations after the Rockefeller or NWLB plans, which provided for elected employee representatives and "joint" meetings with the management. A substantial minority—Goodyear and Dan River Mills were perhaps the best known—adopted Leitch's "industrial democracy" plan, but many of these companies abandoned it in the 1920s because of the complicated procedures it required and declining interest in "democracy" as in industrial relations policy.[118]

A National Industrial Conference Board report published in 1922 explained why company unionism had retained its popularity. At first, the report noted, works councils were "safety valves" to enable management to handle grievances and prevent strikes. But few successful company unions retained this narrow focus. The handling of grievances became the "secondary purpose" of the organization; their "primary purpose" was to enlist the employees' cooperation in the "economical and efficient operation of an industry."[119] The transition was not always easy. One shoe manufacturer explained,

> We are frank to say that so far the majority of their suggestions and requests have been of a rather pseudo-selfish nature, that is, they seem to have asked for and suggested things which would benefit the employees, rather more than the company itself. This we believe is natural and we have encouraged it, at the same time, we have tried to guide them into thinking of things from the company's standpoint.[120]

By 1921–1922 most firms have apparently succeeded. The report noted only two cases, among the more than three hundred studied, where the employee representatives had rejected pay reductions during the recession.[121]

Thus, although the advent of factory organizations seemed at first to represent a sequel to the events of 1909–1914 and to introduce a new era in manager-worker relationships, by 1920 it had become another managerial innovation. The war and postwar boom created unique opportunities for trade union organizers in the manufacturing sector. But when the stimulus to independent union activity disappeared, the opportunities also vanished and the achievements of 1915–1920 proved exceedingly ephemeral. More important, the war situation led many manufacturers, including many who had pioneered in the development of managerial techniques, to realize the importance of collective action among the workers. To control the factory and its labor force, they realized, involved more than improvements in the physical setting, better methods of communication, financial or social incentives to increase production, and the introduction of systematic personnel management. It was also necessary to deal with the worker as a group member. This realization marked an important step toward the human relations approach of the post-World War II period and the end of the formative period of the twentieth-century factory system.

Epilogue

As the preceding essays suggest, the four decades after 1880 were an important transition period in the emergence of twentieth-century industrial management. The growing size and complexity of the factory led manufacturers and engineers to modify or scrap the traditional methods of shop management—the methods that had prevailed since the beginning of the factory system in America. And though their innovations were often primitive by mid-twentieth-century standards, the course of future developments was clear by the beginning of the postwar recession. Even the role of the independent labor union, the major missing element in the factory of 1920, had been foreshadowed in the turmoil of the war years and the awakening of manufacturers to the importance of group activity.

To most manufacturers the management of the factory had been a secondary consideration even before the rise of the large corporation in the late nineteenth century. The routine nature of factory production and the tradition of relying on the first-line supervisors for day-to-day direction effectively removed manufacturers from the shop floor unless an exceptional situation, such as the introduction of a new process or a labor disturbance, demanded their presence. After 1880, however, the size and sophistication of factory operations gradually transformed the relationships between manufacturers, supervisors, and workers.

There was nothing magical about the year 1880; there were antecedents of most features of the new factory system before that date. Nor was there a broad consensus on the reasons for change. Though factory managers seldom discussed their innovations in analytical terms, those who did usually emphasized the importance of the "labor problem." Because of this emphasis many employers who had never been involved in labor disputes became concerned about their relations with their workers and experimented with new administrative techniques. As Taylor demonstrated with considerable success, the best way to encourage management reform was to raise the bogey of labor unrest. Still, manufacturers seldom acted until they were convinced that change would pay tangible returns.

It was no coincidence that John Patterson adopted the slogan "It pays" or that the state inspectors stressed the compatibility of their work and the profit motive. Perhaps some employers acted for social or philanthropic reasons and defended their actions in economic terms to avoid ridicule, but they were a small and intimidated minority.

The results of the changes that occurred between 1880 and 1920 generally fulfilled the manufacturers' expectations. There was general agreement among contemporary observers that the new factory environment was vastly improved. Systematic and scientific management enabled the manager to recognize, if not solve, the problems of directing and coordinating production in the modern factory, and personnel management successfully addressed the labor problem, at least in manufacturing, until the Depression of the 1930s. Ford, Halsey, Taylor, Heinz, Patterson, Porter, and Bloomfield never promised more.

The new factory system was thus the product of many simultaneous developments that occurred in hundreds and in some cases thousands of individual factories. There were few dramatic changes, even fewer turning points; many manufacturers operated in 1920 as they had in 1880. But the cumulative effects were striking. An older manager, foreman, or worker who had been employed in a large plant throughout his career and who looked back after World War I would have been amazed at the differences. The first factory system, the factory system associated with nineteenth-century industrial growth, had disappeared. A new order, different in its broad outline and its details, had emerged.

Notes
Bibliographical Note
Index

Notes

PREFACE

1. This emphasis was common in the older stage theories of industrialization. See N. S. B. Gras, *Industrial Evolution* (Cambridge, Mass., 1930). It is implicit in the more recent writing on the origins of the European factory. See Herman Freudenberger and Fritz Redlich, "The Industrial Development of Europe: Reality, Symbols, Images," *Kyklos* 17 (1964): 372–401; Herman Freudenberger, "Three Mercantilistic Proto-Factories; *Business History Review* 40 (1966): 167–89; and Stanley D. Chapman, "The Textile Factory Before Arkwright: A Typology of Factory Development," *Business History Review* 48 (1974): 451–78. The classic study of the factory system in the United States is Carroll Wright, "The Factory System of the United States," *Tenth Census of the United States,* 1880, vol. 2, *Manufactures,* (Washington, 1883). Also see George Rogers Taylor, *The Transportation Revolution, 1815–1860* (New York, 1951), chap. 11.

2. A contemporary expert, Horace L. Arnold, defined a large plant as one with five hundred or more workers. Horace L. Arnold, *The Complete Cost-Keeper* (New York, 1912), p. 10; see also Sidney Pollard, *The Genesis of Modern Management* (London, 1965), pp. 20–21.

3. Bruce Laurie and Mark Schmitz, "Manufacture and Productivity: The Making of an Industrial Base, Philadelphia, 1850–1880," in *Philadelphia: Work Space, Family and Group Experience in the Nineteenth Century,* ed. Theodore Hershberg (New York, 1981), pp. 53–61.

4. Alfred D. Chandler, Jr., *The Visible Hand: The Managerial Revolution in American Business* (Cambridge, Mass., 1977), p. 241.

CHAPTER 1. THE SETTING

1. Throughout this book I have used the word *manufacturer* to refer to the top manager or managers who had ultimate authority over the operation of the factory. I have made no effort to categorize executives who operated at levels above the plant.

2. See Thomas Dublin, *Women at Work: The Transformation of Work and Community in Lowell, Massachusetts, 1826–1860* (New York, 1979), and Cynthia J. Shelton, *The Mills of Manayunk: Industrialization and Social Conflict in the Philadelphia Region, 1787–1837* (Baltimore, 1986), chap. 3. Also David A. Zonderman, *Aspirations & Anxieties: New England Workers and the Mechanized Factory System, 1814–1850* (New York, 1992).

3. *Twelfth Census of the United States, 1900,* vol. 7, *Manufactures,* pt. 1 (Washington, 1902), table 19, p. lxxxv.

4. Steven J. Ross, *Workers on the Edge: Work, Leisure, and Politics in Industrializing Cincinnati, 1788–1890* (New York, 1985), p. 80; Olivier Zunz, *The Changing Face of Inequality: Urbanization, Industrial Development, and Immigrants in Detroit, 1880–1920* (Chicago, 1982), p. 18. See also Gerald G. Eggert, *Harrisburg Industrializes: The Coming of Factories to an American Community* (University Park, 1993), chaps. 3, 8.

5. George S. Gibb, *The Whitesmiths of Taunton* (Cambridge, Mass., 1946), p. 150.

6. See George Rogers Taylor, *The Transportation Revolution, 1815–1860* (New York, 1951), chap. 11; Caroline Ware, *The Early New England Cotton Manufacture* (New York, 1931); Arthur H. Cole and Harold F. Williamson, *The American Carpet Manufacture* (Cambridge, Mass., 1941), and Arthur H. Cole, *The American Wool Manufacture,* vol. 2 (Cambridge, Mass., 1926).

7. U.S. Department of Commerce, Bureau of the Census, *Historical Statistics of the United States, Colonial Times to 1957,* (Washington, 1960), ser. P 138, p. 413; Solomon Fabricant, *Employment in Manufacturing, 1899–1939* (New York, 1942), pp. 212–14.

8. *Twelfth Census,* vol. 7, *Manufactures,* pt. 1, p. lxxii.

9. McCormick Harvesting Machine Company Papers (State Historical Society of Wisconsin, Madison), ser. 7, Payroll Records.

10. *Twelfth Census of the United States,* vol. 7, *Manufactures,* pt. 1 (Washington, 1902), p. lxxiii.

11. Nathan Rosenberg, "Technological Change in the Machine Tool Industry, 1840–1910," *Journal of Economic History* 33 (1963): 422–23.

12. Richard N. Current, *The Typewriter and the Men Who Made It* (Urbana, 1954), p. 65; Donald R. Hoke, *Ingenious Yankees; The Rise of the American System of Manufactures in the Private Sector* (New York, 1990), chap. 4.

13. Joseph W. Roe, *English and American Tool Builders* (New Haven, 1916), p. 170. Arthur S. Dewing wrote that "Col. Pope gave the [Weed Sewing Machine] Company so many orders that the sewing machine works were gradually transformed into a bicycle factory." Arthur S. Dewing, *Corporate Promotions and Reorganizations* (Cambridge, Mass., 1914), pp. 250ff. See also David A. Hounshell, *From the American System to Mass Production, 1800–1932: The Development of Manufacturing Technology in the United States* (Baltimore, 1984), especially chaps. 2, 5.

14. The Amoskeag increase was due in part to the consolidation of neighboring mills that had been nominally independent but actually owned and managed by Amoskeag officials. See "Manuscript History of the Amoskeag Manufacturing Company and the Amoskeag Company" (Baker Library, Harvard Business School, Cambridge, Mass.), sec. 2. "The experience of the Fall River cotton manufacturers has led them to the conclusion that the most desirable size of a mill . . . is one of 30,000 spindles. . . . Such a mill . . . will have . . . 800 looms . . . [and] employ 325 to 350 operatives." Frederick M. Peck and Henry H. Earl, *Fall River and Its Industries* (Fall River, 1877), p. 110.

15. Peter Temin, *Iron and Steel in Nineteenth Century America* (Cambridge, Mass., 1964), p. 109.

16. The Bethlehem Company may have included miners in its totals. The Cambria figures include men from the Gautier works, a subsidiary. Pennsylvania, Secretary of Internal Affairs, *Annual Report*, vol. 9, 1880 (Harrisburg, 1881), p. 49.

17. The Twelfth Census reported 443 plants with more than 1000 employees. The factory inspectors' reports for Ohio (21 plants), Rhode Island (16), and Connecticut (29) were highly defective, and I was unable to obtain reports for Indiana (16) and New Hampshire (9). Since it is unlikely that more than 20 percent of the 443 plants employed more than 2,000 men, I believe table 3 includes approximately 75 percent of the largest plants in the U.S. However, there are several discrepancies between the inspectors' figures and the census essay that I have been unable to reconcile. *Twelfth Census*, vol. 7, *Manufactures*, pt. I, p. lxxiv.

18. Allan Nevins, *Ford*, vol. 1, *The Times, the Man, the Company* (New York, 1954), pp. 523, 554; Allan Nevins and Frank Ernest Hill, *Ford*, vol. 2, *Expansion and Challenge* (New York, 1957), p. 279.

19. U.S. Immigration Commission, *Reports*, 61st Cong., 2d sess., 1911, vol. 7, pt. 2, p. 238; State of New York, Factory Investigating Commission, *Preliminary Report*, 1912, vol. 3 (Albany, 1912), p. 1353; George F. Stratton, "The Management of Production in a Great Factory," *Engineering Magazine* 34 (January 1908): 569; Stanley Buder, *Pullman* (New York, 1967), p. 224; D. K. Brown, "The Shorter Work Day," *Survey* 37 (January 6, 1917): 360.

20. U.S. Bureau of Labor, *Report on Strike at Bethlehem Steel Works, South Bethlehem, Pennsylvania*, 61st Cong., 2d sess. (1910), pp. 8–10; Arundel Cotter, *The Story of Bethlehem Steel* (New York, 1916), p. 48.

21. Frederick J. Allen and Roy W. Kelly, *The Shipbuilding Industry* (Boston, 1918), p. 228.

22. Harold F. Williamson, *Winchester, The Gun That Won the West* (Washington, 1952), p. 224; Zenas F. Potter, "Penns Grove, a Shipping Place for Sudden Death," *Survey* 36 (February 5, 1916): 539–46, and "War Boom Towns I— Bridgeport," *Survey* 35 (December 4, 1915): 237–41; John Ihlder, "Hopewell, A City Eighteen Months Old," *Survey* 37 (December 2, 1916): 226–30.

23. David B. Tyler, *The American Clyde* (Newark, 1958), p. 107; Allen and Kelly, *Shipbuilding*, p. 9.

24. Paul W. Litchfield, *Industrial Voyage* (Garden City, New York, 1954), p. 181; Harvey S. Firestone, *Men and Rubber* (New York, 1926), p. 245.

CHAPTER 2. THE FACTORY ENVIRONMENT

1. For example, E. Levasseur, *The American Workman* (Baltimore, 1900), Arthur Shadwell, *Industrial Efficiency* (London, 1913), and Henry Pelling, "The American Economy and the Foundation of the British Labour Party," *Economic History Review* 13 (1955): 1–17.

2. See Leonard R. Sayles, *Behavior of Industrial Work Groups* (New York, 1958), p. 149.

3. John Coolidge, *Mill and Mansion* (New York, 1942), p. 29.

4. Commissioner of Labor, *Fourth Annual Report*, 1888 (Washington, 1889), p. 14.

5. Dexter S. Kimball, "Labor-Maintenance Service as a Factor in Management," *Industrial Management* 54 (October 1917): 10.

6. Harold V. Coes, "The Rehabilitation of Existing Plants as a Factor in Production Costs," *Engineering Magazine* 44 (June 1915): 370. This may be an exaggeration; it was, however, the way the General Motors Building in Detroit originated. See Alfred P. Sloan, *My Years with General Motors* (Garden City, 1964), pp. 25–26.

7. *American Machinist* 6 (January 27, 1883): 1.

8. Frederick M. Peck and Henry H. Earl, *Fall River and Its Industries* (Fall River, 1877), pp. 110–11, describe the "standard" Fall River mill.

9. Samuel B. Lincoln, *Lockwood Greene* (Brattleboro, Vt., 1960), pp. 16–37, 192–95; Paul F. McGouldrick, *New England Textiles in the Nineteenth Century* (Cambridge, Mass., 1968), p. 20; George S. Gibb, *The Saco-Lowell Shops* (Cambridge, Mass., 1950), pp. 273, 474–75.

10. The Pemberton Mills in Lawrence, built in 1860, have a good example of the old-style pitched roof. See Historic American Buildings Survey (HABS), *The New England Textile Mill Survey: Selections from the Historic American Buildings Survey,* no. 11 (Washington, 1971), for examples.

11. The Richard Bordon Manufacturing Company, Mill No. 1, built in 1873, was the first large mill "to have a shallow gable roof in preference to the traditional steeply pitched mill roofs." HABS, *Textile Mill Survey,* p. 4; Lincoln, *Greene,* p. 91. Other mills often converted to the flat roof in the following years. See Evelyn H. Knowlton, *Pepperell's Progress* (Cambridge, Mass., 1948), pp. 131–32.

12. See *Engineering News* 42 (May 31, 1900): 361; Harold F. Williamson, *Edward Atkinson* (Boston, 1934), pp. 102–13. Robert B. Gordon and Patrick M. Malone, *The Texture of Industry: An Archeological View of the Industrialization of North America* (New York, 1994), pp. 302–5. The principle of slow-burning construction, introduced in the 1820s, was

> to mass the material in such a way that there shall not be any concealed spaces about the structure, and that the number of projections of timber which are more easily ignited than the flat surfaces shall be reduced as far as possible: that the iron portions of the structure shall not be exposed to the heat of any fire in the contents of the buildings, and furthermore that the isolation of the various portions shall be as complete as is feasible—both as respects one building to another and the various rooms and stories of the same building to each other. (C. J. N. Woodbury, "Methods of Reducing the Fire Loss," *ASME Transactions* 11 (1890): 282)

13. U.S. Industrial Commission, *Report on the Relations and Conditions of Capital and Labor,* vol. 14 (Washington, 1901), p. 735.

14. They claimed they "never had a fire get beyond control where there was a good sprinkler system supplied with ample water at good pressure." Ira H. Woolson, "The Elements of Factory Fire Protection," *Engineering Magazine* 43 (August 1912): 720.

15. Massachusetts, Bureau of Statistics of Labor, *Twelfth Annual Report,* 1881, p. 472; see also "The New Mill of the Willimantic Company," *Scientific American* 44 (March 12, 1881): 169.

16. The first sawtooth roofs appeared in the 1870s; however, 98 of 168 identified in 1906 were built between 1900 and 1906. Fred S. Hinds, "Saw Tooth Skylight in Factory Roof Construction," *ASME Transactions* 28 (1906): 385.

17. *Engineering Record* 60 (December 4, 1909): 632. The Naumkeag Papers at Baker Library contain excellent pictures of the new Naumkeag Mills.

18. J. Leander Bishop, *A History of American Manufacturers from 1608 to 1860* (Philadelphia, 1864), 2:739; William B. Edwards, *The Story of Colt's Revolver* (Harrisburg, 1953), p. 316; J. D. Van Slyck, *New England Manufacturers and Manufactories* (Boston, 1879), 1:184.

19. The Brown & Sharpe proprietors built their factory "after searching the country, and, examining the plans of different shops." *American Machinist* 2 (October 11, 1879): 2. For pictures of the Singer, Elgin, and Baldwin works see Albert Bolles, *Industrial History of the United States* (Peoria, Ill., 1878), pp. 230, 237, 248.

20. Coolidge, *Mill and Mansion,* pp. 101, 211. See also Bolles, *Industrial History,* p. 409.

21. Edwards, *Colt's Revolver,* chap. 4, pp. 44, 50.

22. Alfred D. Chandler, Jr. *The Visible Hand: The Managerial Revolution in American Business* (Cambridge, Mass., 1977), pp. 258–66; Louis C. Hunter, *A History of Industrial Power in the United States, 1780–1930,* vol. 1, *Waterpower in the Century of the Steam Engine* (Charlottesville, 1979), pp. 436–43.

23. "Steel Mill Buildings," Supplement to *Engineering News* 50 (1903): 31.

24. U.S. Bureau of Labor, *Conditions of Employment in the Iron and Steel Industry in the United States,* 62nd Cong., 1st sess., 1912 (Washington, 1913), 3:470.

25. Warren C. Scoville, *Revolution in Glassmaking: Entrepreneurship and Technological Change in the American Industry, 1880–1920* (Cambridge, Mass., 1948), p. 76. A pottery plant was "a large brick building of from two to four stories in height, through the roof of which protrudes massive, conical-shaped chimneys. These are in reality the tops of the great kilns within, and proclaim to the eye the character as well as the magnitude of the business carried on." Ohio, Bureau of Labor Statistics, *Nineteenth Annual Report,* 1895, p. 26. See also U.S. Department of Commerce, *The Pottery Industry,* Miscellaneous Series no. 21 (Washington, 1915), pp. 323, 325–27.

26. Carl Condit, *American Building Art* (New York, 1960), 1:19; Lincoln, Greene, pp. 296–97. Many of the buildings listed in the HABS, *Textile Mills Survey,* including many built in the 1850s and 1860s, had cast iron columns. For the use of iron columns in Paterson, New Jersey, cotton mills built between the 1850s and 1870s, see L. R. Trumbull, *A History of Industrial Paterson* (Paterson, 1882), pp. 180, 277.

27. *American Machinist* 30 (November 7, 1907): 684.

28. L. P. Alford, "Advances in Factory Construction," *American Machinist* 30 (Nov. 7, 1907): 705; see also Carl Condit, "The First Reinforced Concrete Skyscraper," *Technology and Culture* 9 (January 1968): 1–33.

29. *Engineering News* 47 (January 18, 1912): 137.

30. Frank W. Reynolds, "The Development of the Textile Industries of the United States," *ASME Transactions* 33 (1911): 977.

31. George P. Carver, "Concrete Building Work for the Shoe Machinery Company, Beverly, Massachusetts," *Engineering News* 53 (May 27, 1905): 537–38; also L. P. Alford, "Largest Concrete Machine Shop in the World," *American Machinist* 30 (May 23, 1907): 723–29.

32. "Report to Directors of Packard Company, August 31, 1911," Studebaker-Packard Papers (Syracuse University Library, Syracuse, New York).

33. Grant Hildebrand, *The Architecture of Albert Kahn* (Cambridge, Mass., 1974), p. 39; see also Christy Borth, *Masters of Mass Production* (New York, 1954), pp. 451–52.

34. Allan Nevins, *Ford*, vol. 1, *The Times, the Man, the Company* (New York, 1954), pp. 451–52.

35. See, for example, Nathan Rosenberg, *Technology and American Economic Growth* (New York, 1973), chap. 4; David Jeremy, "Innovation in American Textile Technology during the Early 19th Century," *Technology and Culture* 14 (January 1973): 40–76; Paul Strassman, *Risk and Technological Innovation: American Manufacturing Methods during the Nineteenth Century* (Ithaca, 1959); Hounshell, *From the American System.*

36. *Engineering News* 44 (July 12, 1900): 19; Hunter, *A History of Industrial Power*, vol. 1, pp. 456–71.

37. Hunter, *A History of Industrial Power*, vol. 1, p. 436. See also John B. Armstrong, *Factory under the Elms* (Cambridge, Mass., 1969), p. 140.

38. Coleman Sellers, "American Supremacy in Applied Mechanics, III," *Engineering Magazine* 2 (February 1892): 627. See also Fred H. Colvin, *60 years with Men and Machines* (New York, 1947) p. 20–23.

39. Victor S. Clark, *History of Manufactures in the United States*, vol. 2, *1860–1893* (New York, 1949), p. 389; George W. Browne, comp., *The Amoskeag Manufacturing Company of Manchester, New Hampshire: A History* (Manchester, N.H., 1915), pp. 109–10. Other New England textile firms followed a similar policy. See Allen H. Fenichel, "Growth and Diffusion of Power in Manufacturing, 1838–1919," in National Bureau of Economic Research, *Output, Employment, and Productivity in the U.S. after 1800* (New York, 1966), pp. 475–78.

40. U.S. Congress, Senate, *Report on Condition of Woman and Child Wage-Earners in the United States*, 61st Cong., 2d sess., doc. 645, vol. 1 (Washington, 1910), pp. 357–58. See Knowlton, *Pepperell's Progress*, p. 54, and Peck and Earl, *Fall River*, p. 110, for similar descriptions.

41. But see Peck and Earl, *Fall River*, pp. 110–11.

42. Merrimack Manufacturing Company Papers (Baker Library, Harvard Business School, Cambridge, Mass.), vol. 60, (April 1919), pp. 6–12.

43. Record of Amoskeag Employee Representation (1923), Amoskeag Papers (Baker Library, Harvard Business School, Cambridge, Mass.), vol. 5, C-28.

44. See H. L. Gantt, "The Mechanical Engineer and the Textile Industry," *ASME Transactions* 32 (1910): 504–5 esp.; also Daniel Nelson and Stuart Campbell, "Taylorism versus Welfare Work in American Industry: H. L. Gantt and the Bancrofts," *Business History Review* 46 (Spring 1972): 10.

45. Frederick J. Allen, *The Shoe Industry* (Boston, 1916), pp. 116, 119.

46. Sanford E. Thompson, "The Boot and Shoe Industry," in American Engineering Council, Committee on Elimination of Waste in Industry, *Waste in Industry* (Washington, 1921), p. 133.

47. U.S. Bureau of Labor, *Conditions of Employment*, 3:50–51.

48. Phyllis Bate, "The Development of the Iron and Steel Industry of the Chicago Area, 1900–20" (Ph.D. Diss., University of Chicago, 1948), p. 152.

49. *Engineering News* 24 (November 1, 1890): 388; Clark, *History of Manu-*

factures, 2:266. Steam locomotives replaced the mules at the Portsmouth (Ohio) Steel Company because "too many mules were being killed in the handling of heavy steel products." Frank H. Rowe, *History of the Iron and Steel Industry in Scioto County, Ohio* (Columbus, 1938), p. 56.

50. See Michael Nuwer, "From Batch to Flow: Production Technology and Work-Force Skills in the Steel Industry, 1880–1920," *Technology and Culture* 29 (October 1988): 808–838; David Brody, *Steelworkers in America* (Cambridge, Mass., 1960), p. 11.

51. See Charles B. Kuhlmann, *The Development of the Flour-Milling Industry in the United States* (Boston, 1929), pp. 24–25, 96–97; Siegfried Giedion, *Mechanization Takes Command* (New York, 1948), pp. 94–95, 216–17.

52. Chandler, *The Visible Hand,* pp. 249–53.

53. Quoted in David B. Tyler, *The American Clyde* (Newark, 1958), p. 38. Also see John G. B. Hutchins, *The American Maritime Industries and Public Policy, 1789–1914* (Cambridge, Mass., 1941): 460, 468.

54. Colvin, *60 Years,* pp. 92–93, 98–99. The manufacture of gun powder "did not take place in a single building under one roof, or move in a systematic 'flow pattern.' . . . Each step took place in a separate structure; the buildings were usually considerable distances apart and had no sequential relationship." Norman B. Wilkinson, "In Anticipation of Frederick W. Taylor: A Study of Work by Lammot DuPont, 1872," *Technology and Culture* 6 (Spring 1965): 213.

55. U.S. Congress, Senate, *Woman and Child,* 3:83. For parallel activities in the plate and window glass divisions, see Pearce Davis, *The Development of the American Glass Industry* (Cambridge, Mass., 1949), p. 168.

56. The Baldwin works had a second-story blacksmith shop for "light work." In 1897 it was described as "unusual" but very satisfactory. *American Machinist* 20 (October 1897): 808–10. However, see Shadwell, *Industrial Efficiency,* pp. 255, 322.

57. Horace L. Arnold, "Modern Machine-Shop Economics, II," *Engineering Magazine* 9 (May 1896): 264; see Edwards, *Colt's Revolver,* frontispiece and pp. 316–17.

58. *American Machinist* 2 (October 11, 1897): 2; *American Machinist* 7 (March 1884): 2–3; Henry Hess, "Works Design as a Factor in Manufacturing Economy," *Engineering Magazine* 27 (July 1904): 509; Arnold, "Modern Machine-Shop Economics, II," p. 280; Shadwell, *Industrial Efficiency,* p. 235.

59. Massachusetts Bureau of Statistics of Labor, *Sixteenth Annual Report,* 1885, p. 10. For similar operations see Van Slyck, *New England Manufacturers,* 2:654.

60. Frederic B. Warren, "A Railroad University, Altoona, and its Methods," *Engineering Magazine* 33 (May 1907): 74.

61. Arthur A. Bright, *The Electric-Lamp Industry* (New York, 1949), p. 10; Gordon and Malone, *The Texture of Industry,* pp. 316–17.

62. *History of the Baldwin Locomotive Works, 1831–1923* (Philadelphia, 1923), p. 82.

63. Harold C. Passer, *The Electrical Manufacturers* (Cambridge, Mass., 1953), pp. 302–5.

64. Louis C. Hunter and Lynwood Bryant, *A History of Industrial Power in the United States, 1780–1930,* vol. 3, *The Transmission of Power* (Cambridge,

1991), p. 234; Charles M. Riply, *Romance of a Great Factory* (Schenectady, 1919), p. 77.

65. Richard B. DuBoff, "The Introduction of Electric Power in American Manufacturing," *Economic History Review* 20 (1967): 510.

66. Ibid. An excellent treatment of the subject. See also Fenichel, "Growth and Diffusion of Power." Electric lighting also aroused the curiosity of social scientists in industrial conditions and was a major factor in the rise of both industrial psychology and industrial sociology. For an early summary of the academicians' interests see George M. Price, *The Modern Factory* (New York, 1914), chap. 5.

67. Lief provides the following description of preparations for the 1910 Firestone Tire & Rubber Company plant: "Patiently, with a scale model of the new plant, Firestone concentrated for many months on ways of arranging the most efficient layout. By passing a string—representing work material—from one department to another, from floor to floor, he studied the movement of the material through the miniature factory." Alfred Lief, *The Firestone Story* (New York, 1951), p. 56. The Gary and Aliquippa steel works received the same type of attention. See Isaac James Quillen, "Industrial City, A History of Gary, Indiana, to 1929" (Ph.D. Diss., Yale University, 1942), p. 198.

68. See Charles Day, "Metal-Working Plants, Their Machine-Tool Equipment," *Engineering Magazine* 39 (June–July 1910): 364–76, 535–48.

69. Horace L. Arnold and Fay Leone Faurote, *Ford Methods and the Ford Shops* (New York, 1919), p. 368.

70. See "A Comparison of Methods of Automobile Manufacture," *Industrial Engineering and the Engineering Digest* 7 (February 1910): 87–94.

71. Hounshell, *From the American System*, pp. 252–54.

72. Hounshell, *From the American System*, pp. 217–39.

73. Hounshell, *From the American System*, pp. 244–55. See also Nevins, *Ford,* 1:464–65, 470–74; Arnold and Farote, *Ford,* pp. 95–106, 140–51; Keith Sward, *The Legend of Henry Ford* (New York, 1968), chap. 8.

74. See Forrest Cardullo, "Safety and Welfare Work," *Machinery* 22 (November 1915): 196, for a picture of the Pierce Arrow assembly room. However, after 1915 most auto makers adopted the moving assembly line. For Studebaker see Reminiscences of M. F. Wollering, Ford Archives (Henry Ford Museum, Dearborn, Michigan), pp. 41–49; for Willys-Overland see Edward K. Hammond, "Automobile Factory Transportation Systems," *Machinery* 26 (September 1919): 2–7; John B. Rae, *American Automobile Manufacturers* (Philadelphia, 1959), p. 104.

75. See Daniel Nelson, *American Rubber Workers and Organized Labor, 1900–1941* (Princeton, 1988), chap. 3; Glenn D. Babcock, *History of the United States Rubber Company: A Case Study in Corporate Management* (Bloomington, 1966), pp. 292–95.

76. Arnold, *Ford,* p. 331; Charles R. Walker, Robert H. Guest, and Arthur N. Turner, *The Foreman on the Assembly Line* (Cambridge, Mass., 1956).

77. See chapter 5.

78. William C. Hanson, "Attitude of Massachusetts Manufacturers Toward the Health of Their Employees," *BLS Bulletin* 96 (1911): 488–89.

79. The clothing industry in the major eastern cities, notably New York, was characterized by sweatshop conditions. But in other cities—Newburgh and Rochester, New York; Cleveland; and to a lesser degree Chicago—larger firms and better conditions prevailed.

80. Hannah R. Sewall, "Child Labor in the United States," *Bureau of Labor Bulletin* 52 (May 1904): 506.

81. U.S. Industrial Commission, *Report,* 7:253.

81. "Even in the South, where so much is new, there were many old mills, survivals from the beginning of the cotton industry, when cheap construction and old machinery were considered economical." Sewall, "Child Labor," p. 507; also U.S. Congress, Senate, *Woman and Child,* 1:359.

83. Ralph W. Hidy and Muriel E. Hidy, *History of Standard Oil Company (New Jersey), Pioneering in Big Business, 1882–1911* (New York, 1955), p. 597.

84. U.S. Congress, Senate, *Woman and Child,* 18:35.

85. See George M. Kober, "Industrial Hygiene," *BLS Bulletin* 75 (1908): 473; "Causes of Death by Occupation," *BLS Bulletin* 207 (1917): 24–78.

86. See Sewall, "Child Labor," pp. 528–31; see also John R. Commons et al., eds., *A Documentary History of American Industry Society,* vol. 8 (New York, 1958), for pre–Civil War investigations of the impact of factory work on operatives' health in Massachusetts.

87. U.S. Congress, Senate, *Woman and Child,* 1:583–84.

88. For debate on the effects of lint see Holland Thompson, *From the Cotton Field to the Cotton Mill* (New York, 1906), p. 2227, and Sue Ainslie Clark and Edith Wyatt, *Making Both Ends Meet* (New York, 1911), p. 251.

89. Constance M. Green, *Holyoke, Massachusetts* (New York, 1939), p. 103.

90. See Massachusetts Bureau of Statistics of Labor, *Thirteenth Annual Report,* 1882, p. 221; U.S. Congress, Senate, *Woman and Child,* 1:362; Thomas R. Smith, *The Cotton Textile Industry of Fall River, Massachusetts* (New York, 1944), pp. 58–59; John K. Towles, "Factory Legislation in Rhode Island," *American Economic Association Quarterly* 9 (1908): 90–91.

91. John A. Fitch, *The Steel Workers* (New York, 1910), pp. 62–63.

92. U.S. Bureau of Labor, *Conditions of Employment,* 3:24.

93. Horace L. Arnold, "Modern Machine-Shop Economics, IV," *Engineering Magazine* 60 (July 1896): 692.

94. Bishop, *Manufactures* 2:749.

95. Joseph Horner, "The Equipment of the Foundry," *Cassier's Magazine* 24 (June 1903): 505.

96. State of New York, Factory Investigating Commission, *Preliminary Report,* 1912 (Albany, 1912), 3:1278.

97. For comments on the foundries of the American Locomotive Company and General Electric see *Iron Molders Journal* 39 (March 1903): 174; see also Arnold, *Ford Methods,* pp. 327–28.

98. State of New York, Factory Investigating Commission, *Preliminary Report,* 2:755; see also David Brody, *The Butcher Workmen* (Cambridge, Mass., 1964), pp. 6–7.

99. "Vocational Education Survey of Richmond, Virginia," *BLS Bulletin* 162

(1915): 259; U.S. Dept. of Commerce, *Pottery Industry,* p. 323; "Industrial Poisons," *BLS Bulletin* 179 (1915): 8–9; John D. Gaffey, *The Productivity of Labor in the Rubber Tire Manufacturing Industry* (New York, 1940), pp. 103–4.

100. Henry I. Snell, "Heating Machine and Other Large Workshops," *Cassier's Magazine* 23 (Nov., 1902): 271.

101. "The Brown and Sharp Manufacturing Company," *Scientific American* 41 (November 1, 1870): 273.

102. *American Machinist* 18 (June 20, 1895): 488.

103. Quoted in George F. Kenngott, *The Record of a City* (New York, 1912), p. 98.

104. "Employers Welfare Work," *BLS Bulletin* 123 (1913): 27.

105. U.S. Congress, Senate, *Woman and Child,* 19:287. For a similar description see Towles, "Rhode Island," pp. 92–93.

106. Lucian W. Chaney and Hugh S. Hanna, "Accidents and Accident Prevention in Machine Building," *BLS Bulletin* 216 (1917): 67.

107. Crystal Eastman, *Work Accidents and the Law* (New York, 1916), p. 84.

108. See Frederick L. Hoffman, "Industrial Accidents," *BLS Bulletin* 78 (1908): 417–20.

109. Eastman, *Work Accidents,* p. 86.

110. U.S. Congress, Senate, *Woman and Child,* 1:383.

111. Chaney and Hanna, "Accidents," pp. 29, 32–35, 45; see also "Accidents and Accident Prevention," *BLS Bulletin* 256 (1919): 10–11, 61.

112. U.S. Bureau of Labor, *Conditions of Employment* 4:11.

113. Lucian W. Chaney and Hugh S. Hanna, "The Safety Movement in the Iron and Steel Industry, 1907 to 1917," *BLS Bulletin* 234 (1918): 16–22. Less than one-quarter of the workers killed in the Pittsburgh area in 1907 bore any responsibility for their misfortune. See Eastman, *Work Accidents,* pp. 51, 86.

114. Chaney and Hanna, "Accidents," p. 67. As late as 1910 a National Association of Manufacturers survey of ten thousand manufacturers found that 78.5 percent had no systematic relief plans. Robert Asher, "Workmen's Compensation in the United States, 1880–1935" (Ph.D. Diss., University of Minnesota, 1971), p. 218.

115. State of New York, Factory Investigating Commission, *Preliminary Report* 3:1353.

116. U.S. Commissioner of Labor, *Twenty-Third Report,* 1908, pp. 388–89, 399.

117. Old-age pensions were an offshoot of the relief programs, but only two manufacturers are known to have introduced them before 1905 and only a few others before the 1920s. Murray W. Latimer, *Industrial Pension Systems in the United States* (New York, 1932), 1:39; see also Charles R. Henderson, *Industrial Insurance in the United States* (Chicago, 1909), pp. 65–80.

118. "Safety First, No. 1," 1916, Phoenix Iron Company Papers, Eleutherian Mills Historical Library, Wilmington, Delaware.

119. For examples of "unsystematic relief" see Pennsylvania, Secretary of Internal Affairs, *Annual Report,* vol. 15, 1887, B9–B17.

120. Eastman, *Work Accidents,* pp. 155–56.

121. Mary K. Conyington, "Effects of Workmen's Compensation Laws in Di-

minishing the Necessity of Industrial Employment of Women and Children," *BLS Bulletin* 217 (1917): 102, 107; Eastman, *Work Accidents,* pp. 121–22.

122. John Kilburn to L. M. Sargent, January 2, 1890, Lawrence Manufacturing Company Papers, (Baker Library, Harvard Business School, Cambridge, Mass.), GO-1; L. A. Aumann to American Mutual Liability Insurance Company, April 1, 1899, July 11, 1900, Dwight Manufacturing Company Papers (Baker Library, Harvard Business School, Cambridge, Mass.), HL-1. For additional examples, see Carl Gersuny, *Work Hazards and Industrial Conflict* (Hanover, 1981), chaps. 2, 3, 4.

123. L. A. Aumann to American Mutual Liability Insurance Company, March 14, 1898, Dwight Papers, HL-1.

124. L. A. Aumann to American Mutual Liability Insurance Company, September 10, 1901, Dwight Papers, HL-1.

125. John Kilburn to L. M. Sargent, June 14, 1888, August 14, 1888, Lawrence Papers, GO-1.

126. Gerd Korman, *Industrialization, Immigrants, and Americanizers* (Madison, 1967), p. 71; U.S. Congress, Senate, Commission on Industrial Relations, *Final Report and Testimony,* 64th Cong., 1st sess. (Washington, 1916), 3:2886.

127. Elizabeth Brandeis, "Labor Legislation," in Commons, *History of Labor,* 3:574.

128. William D. Haynie to John M. Mayhew, May 11, 1900, McCormick Papers, ser. SC, box 29; Bate, "Iron and Steel," p. 153.

129. Charles A. Gulick, *Labor Policy of the United States Steel Corporation* (New York, 1924), pp. 138–39; U.S. Bureau of Labor, *Conditions of Employment,* 4:241–42. For general accounts see Brody, *Steelworkers,* pp. 158–67, and Korman, *Industrialization,* chap. 5.

130. See State of New York, Factory Investigating Commission, vol. 2, 1912, pp. 489–93; see also chapter 7.

131. See Gulick, *U.S. Steel,* pp. 138–50; Robert J. Young, "Practical Safeguards and Means of Preventing Industrial Accidents," *American Labor Legislation Review* 1 (December 1911): 25–44. See Price, *The Modern Factory,* chaps. 3 and 4, for specific safety devices.

132. Arthur H. Young, "Practical Aspects of the Safety Movement," *Industrial Management* 54 (October 1917): 33; for the day-to-day trials of a new safety program see "Safety First, no. 1," 1916, Phoenix Iron Company Papers.

133. Fitch, *Steel Workers,* pp. 198–99.

134. Chaney and Hanna, "Accidents," p. 52.

CHAPTER 3. THE FOREMAN'S EMPIRE

1. Thomas H. Patten, Jr., *The Foreman: Forgotten Man of Management* (New York, 1968), chap. 2. I have used the terms *foreman* and *supervisor* to designate various types of first-line shop managers. Except in a few cases where distinctions are significant, I have emphasized the function rather than the name.

2. See Charles W. Dennet, "Overseers and the Overseen," in New England Cotton Manufacturers' Association, *Transactions, Annual Meeting,* 1901, pp. 312–13. A description of a shoe factory foreman in 1920 is applicable: "Often

he is paid a salary inadequate to stimulate him to do his best. He has not the training for all his varied duties, nor the time to carry them out. In one instance the number of applications for jobs in one day would have taken more than the entire time of the foreman if he had spent fifteen minutes with each applicant." Sanford E. Thompson, "The Boot and Shoe Industry," in American Engineering Council, Committee on Elimination of Waste in Industry, *Waste in Industry* (Washington, 1924), p. 154.

3. Leonard R. Sayles, *Behavior of Industrial Work Groups* (New York, 1958), p. 93.

4. For illustrations of these distinctions, see Michael Nuwer, "From Batch to Flow: Production Technology and Work Force Skills in the Steel Industry, 1880–1920," *Technology and Culture* 29 (October 1988): 808–38; Philip Scranton, "Diversity in Diversity: Flexible Production and American Industrialization, 1880–1930," *Business History Review* 65 (Spring 1991): 27–90.

5. See the discussion of the modern foreman's duties in Charles R. Walker, Robert H. Guest, and Arthur N. Turner, *The Foreman on the Assembly Line* (Cambridge, Mass., 1956), esp. pp. 9–11, 53, 144.

6. Felicia J. Deyrup, *Arms Makers of the Connecticut Valley* (Northampton, Mass., 1948); Merritt Roe Smith, *Harpers Ferry Armory and the New Technology* (Ithaca, 1977).

7. Many industries used different techniques in different departments or shops, complicating the job of categorization. Brewing, for example, was a continuous-process industry, but most brewery employees were coopers, bottlers, or teamsters. See Thomas C. Cochran, *The Pabst Brewing Company* (New York, 1948), pp. 203–4, 251. Petroleum refining was similar. See Ralph W. Hidy and Muriel E. Hidy, *History of Standard Oil Company (New Jersey), Pioneering in Big Business, 1882–1911* (New York, 1955), p. 592.

8. See Patten, *The Foreman,* chap. 3.

9. Joseph A. Litterer, "Systematic Management: The Search for Order and Integration," *Business History Review* 25 (1961): 468.

10. Quoted in Harold F. Williamson, *Winchester, The Gun That Won the West* (Washington, 1952), p. 86.

11. Sidney Pollard, *The Genesis of Modern Management* (London, 1965), pp. 51–62.

12. Williamson, *Winchester,* pp. 478–79; John Buttrick, "The Inside Contract System," *Journal of Economic History* 12 (Summer 1952): 207–8. See also Ernest J. Englander, "The Inside Contract System of Production and Organization; A Neglected Aspect of the History of the Firm," *Labor History* 28 (Fall 1987): 429–46.

13. Henry Roland, "Six Examples of Successful Shop Management, V," *Engineering Magazine* 12 (March 1897): 1000. Also Charles Fitch, "Report on the Manufactures of Interchangeable Mechanism," *Tenth Census, Manufactures of the United States* (Washington, 1883), p. 6.

14. Buttrick, "Inside Contract," pp. 216–17; John Converse, "Progressive Non-Union Labor," *Cassier's Magazine* 23 (March 1903): 663–65; "The Labor Situation at the Baldwin Works," *Iron Trade Review* 36 (February 12, 1903): 41. But the Baldwin contractors came under increased pressure after 1915. See Samuel

M. Vauclain Papers (Historical Society of Pennsylvania, Philadelphia), esp. John P. Sykes to S. M. Vauclain, October 6, 1919, Vauclain Papers, no. 2.

15. Thomas R. Navin, *The Whitin Machine Works Since 1831* (Cambridge, Mass., 1950), p. 146.

16. Payroll, Job Time Book (1901–1905), Whitin Machine Works Papers (Baker Library, Harvard Business School, Cambridge, Mass.), HA-1.

17. Henry Roland, "Six Examples of Successful Shop Management," *Engineering Magazine* 12 (October 1896): 76.

18. See Navin, *Whitin,* pp. 140–49. At Winchester costs increased. Williamson, *Winchester,* p. 138.

19. U.S. Commissioner of Labor, *Regulation and Restriction of Output, Eleventh Special Report* (Washington, 1904), p. 135.

20. Unions, particularly in the metals and machinery industries, also opposed it. See Commissioner of Labor, *Regulation and Restriction,* p. 19.

21. A Fall River spinner reported that he could not find work because he did not have a son to assist him. U.S. Congress, Senate, Committee on Education and Labor, *The Relations Between Labor and Capital,* vol. 3 (Washington, 1885), p. 451.

22. Melvin T. Copeland, *The Cotton Manufacturing Industry of the United States* (Cambridge, Mass., 1912), pp. 2–3; Jacquelyn Dowd Hall, James Leondis, Robert Korstad, Mary Murphy, LuAnn Jones, Christopher B. Baly, *Like a Family: The Making of a Southern Cotton Mill World* (Chapel Hill, 1987), pp. 60–62.

23. U.S. Industrial Commission, *Report on the Relations and Conditions of Capital and Labor,* vol. 14 (Washington, 1901), pp. 645–46; U.S. Dept of Commerce, *The Pottery Industry,* Miscellaneous Series, no. 21 (Washington, 1915), pp. 278–89, 312; F. Thistlethwaite, "The Atlantic Migration of the Pottery Industry," *Economic History Review* 11 (1958–1959): 274.

24. See U.S. Congress, Senate, *Report on Condition of Woman and Child Wage-Earners in the United States,* 61st Cong., 2d sess., doc. 645, vol. 3 (Washington, 1911), p. 139. The potters and glass workers' unions opposed this arrangement. See Walter E. Weyl and A. M. Sakolski, "Conditions of Entrance to the Principal Trades," *Bureau of Labor Bulletin* 67 (November 1906): 749–50.

25. Jesse S. Robinson, *The Amalgamated Association of Iron, Steel, and Tin Workers* (Baltimore, 1920), p. 130.

26. John A. Fitch, *The Steel Workers* (New York, 1910), pp. 99–100; Francis G. Couvares, *The Remaking of Pittsburgh; Class and Culture in an Industrializing City, 1877–1919* (Albany, 1984), chap. 2.

27. See Peter Temin, *Iron and Steel in Nineteenth Century America* (Cambridge, Mass., 1964), p. 133; Nuwer, "From Batch to Flow," pp. 808–38.

28. Frank T. Stockton, *The International Molders Union of North America* (Baltimore, 1921), pp. 179–85.

29. Benson Soffer, "A Theory of Trade Union Development: The Role of the 'Autonomous' Workman," *Labor History* 1 (Spring 1960): 141–63.

30. George S. Gibb, *The Whitesmiths of Taunton* (Cambridge, Mass., 1946), p. 284.

31. S. H. Bunnel, "Planning the Work in a Shop," *American Machinist* 30 (July 11, 1907): 50.

32. Quoted in Gerd Korman, *Industrialization, Immigrants, and Americanizers* (Madison, 1967), p. 64.

33. Fitch, *Steel Workers*, pp. 29–30, 43–44.

34. Whiting Williams, *What's on the Worker's Mind* (New York, 1920), p. 57.

35. In the smaller mills or departments, overseers often made repairs themselves. See, e.g., Evelyn H. Knowlton, *Pepperell's Progress* (Cambridge, Mass., 1948), pp. 160–61.

36. U.S. Congress, Senate, *Labor and Capital*, 3:8.

37. J. W. Cumnock to Overseer, July 13, 1892; Cumnock to F. L. Simpson, May 25, 1896; Cumnock to Samuel C. George, Nov. 11, 1891; Cumnock to Mr. Jay, September 19, 1892, Dwight Manufacturing Company Papers (Baker Library, Harvard Business School, Cambridge, Mass.), MD-1, 2.

38. Employers agreed with the treasurer of a Fall River mill: "Most of what we call second hands, overseers, and a large part of the superintendents, if not all of them, come up from small beginnings, most of them beginning as boys. Many have acquired knowledge of the business, and as soon as they become proficient they have been advanced." U.S. Industrial Commission, *Report*, vol. 15, 1901, p. 561. This policy did not apply to women. See U.S. Congress, Senate, *Woman and Child*, 1:590.

39. Fitch, *Steel Workers*, p. 142.

40. "Vocational Educational Survey of Minneapolis, Minnesota," *BLS Bulletin* 199 (1916): 237.

41. See Monte A. Calvert, *The Mechanical Engineer in America, 1830–1910* (Baltimore, 1967).

42. U.S. Congress, House of Representatives, *Hearings before the Committee on Investigation of United States Steel Corporation* (Washington, 1912), p. 2924.

43. See U.S. Congress, Senate, *Woman and Child,* 6:66; Massachusetts Bureau of Statistics of Labor, *Thirteenth Report,* 1883, p. 338; also U.S. Congress, Senate, *Labor and Capital,* 1:444; and Rowland T. Berthoff, *British Immigrants in Industrial America, 1790–1950* (Cambridge, Mass., 1953), p. 35. On child abuse see New York, Bureau of Statistics of Labor, *Second Annual Report,* 1884, pp. 71–79.

44. Massachusetts Bureau of Statistics of Labor, *Thirteenth Report,* 1883, p. 306.

45. Quoted in Robert Sidney Smith, *Mill on the Dan* (Durham, N.C., 1960), p. 261.

46. Harold S. Robert, *The Rubber Workers* (New York, 1944), p. 60.

47. For the early textile industry see "Regulations," 1837, Nashua Manufacturing Company Papers (Baker Library, Harvard Business School, Cambridge, Mass.), BO-1; also Massachusetts Bureau of Statistics of Labor, *Thirteenth Report,* 1883, p. 227; E. Levasseur, *The American Workman* (Baltimore, 1900), pp. 171–72. Florence Kelley complained that "even where strict rules are enforced they are not for the purpose of guarding against unchaste conversation and other immoral practices, but rather to compel greater diligence at the loom or bench," Pennsylvania, Secretary of Internal Affairs, *Annual Report*, vol. 15, 1886, p. 14.

48. See E. P. Thompson, "Time, Work-Discipline, and Industrial Capitalism,"

Past and Present 38 (December 1967): 56–97; Herbert G. Gutman, "Work, Culture, and Society in Industrializing America, 1815–1919," *American Historical Review* 78 (June 1973): 531–71.

49. See Daniel Nelson, "The New Factory System and the Unions: The NCR Company Dispute of 1901," *Labor History* 15 (Winter 1974): 89–97.

50. See William T. Hutchinson, *Cyrus Hall McCormick* (New York, 1935), p. 695; U.S. Bureau of Labor, *Report on Strike at Bethlehem Steel Works, South Bethlehem, Pennsylvania,* 61st Cong., 2d sess. (Washington, 1910), p. 15; Hidy and Hidy, *History of Standard Oil* (New Jersey), p. 598. In the southern textile industry overseers supposedly were "often overruled." Holland Thompson, *From the Cotton Field to the Cotton Mill* (New York, 1906), p. 205.

51. Adjustments, I, October 24, 1918, Amoskeag Papers (Baker Library, Harvard Business School, Cambridge, Mass.), CA-1.

52. Roland, "Six Examples," pp. 76–78.

53. Quoted in Thomas L. Norton, *Trade Union Policies in the Massachusetts Shoe Industry, 1919–1929* (New York, 1932), p. 47; also see Sanford Thompson, "The Boot and Shoe Industry," in *Waste in Industry,* p. 159; Hugh Allen, *The House of Goodyear* (Akron, 1936), p. 179.

54. See Robert Ozanne, *Wages in Practice and Theory: McCormick and International Harvester, 1860–1960* (Madison, 1968), chaps. 3, 4, 8.

55. Allen Nevins, *Ford,* vol. 1: *The Times, the Man, the Company* (New York, 1954), p. 551. Also Daniel M. G. Raff, "Ford Welfare Capitalism in Its Economic Context," *Masters to Managers: Historical and Comparative Perspectives on American Employers,* ed. Sanford M. Jacoby (New York, 1991), pp. 90–110.

56. Because it contributed to the "driving system," craft unions often opposed piecework and accepted it only when "protestation appears useless." Thomas S. Adams and Helen L. Sumner, *Labor Problems: A Text Book* (New York, 1905), p. 259. The Molders and Machinists were particularly intransigent. In 1909 the Machinists' president reported that "at least fifty percent" of the Machinists' strikes were against piecework. *Machinists Monthly Journal* 21 (October 1909): 928. But this policy was later described as the unions' "greatest single mistake." Sumner Slichter, *Union Policies and Industrial Management* (Washington, 1941), p. 308.

57. Henry Roland, "Six Examples of Successful Shop Management, IV," *Engineering Magazine* 12 (February 1897): 832.

58. U.S. Commissioner of Labor, *Regulation and Restriction,* p. 81.

59. Quoted in Hugo Diemer, "The Commercial Organization of the Machine Shop, IV," *Engineering Magazine* 19 (September 1900): 897.

60. U.S. Commissioner of Labor, *Regulations and Restriction,* p. 18.

61. John R. Commons, "Labor Conditions in Slaughtering and Meat Packing," in *Trade Unionism and Labor Problems,* ed. John R. Commons (New York, 1905), p. 241.

62. U.S. Commissioner of Labor, *Regulation and Restriction,* p. 28.

63. Slichter, *Union Policies,* chaps. 2–11; Lloyd Ulman, *The Rise of the National Trade Union* (Cambridge, Mass., 1955), chaps. 15–17. See also Robinson, *Amalgamated Association,* chaps. 6–11; Stockton, *Molders,* chaps. 9–13; U.S.

Dept. of Commerce, *The Pottery Industry*, chap. 3; Pearce Davis, *The Development of the American Glass Industry* (Cambridge, Mass., 1949), chap. 7; Warren C. Scoville, *Revolution in Glassmaking: Entrepreneurship and Technological Change in the American Industry, 1880–1920* (Cambridge, Mass., 1948), pp. 200–239.

64. Robinson, *Amalgamated Association*, p. 114.

65. U.S. Dept. of Commerce, *Historical Statistics of the United States* (Washington, 1957), ser. P 138, p. 413, and ser. D 749–56, p. 98.

66. U.S. Dept. of Commerce, *The Pottery Industry*, p. 199.

67. For representative examples see Robert Ozanne, *A Century of Labor Management Relations at McCormick and International Harvester* (Madison, 1967), pp. 20–25; Melvyn Dubofsky, *We Shall Be All* (Chicago, 1969), pp. 227–62; David Brody, *Steelworkers in America* (Cambridge, Mass., 1960), chaps. 3, 12; Roberts, *Rubber Workers*, pp. 38–78; Joseph F. Wall, *Andrew Carnegie* (New York, 1970), pp. 526–38. The papers of manufacturers generally contain little material on labor or shop management problems except for strikes. See, e.g., T. J. Coolidge to H. E. Straw, March 15, 1886, Amoskeag Papers, GA; Cyrus H. McCormick Diary, McCormick Papers, 4C, boxes 1 and 2; Samuel M. Vauclain Papers, box 1.

68. See Philip Taft and Philip Ross, "American Labor Violence: Its Causes, Character, and Outcome," in *The History of Violence in America*, ed. Hugh Davis Graham and Ted Robert Gurr (New York, 1969), pp. 281–344.

69. H. M. Gitelman, "Perspectives on American Industrial Violence," *Business History Review* 47 (1973): 8–16.

70. See Taft and Ross, "American Labor Violence."

71. The best work is Joseph A. Litterer, "Systematic Management: Design for Organizational Recoupling in American Manufacturing Firms," *Business History Review* 37 (Winter 1963): 369–91. Although other authors have applied the term "systematic management" to other aspects of the management movement, I have followed Litterer's usage and assumed the term to be "systematic shop management." See also Litterer, "Systematic Management: The Search for Order and Integration," pp. 461–76, and "The Emergence of Systematic Management as Indicated by the Literature of Management from 1870 to 1900" (Ph.D. Diss., University of Illinois, 1950); and Leland H. Jenks, "Early Phases of the Management Movement," *Administrative Science Quarterly* 5 (December 1960): 421–47.

72. See Hugo Diemer, "A Combined Bonus and Premium System," *Engineering Magazine* 29 (August 1905): 730.

73. Jenks, "Early Phases," pp. 428–30.

74. Frederick W. Taylor, "A Piece Rate System: A Step Toward Partial Solution of the Labor Problem," *ASME Transactions* 16 (1895): 860–61.

75. Litterer, "Emergence," p. 64.

76. Ibid., p. 66.

77. John R. Dunlap, "The Literature of Industrial Management," *Engineering Magazine* 49 (May 1915): 166.

78. Litterer, "Design for Organizational Recoupling," p. 370. See also JoAnne Yates, *Control Through Communication: The Rise of System in American Management* (Baltimore, 1989).

79. Henry P. Kendall, "Types of Management: Unsystematized, Systematized, and Scientific," in Dartmouth College Conferences, *Addresses and Discussions at the Conference on Scientific Management Held October 12–14, 1911* (Hanover, N.H., 1912).

80. Litterer, "Design for Organizational Recoupling," pp. 376–83.

81. Kendall, "Unsystematized, Systematized, and Scientific Management," p. 120. See also H. Thomas Johnson, "Early Cost Accounting for Internal Management Control, Lyman Mills in the 1850's," *Business History Review* 46 (1972): 466–74, and H. Thomas Johnson and Robert S. Kaplan, *Relevance Lost: The Rise and Fall of Management Accounting* (Boston, 1987), chaps. 2, 3.

82. Samuel Paul Garner, *Evolution of Cost Accounting to 1925* (University, Ala., 1954), pp. 98, 114–15.

83. Garner, *Evolution of Cost Accounting,* pp. 187–88; Mariann Jelinek, "Toward Systematic Management: Alexander Hamilton Church," *Business History Review* 54 (Spring 1980): 63–79.

84. Kendall, "Unsystematized, Systematized, and Scientific Management," pp. 120–22.

85. Litterer, "Design for Organizational Recoupling," pp. 376–83.

86. Ibid., J. Slater Lewis, *The Commercial Organization of Factories* (London, 1896); Horace L. Arnold, *The Complete Cost Keeper* (New York, 1912).

87. See Seymour Melman, "The Rise of Administrative Overhead in the Manufacturing Industries of the United States, 1899–1947," *Oxford Economic Papers* 3 (1951): 90–91.

88. Henceforth "incentive wage" refers to the profit-sharing, premium, and bonus wage plans that employers introduced in the 1880s and after but not to the conventional or straight piece rate systems that had long been used.

89. For antecedents of the premium see U.S. Commissioner of Labor, *Regulation and Restriction,* p. 126; see also A. Hamilton Church, "Practical Principles of Rational Management, IV," *Engineering Magazine* 45 (April 1913): 28–29.

90. Frederick W. Taylor to Henry R. Towne, August 8, 1896, Frederick W. Taylor Papers (Stevens Institute of Technology, Hoboken, New Jersey), 63A.

91. Henry Roland, "Six Examples of Successful Shop Management, III," *Engineering Magazine* 12 (December 1896): 402.

92. Henry R. Towne, "Gain Sharing," *ASME Transactions* 10 (1889): 618.

93. Roland, "Six Examples, III," pp. 404–6; Henry R. Towne, "Discussion," *ASME Transactions* 8 (1887): 29–92.

94. Henry R. Towne, "Discussion," *ASME Transactions* 8 (1887): 644–66.

95. *American Machinist* 22 (March 9, June 29, 1899): 516, 179; Frederick A. Halsey, "Discussion," *ASME Transactions* 41 (1919): 170.

96. Frederick A. Halsey, "The Premium Plan of Paying for Labor," *ASME Transactions* 22 (1891): 758. For his criticism of welfare work see Halsey, "The National Cash Register Company's Experiment," *American Machinist* 24 (June 20, 1901): 688–89.

97. Halsey, "Premium Plan," p. 763.

98. Halsey, "Premium Plan," p. 761.

99. *American Machinist* 22 (March 9, 1899): 179.

100. Horace B. Drury, *Scientific Management* (New York, 1915), pp. 48–49.

In 1899 Halsey wrote that at least eighteen establishments had adopted the premium. *American Machinist* 22 (September 7, 1899): 844. By 1902 there were at least thirty-eight. "Shops Using the Premium Wage System," *Iron Trade Review* 35 (July 3, 1902): 64. The following year Frank Richards, a critic, wrote that "perhaps two per cent of the machine work in the United States is done under the premium plan." (Frank Richards, "Is Anything the Matter with Piece Work?" *ASME Transactions* 25 [1903–4]: 70).

101. James O'Connell, "Piece-Work Not Necessary for Best Results in the Machine Shop," *Engineering Magazine* 19 (June 1900): 373–74. See also *Proceedings of Eighth Convention, International Association of Machinists, 1899,* pp. 336, 390–91, 403–4. The *Machinists' Monthly Journal* contained many articles on the union's fight against piecework and the problems it involved. See also Slichter, *Union Policies,* pp. 306–8, and Mark Perlman, *The Machinists* (Cambridge, Mass., 1961), p. 43.

102. Halsey, "Premium Plan," p. 761.

103. Frederick A. Halsey, "Discussion," *ASME Transactions* 24 (1903): 1466.

104. Quoted in George S. Gibb, *The Saco-Lowell Shops* (Cambridge, Mass., 1950), p. 324.

105. Charles E. Sorenson, *My Forty Years with Ford* (New York, 1956), p. 41.

CHAPTER 4. THE RISE OF SCIENTIFIC MANAGEMENT

1. See Leland H. Jenks, "Early Phases of the Management Movement," *Administrative Science Quarterly* 5 (December 1960): 425–27.

2. This phrase is from Taylor's first important work on management, "A Piece Rate System: A Step Toward Partial Solution of the Labor Problem," *ASME Transactions* 16 (1895): 856–93.

3. See Daniel Nelson, *Frederick W. Taylor and the Rise of Scientific Management* (Madison, 1980), chap. 2. See also the introductory chapter in *A Mental Revolution; Scientific Management Since Taylor,* ed. Daniel Nelson (Columbus, 1992).

4. See the Midvale file, no. 71, and the Taylor Scrapbooks, nos. 1 and 2, Frederick W. Taylor Collection (Stevens Institute of Technology, Hoboken, N.J.).

5. Taylor Scrapbooks, nos. 1 and 2, Taylor Collection; Frank Barkley Copley, *Frederick W. Taylor, The Father of Scientific Management,* 2 vols. (New York, 1923).

6. See Carl G. Barth's introduction to Taylor Scrapbook no. 2, Taylor Collection; Frederick W. Taylor, "Shop Management," *ASME Transactions* 24 (1903): 1396–99; Frederick W. Taylor, "On the Art of Cutting Metals," *ASME Transactions* 28 (1906): 34–40.

7. See Barth's introductions to Taylor Scrapbooks, nos. 1 and 2; see also the Taylor–Sanford E. Thompson correspondence, files 124A, 124B, Taylor Collection.

8. This statement is based on the report of a Philadelphia local of the International Association of Machinists. See *Monthly Journal,* 6 (November 1894): 430–31.

9. For information on Taylor's fortune, see Nelson, *Taylor,* pp. 104–11. Taylor's discoveries insured his prominence among fellow engineers and led to the

presidency of the ASME in 1906–1907. See Frederick R. Hutton, *A History of the American Society of Mechanical Engineers from 1880 to 1915* (New York, 1915), and Edwin T. Layton, Jr., *The Revolt of the Engineers* (Cleveland, 1972), chap. 7.

10. Taylor-Thompson Correspondence, files 124 and 125, Taylor Collection.

11. Barth introduction to Taylor Scrapbook no. 3, Taylor Collection; Copley, *Taylor*, 1:364–65.

12. Barth introduction to Taylor Scrapbook no. 3, Taylor Collection; for a detailed account of the Taylor accounting system in a plant where it was installed see Horace L. Arnold, *The Factory Manager and Accountant* (London, 1910), chap. 3.

13. See, for example, "Recollections of Coleman DuPont," file 14F, Taylor Collection.

14. Taylor invariably began his articles and talks with a discussion of "soldiering," or restriction of output, which he attributed to poor management. See Taylor, "A Piece Rate System," pp. 860–63; Taylor, "Shop Management," pp. 1349–52; U.S. House of Representatives, *Hearings Before Special Committee to Investigate the Taylor and Other Systems of Shop Management*, 62nd Cong., 2d sess. (Washington, 1912), 3:8–25 (pagination for Taylor's testimony is from the more readily available reprint, Taylor, *Scientific Management* [New York, 1947]); Frederick W. Taylor, *The Principles of Scientific Management* (New York, 1912), pp. 13–18.

15. Taylor, "Shop Management," pp. 1391–97.

16. For accounts of the origins of the task and bonus system see Taylor, "Shop Management," pp. 1376–78; Taylor, *Principles*, pp. 39–42; Henry Laurence Gantt, *Work, Wages, and Profits* (New York, 1913), pp. 104–13; and L. P. Alford, *Henry Laurence Gantt, Leader in Industry* (New York, 1934), pp. 87–91.

17. Taylor, "Testimony," pp. 66–77; Taylor, *Principles*, pp. 80–81.

18. Edna Yost, *Frank and Lillian Gilbreth, Partners for Life* (New Brunswick, 1949), pp. 219–22.

19. J. M. Dodge to Frederick W. Taylor, January 18, 1915; Frederick W. Taylor to J. M. Dodge, January 27, 1915, Taylor Collection, File 58B.

20. Taylor, "Testimony," pp. 260–61.

21. Frank B. Gilbreth and Lillian M. Gilbreth, "An Indictment of Stop Watch Time Study," *Bulletin of the Taylor Society* 6 (June 1921): 91, and Carl Barth, "Discussion," ibid., pp. 108–10.

22. See Henry Kendall, "Types of Management: Unsystematized, Systematized, and Scientific," in Dartmouth College Conferences, *Addresses and Discussions at the Conference on Scientific Management Held October 12–14, 1911* (Hanover, N.H., 1912), pp. 112–41.

23. Taylor would add that fairness and the "proper personal relations" were also necessary. In 1903 he wrote: "The employer who . . . is never known to dirty his hands or clothes, and who either talks to his men in a condescending or patronizing way, or else not at all, has no chance whatever of ascertaining [the employees'] real thoughts or feelings." Taylor, "Shop Management," p. 1447. Taylor prided himself on his ability to use profanity and to maintain close personal relationships with workmen.

24. Taylor, "Shop Management," pp. 1404, 1455.

25. Ibid., p. 1394.

26. Taylor, "A Piece Rate System," p. 892.

27. Taylor, *Principles,* pp. 46–47. There were several efforts to test this assertion. See Josephine Goldmark, *Fatigue and Efficiency* (New York, 1912), and Sue Ainslie Clark and Edith Wyatt, *Making Both Ends Meet* (New York, 1911).

28. Frank B. Copley, "Frederick W. Taylor, Revolutionist," *Outlook* 3 (September 1, 1914): 42.

29. Taylor, "A Place Rate System," p. 881.

30. Taylor, "Testimony," p. 641; see also "Shop Management," p. 1454.

31. Taylor's relations with the unions are treated at length in Milton J. Nadworny, *Scientific Management and the Unions, 1900–32* (Cambridge, Mass., 1955), and Hugh G. J. Aitken, *Taylorism at Watertown Arsenal* (Cambridge, Mass., 1960).

32. Frederick W. Taylor to J. M. Dodge, February 25, 1915, Taylor Collection.

33. Frederick W. Taylor to David Van Alstyne, December 27, 1906, Taylor Collection, file 138.

34. Taylor used the same outline for all his works on management, varying only the details and examples and his emphasis on the "principles" of scientific management. He began with a description of the defects of conventional management, introduced time and motion study, and then noted the other features of his system. His refinements of systematic management (cost keeping, tool room operations, improvements in belting, etc.) received less attention in each subsequent publication—that is, as Taylor became better known and attracted a wider audience. See Charles D. Wrege and Anne Marie Stotka, "Cooke Creates a Classic," *Academy of Management Review* 3 (October 1978): 736–49. For contrasts between the theory and actual practice of scientific management, compare Taylor's writings with C. Bertrand Thompson's detailed manual, *The Taylor System of Scientific Management* (New York, 1917). Also see Hathaway's account of the introduction of scientific management at Tabor. Interstate Commerce Commission, *Evidence Taken by the Interstate Commerce Commission in the Matter of Proposed Advances in Freight Rates by Carriers, Aug. to Dec., 1910,* 61st Cong., 3d sess. (Washington, 1911), 4:2660–67.

35. There are numerous statements of this view in U.S. Congress, House of Representatives, *Hearings,* vols. 1 and 2.

36. Summer Slichter describes union policies toward incentive wage plans in *Union Policies and Industrial Management* (Washington, 1941), pp. 296–309; Nadworny, *Scientific Management and the Unions,* chap. 4, traces the opposition to Taylor and his system.

37. Nadworny, *Scientific Management and the Unions,* pp. 114–16.

38. Sudhir Kakar, *Frederick Taylor: A Study in Personality and Innovation* (Cambridge, 1970), chap. 9.

39. See Nelson, *Taylor,* chaps. 5–8; Samuel Haber, *Efficiency and Uplift* (Chicago, 1964), and R. E. Callahan, *Education and the Cult of Efficiency* (Chicago, 1962).

40. Frederick W. Taylor to Carl Barth, November 15, 1909, Taylor Collection, file 113B.

41. Frederick W. Taylor to Richard H. Rice, March 9, 1905, Taylor Collection, file 120B.

42. Frederick W. Taylor to Carl Barth, November 15, 1909, and December 23, 1910, Taylor Collection, file 113B.

43. Frederick W. Taylor to Henry L. Gantt, May 10, 1991, Taylor Collection, file 121B.

44. See Taylor's correspondence with Watson E. Goodyear, E. Gower Guthrie, E. Nusbaumer, and Douglas H. Vetch, Taylor Collection, file 137.

45. Frederick W. Taylor to Henry L. Gantt, August 27, 1909, Taylor Collection, file 121A.

46. Frederick W. Taylor to Henry L. Gantt, April 13, 1908, Taylor Collection, file 120B.

47. Frederick W. Taylor to Carl Barth, November 25, 1910, Taylor Collection, file 113B.

48. Harrington Emerson to Edwin Emerson, December 19, 1899, February 14, 1900, May 15, 1900, May 30, 1901, Emerson Family Papers (New York Public Library, New York City).

49. Harrington Emerson, "Discussion," *ASME Transactions* 24 (1903): 1463.

50. Harrington Emerson, *Efficiency as a Basis for Operations and Wages* (New York, 1919); U.S. Congress, Senate, Commission on Industrial Relations, *Final Report and Testimony,* 64th Cong., 1st sess. (Washington, 1916), 4:822–32.

51. Nadworny, *Scientific Management and the Unions,* p. 28.

52. Frederick W. Taylor to Henry L. Gantt, January 3, 1910, Taylor Collection, file 121A.

53. See Lillian M. Gilbreth to Harlow S. Person, January 3, 1927, Frank B. Gilbreth Papers (Purdue University, Lafayette, Indiana); also Frank B. Gilbreth, *Motion Study* (New York, 1911), and Taylor, *Principles,* pp. 77–85.

54. Frederick W. Taylor to Frank B. Gilbreth, February 3, 1908, Taylor Collection, file 59A.

55. Frank B. Gilbreth to Frederick W. Taylor, February 6, 1908, Taylor Collection, file 59A. Thompson also suspected Gilbreth of being an opportunist. His attitude may have influenced Taylor's reassessment of Gilbreth's motives in 1912–1914. Sanford E. Thompson to Taylor, January 11, 1908, Taylor Collection, file 126C.

56. Frank B. Gilbreth to Sanford E. Thompson, April 21, 1908; Sanford E. Thompson to Frank B. Gilbreth, April 22, 1908; Frederick W. Taylor to Frank B. Gilbreth, April 27, 1908, all in Taylor Collection, file 59A; Nadworny, *Scientific Management and the Unions,* p. 22.

57. Frank B. Gilbreth to Sanford Thompson, May 1, 1908, Taylor Collection, file 59a.

58. See Layton, *Revolt of the Engineers,* chap. 7, for Taylor's relationship with the ASME.

59. Taylor to Gantt, November 11, 1910, to C. W. Rice, November 11, 1910, to E. C. Wolf, February 20, 1915, all in Taylor Collection, file 6; and the Taylor-H. F. J. Porter correspondence, 1911, Taylor Collection, file 5. See also Rob-

ert Thurston Kent, "The Promotion of Efficiency," *Industrial Engineering and Engineering Digest* 11 (March 1912): 284–85, and Charles Buxton Going, "The Efficiency Movement, An Outline," *Transactions of the Efficiency Society* 1:12–20.

60. Alford, *Gantt*, p. 156.

61. Gantt, *Work, Wages, and Profits*, p. 156.

62. Frederick W. Taylor to Henry L. Gantt, June 14, 1909, Taylor Collection, file 121A.

63. Frank B. Gilbreth to Frederick W. Taylor, Aug. 25, 1911, Oct. 27, 1911; Frederick W. Taylor to Frank B. Gilbreth, Aug. 30, 1911, Oct. 23, 1911; all in Taylor Collection, file 59A. Also see Milton J. Nadworny, "Frederick Taylor and Frank Gilbreth: Competition in Scientific Management," *Business History Review* 31 (Spring 1957): 23–24.

64. Frank B. Gilbreth to Joseph W. Roe, March 4, 1912, Gilbreth Papers.

65. Frank B. Gilbreth to Frederick W. Taylor, April 18, 1912, Taylor Collection, file 59B.

66. Frederick W. Taylor to Frank B. Gilbreth, July 23, 1912, Taylor Collection, file 59B.

67. Frank B. Gilbreth to Frederick W. Taylor, August 20, 1912, April 3, 1913, Taylor Collection, file 59B; Nadworny, "Taylor and Gilbreth," pp. 23–34.

68. Frank B. Gilbreth to Frederick W. Taylor, September 15, 1913, Gilbreth Papers.

69. J. M. Dodge to Frank B. Gilbreth, December 11, 1912, Gilbreth Papers.

70. Carl G. Barth and Dwight V. Merrick, "Discussion," *ASME Transactions* 34 (1912): 1205.

71. See Frederick W. Taylor and Frank B. Gilbreth, March 11, 1914, Taylor Collection, file 59A; Frank B. Gilbreth to Frederick W. Taylor, July 17, 1914, Gilbreth Papers.

72. Frederick W. Taylor to Henry L. Gantt, August 7, 1914, Taylor Collection, file 121B.

73. Frank B. Gilbreth to Lillian M. Gilbreth, April 6, 1914, Gilbreth Papers.

74. See H. K. Condit, "Management Methods and Principles of Frank B. Gilbreth, Inc.," *American Machinist* 58 (January 4, February 22, March 22, May 3, 1923): 33–35, 293–95, 443–47, 665–67; 59 (July 5, August 30, 1923): 25–27, 329–34; and Brian Price, "Frank and Lillian Gilbreth and the Motion Study Controversy, 1907–1930," in Nelson, *A Mental Revolution*, 58–76.

75. J. M. Dodge to Frank B. Gilbreth, April 17, 1992, Gilbreth Papers.

76. C. B. Thompson, *The Theory and Practice of Scientific Management* (Boston, 1917), pp. 37–40; Majority Report of Sub-Committee on Administration, "The Present State of the Art of Industrial Management," *ASME Transactions* 34 (1912): 1150.

77. U.S. Congress, Senate, Commission on Industrial Relations, *Final Report* 1:792, 822; Horace B. Drury, *Scientific Management* (New York, 1915), p. 145.

78. Thompson, *Theory and Practice*, p. 50.

79. Robert F. Hoxie, *Scientific Management and Labor* (New York, 1918), p. 26. Two years before, when asked by a congressman how many firms had intro-

duced his system, Taylor had replied that "not one" had done so "in its entirety." Taylor, "Testimony," p. 280.

80. For details, see Nelson, *Taylor,* chap. 6.

81. These were the Lewis F. Shoemaker, Company, F. B. Stearns Company, Universal Winding Company, Franz Premier Company, Goldie & McCulloch, Burgess Sulphite Company, Williamson Brothers, Westinghouse Electric, Standard Roller Bearing Company, Bausch & Lomb, Lowell Machine Works, Barcalo Company, Acme Wire Company, F. R. Patch Company, Williams & Wilkins, Sewell Clapp Company, Plymouth Cordage Company, Robins Conveying Belt and the American Locomotive Company shops (where Gantt worked in 1902 and Emerson in 1907). There are also references to at least three other firms, the Manhattan Press, Chester Steel Castings Company, and the Erie Forge Company, in the Taylor Collection, but there is so little information about them that I have not included them in table 4.

82. Frederick W. Taylor to H. K. Hathaway, February 3, 1914, Taylor Collection, file 123A. Taylor and Emerson corresponded frequently during this period. Emerson wrote that "I would rather have your approval . . . that of [sic] any other man living or dead." Emerson to Taylor, November 17, 1905, Taylor Collection, file 58C. Also Harrington Emerson, "Discussion," *ASME Transactions* 24 (1903): 1463, and "Discussion," *ASME Transactions* 25 (1903–1904): 73. Parkhurst was close to Gilbreth and Robert Thurston Kent though not to the other Taylor associates. His *Applied Methods of Scientific Management* first appeared in Kent's *Industrial Engineering and Engineering Digest* in 1911. He discussed his exclusion from the Taylor circle in a conversation with Gilbreth in 1915 (Frank B. Gilbreth to Lilliam M. Gilbreth, September 24, 1915, Gilbreth Papers).

83. By 1910 many progressive firms had installed detailed cost accounting systems. After his retirement Taylor increasingly deemphasized the importance of costkeeping to scientific management. Copley, *Taylor,* 1:365–71; 2:375–77.

84. As Table 4 suggests, scientific management was introduced in many industries and plants employing radically different production methods. For Taylor's comments on the textile industry see "A Piece Rate System," p. 867.

85. Many of the firms listed in table 4—such as Remington, Pullman, Link-Belt, Cheney Brothers, Plimpton Press, Ferracute Machine, Joseph & Feiss, and Yale & Towne—were well known for their advanced methods and equipment. See H. L. Gantt's "Discussion" in Sub-Committee on Administration, "Present State of the Art," p. 180.

86. R. R. Keely to Frederick W. Taylor, May 14, 1914, Taylor Collection, file 137C; Carl Barth to J. S. Runnels, March 6, 1913, Carl G. Barth Papers (Baker Library, Harvard Business School, Cambridge, Mass.), drawer 2.

87. Gantt reported in 1914 that he typically spent a year or more on his jobs "setting [the] house in order." U.S. Congress, Senate, Commission on Industrial Relations, *Final Report,* 1:956. For an able critique of Emerson's work see Fred H. Colvin, "How Bonus Works on the Santa Fe, II," *American Machinist* 36 (Feb. 1, 1912): 168.

88. "Scheduling Locomotive Repair Work on the Canadian Pacific Railway," *Industrial Engineering and Engineering Digest* 8 (November 1910): 38–83; *Rail-*

way Age Gazette 50 (April 7, 1911): 836–37; Hollis Godfrey to Frederick W. Taylor, May 4, 1912, Taylor Collection, file 59B2; Holden A. Evans, *Cost Keeping and Scientific Management* (New York, 1911), pp. 186–231.

89. George D. Babcock and Reginald Trautschold, *The Taylor System in Franklin Management* (New York, 1917), p. 77.

90. Wilfred Lewis, "An Object Lesson in Efficiency," *Industrial Engineering and Engineering Digest* 9 (May 1911): 383. The Barth Papers contain numerous planning department forms from the Tabor Company. "Tabor Manufacturing Company," drawer 2; see also "Barcalo Manufacturing Company Report of Philadelphia Trip, Nov. 25, 1912," Taylor Collection, file 138B. The Link-Belt planning department is described in "Methods of Management That Made Money," *Industrial Engineering and Engineering Digest* 9 (January 1911): 23–25; and James M. Dodge, "A History of the Introduction of a System of Shop Management," *ASME Transactions* 27 (1906): 720–25; Aitken, *Taylorism*, pp. 96–100, 125–34.

91. H. M. Wilcox, "Organization and System in the Cartridge Department of the Winchester Repeating Arms Company for the Control of Mass Production," December 1, 1917, Barth Papers, drawer 2. Williamson notes only time study. Harold F. Williamson, *Winchester, The Gun That Won the West* (Washington, 1952), p. 232.

92. See Taylor, "Shop Management," pp. 1392–94, 1418–21. In *The Principles of Scientific Management* Taylor, apparently influenced by Gantt's characterizations, called the "gang" and "speed" bosses and the inspectors "teachers." See *Principles*, pp. 123–24.

93. The leaders included the Plimpton Press, Joseph & Feiss, Eastern Manufacturing Company, and Cheney Brothers. Henry Kendall, general manager of Plimpton Press and supporter of scientific management, was responsible for the introduction of formal personnel work there. Richard A. Feiss's role is described later. In the other cases, however, the two developments were distinct. See, e.g., Sanford E. Thompson et al., "Development of Scientific Methods of Management in a Manufacturing Plant," *ASME Transactions* 39 (1917): 129.

94. Time study men from Tabor and Link-Belt often assisted Barth and Hathaway. Sanford E. Thompson's partner William O. Lichtner also was employed on several jobs. See Dwight Merrick, *Time Studies as a Basis for Rate Setting* (New York, 1920), and William O. Lichtner, *Time Study and Job Analysis* (New York, 1921).

95. Frank B. Gilbreth to Frederick W. Taylor, September 15, 1913, Gilbreth Papers; H. N. Stronch, "A Report on the Operation of Scientific Management at the New England Butt Company," October 18, 1913, Gilbreth Papers, "Micro-Motion Study," *Industrial Engineering and Engineering Digest* (January 1913): 1–4; "A New Development in Factory Study," *Industrial Engineering and Engineering Digest* 13 (February 1913): 58–61; "Discussion," *ASME Transactions* 34 (1912): 1182–87.

96. C. B. Thompson, *Theory and Practice*, p. 79.

97. Gantt, *Work, Wages, and Profits*, chap. 7.

98. Clark and Wyatt, *Making Both Ends Meet*, p. 261. Also see Daniel Nelson and Stuart Campbell, "Taylorism versus Welfare Work in American Industry:

H. L. Gantt and the Bancrofts," *Business History Review* 46 (Spring 1972): 12–13. Keely encountered a similar problem at the Baird Machine Works. R. R. Keely to Frederick W. Taylor, April 9, April 22, 1914, Taylor Collection, file 137D.

99. Carl Barth to Frederick W. Taylor, August 13, 1908, Taylor Collection, file 113A. For similar experiences at Amoskeag see "Planning Office Papers," Amoskeag Company Papers (Baker Library, Harvard Business School, Cambridge, Mass.), DG-1, and at Forbes Lithograph, see Barth to Frederick W. Taylor, July 18, 1911, Taylor Collection, file 113C.

100. See Clark and Wyatt, *Making Both Ends Meet;* also compare U.S. Commission on Industrial Relations, *Report,* 1:1016–17 and "Discussion," *AMSE Transactions* 30 (1908): 1049–50, regarding the Brighton Mills.

101. Stanley B. Mathewson, *Restriction of Output among Unorganized Workers* (New York, 1931), pp. 74–77.

102. See Clark and Wyatt, *Making Both Ends Meet,* for the statements of workers of the Sayles Bleachery and Brighton Mills.

103. H. L. Gantt to Frederick W. Taylor, September 23, 1911, Taylor Collection, file 121B; Amoskeag Manufacturing Company, "History 1805–1948," n.d. (Baker Library, Harvard Business School, Cambridge, Mass.), pt. 4; *Adjustments,* vol. 1, Amoskeag Papers, CA-1.

104. See Alford, *Gantt,* chap. 8; Nelson and Campbell, "Taylorism versus Welfare Work," pp. 12–15; "Canadian Pacific Shop Management," *American Machinist* 35 (December 21, 1911): 1164–67; E. Robertson to J. Christian Barth, January 31, 1912, Barth Papers, drawer 2; Frederick W. Taylor to Carl Barth, March 28, 1907, March 31, 1910, Taylor Collection, file 113A; Henry R. Towne to Kempton P. A. Taylor, August 11, 1915, Taylor Collection, file 14AA; Henry R. Towne to Frank B. Copley, May 2, 1921, Taylor Collection, file 14AA; Nadworny, "Frederick Taylor and Frank Gilbreth," pp. 23–24; C. B. Thompson to Frederick W. Taylor, December 28, 1914, Taylor Collection, file 52G; Frederick W. Taylor to Morris L. Cooke, June 6, 1911, Taylor Collection, file 116B; S. E. Thompson et al., "Development of Scientific Methods," p. 129; Evans *Cost Keeping,* pp. 142, 234; Holden A. Evans, *One Man's Fight for a Better Navy* (New York, 1940), pp. 179–80; Frederick W. Taylor to Henry Kendall, Feb. 26, 1913, Taylor Collection, file 137D; Frederick W. Taylor to H. K. Hathaway, December 15, 1913, Taylor Collection, file 122C; Carl Barth to Frederick W. Taylor, July 18, 1908, Taylor Collection, file 113C; Henry Kendall to Kempton P. A. Taylor, August 18, 1915, Taylor Collection, file 14P. H. H. Vaughan, Gantt's employer at the Canadian Pacific shops, was the only member of the ASME's 1912 Sub-Committee on Administration who refused to sign the famous report "The Present State of the Art of Industrial Management," which generally endorsed the Taylor System. "Present State of the Art of Industrial Management," pp. 1151–52.

105. C. B. Thompson, *Theory and Practice,* pp. 100–101. There were strikes at the Sayles Bleachery, Mare Island Shipyard, and Watertown Arsenal. Workers at several American Locomotive Company shops struck after Gantt had completed his work and Emerson had been employed to install his wage plan. See Alford, *Gantt,* pp. 108, 116; Evans, *One Man's Fight,* pp. 202–4; Aitken, *Taylorism,* chap. 4; and Nadworny, *Scientific Management and the Unions,* pp. 27–28.

106. The exact nature of the workers' complaints at the Sayles Bleachery are

unclear. Alford reported that the employees wanted a wage increase in return for accepting Gantt's reforms. At Mare Island and at Watertown Arsenal the strikes occurred when the experts subjected the workers to time study (Watertown) and the incentive wage (Mare Island) before they introduced other shop reforms. The work stoppages were thus against not scientific management but isolated features of it. They confirmed Taylor's frequent prediction that scientific management improperly applied would lead to labor troubles. See Aitken, *Taylorism,* chap. 4, and Evans, *One Man's Fight,* pp. 202–3. For evidence that scientific management improved labor-management relations see H. K. Hathaway to Frederick W. Taylor, March 13, 1910, Taylor Collection, file 122A; Drury, *Scientific Management,* p. 129; Lewis, "Object Lesson in Efficiency," p. 381; U.S. Congress, Senate, Commission on Industrial Relations, *Final Report,* 4:3176–77.

107. See, for example, *Hearings before the Special Committee* 3:1443–52.

108. The best source on Taylor's relations with his followers is Nadworny, *Scientific Management and the Unions,* chaps. 3–5.

109. H. K. Hathaway to Oberlin Smith, October 30, 1906; Oberlin Smith to H. K. Hathaway, January 7, 1907, Taylor Collection, file 138G; Parkhurst, *Applied Methods.*

110. Charles H. Fry, "Shop Betterment on the Santa Fe," *The Railroad Gazette* 41 (November 30, 1906): 479–80; Charles Buxton Going, "Methods of the Santa Fe, Efficiency in the Manufacture of Transportation," II, *Engineering Magazine* 37 (April 1909): 9–36; (May 1909): 225–48; (June 1909): 337–60.

111. Taylor wrote in December 1911 that the Santa Fe Shops "were about one-quarter way toward scientific management"—his most generous statement about Emerson since 1907. Frederick W. Taylor to William Crozier, December 8, 1911, Taylor Collection, file 185B.

112. David J. Goldberg, "Richard A. Feiss, Mary Barnett Gilson, and Scientific Management at Joseph & Feiss, 1909–1925," in Nelson, *A Mental Revolution,* pp. 40–57. Mary G. Gibson, *What's Past is Prologue* (New York, 1940), p. 57. Taylor described the Joseph & Feiss factory as the "best plant anywhere" (Frederick W. Taylor to H. L. Gantt, Nov. 23, 1914, Taylor Collection, file 121B).

113. Gilson, *What's Past is Prologue,* pp. 58–59, 81; Richard A. Feiss, "Personal Relationship as a Basis of Scientific Management," *Bulletin of the Taylor Society* 1 (November 1915): 5–15.

CHAPTER 5. RECRUITING THE FACTORY LABOR FORCE

1. U.S. Bureau of Labor, *Conditions of Employment in the Iron and Steel Industry in the United States,* 62nd Cong., 1st sess., 1912 (Washington, 1913), 3:140. In the steel industry skilled workers were often selected by employment agents. For a fascinating contemporary critique of the operation of the informal system see "Viator," "The New Man in the Shop," *Iron Trade Review* 17 (December 13, 1884): 787.

2. U.S. Congress, Senate, Commission on Industrial Relations, *Final Report and Testimony,* 64th Cong., 1st sess. (Washington, 1916), 1:3463–64.

3. Samuel J. Marquis, Testimony, November 23, 1920, Ford Archives (Henry Ford Museum, Dearborn, Mich.), acc. 293, box 1.

4. Walter Licht, *Getting Work: Philadelphia, 1840–1950* (Cambridge, 1992), chap. 2. Prejudice against the "new" immigrants and other groups that made up the unskilled labor force was widespread. See John Higham, *Strangers in the Land* (New Brunswick, N.J., 1955), chaps. 3–4. "In the up-state factors it [prejudice] is so extreme that they speak of the Americans as the 'white help' and of the foreigners as a separate class." State of New York, Factory Investigating Commission, *Preliminary Report,* 1912 (Albany, 1912), 3:1636.

5. For the evaluations of employers in Fall River, New Bedford, Manchester, and Cohoes, New York, see U.S. Immigration Commission, *Reports,* 61st Cong., 2d sess. (Washington, 1911), vol. 10, pt. 3, p. 179; also Hugo Munsterberg, *Psychology and Industrial Efficiency* (Boston, 1913), p. 131.

6. See Broadus Mitchell, *The Rise of the Cotton Mills in the South* (Baltimore, 1921), p. 188; also Jack Blicksilver, *Cotton Manufacturing in the Southeast* (Atlanta, 1959), p. 68; U.S. Congress, Senate, *Report on Condition of Woman and Child Wage-Earners in the United States,* 61st Cong., 2d. sess., doc. 645, vol. 16 (Washington, 1912), p. 19.

7. See U.S. Congress, Senate, Committee on Education and Labor, *The Relations between Labor and Capital,* vol. 4 (Washington, 1885), pp. 469–70, and Immigration Commission, *Reports,* vol. 9, pt. 2, pp. 151–52, 203–4, for the iron and steel industry, and U.S. Congress, Senate, *Woman and Child,* 3:171, for glass. For the impact of discrimination on the black worker see Timothy Smith, "Native Blacks and Foreign Whites: Varying Responses to Educational Opportunity in America, 1880–1950," *Perspectives in American History* 6 (1972): 332–35.

8. Shelby M. Harrison listed four basic "unorganized" methods: "application at the gate," "going back to previous employer," "contact made by acquaintances," and "waiting list or application file." Shelby M. Harrison et al., *Public Employment Offices* (New York, 1924), pp. 36–44. Also see Charlotte Erickson, *American Industry and the European Immigrant, 1860–1885* (Cambridge, Mass., 1957).

9. For the relationship between American economic growth and European immigration see Richard A. Easterlin, "Influences in European Overseas Emigration Before World War I," *Economic Development and Cultural Change* 9 (1961): 331–49.

10. See Monte A. Calvert, *The Mechanical Engineer in America, 1850–1910* (Baltimore, 1967), chap. 4. See also the series of reminiscences by W. S. Rogers, entitled "Sketches of an Apprenticeship" that appeared in the *American Machinist* 13 (August–December 1890) and 14 (January–March 1891).

11. U.S. Commissioner of Labor, *Regulation and Restriction of Output, Eleventh Special Report* (Washington, 1904), p. 147.

12. F. Thistlethwaite, "The Atlantic Migration of the Pottery Industry," *Economic History Review* 11 (1958–59): 264–65.

13. Rowland T. Berthoff, *British Immigrants in Industrial America, 1790–1950* (Cambridge, Mass., 1953), p. 23; Margaret F. Byington, *Homestead: The Households of a Mill Town* (New York, 1910), p. 6.

14. Quoted in Berthoff, *British Immigrants,* p. 38.

15. U.S. Congress, Senate, *Labor and Capital,* vol. 3 (1885), p. 496, but also Erickson, *Industry and Immigrant,* p. 57.

16. John Bodnar, *The Transplanted; A History of Immigrants in Urban America* (Bloomington, 1985), chap. 2; Bodnar, *Immigration and Industrialization: Ethnicity in an American Milltown, 1870–1940* (Pittsburgh, 1977), pp. 26–27, 36–37; Alan Pred, *The Spatial Dynamics of United States Urban-Industrial Growth* (Cambridge, Mass., 1966), pp. 39–79.

17. Immigration Commission, *Reports,* vol. 9, pt. 2, pp. 44–45.

18. See U.S. Immigration Commission, *Reports, Immigrants in Industries,* vol. 22, pt. 9, p. 377; vol. 25, pt. 15, p. 488.

19. See the testimony of John Fitch regarding Eastern European immigrant steel workers. U.S. Congress, House of Representatives, *Hearings before the Committee on Investigation of the United States Steel Corporation* (Washington, 1912), pp. 2922–23.

Portuguese workers first came to New Bedford as sailors on whaling ships. Dutch workers were employed at the Whitin Company after they accompanied a herd of cattle. Immigration Commission, *Reports,* vol. 10, pt. 3, pp. 41–42, 299; Thomas R. Navin, *The Whitin Machine Works since 1831* (Cambridge, Mass., 1950), pp. 152–63. For the larger context, see E. Bodnar, *The Transplanted.*

20. See Tamara K. Hareven, *Family Time and Industrial Time: The Relationship Between the Family and Work in a New England Industrial Community* (New York, 1982).

21. Historians who have studied mobility in nineteenth-century cities have raised doubt about the "promise of mobility." See Stephan Thernstrom, *Poverty and Progress* (Cambridge, Mass., 1964). See also E. P. Hutchinson, *Immigrants and Their Children, 1850–1950* (New York, 1956), pp. 138–39, 202–3.

22. John R. Commons, "Labor Conditions in Slaughtering and Meat Packing," in *Trade Unionism and Labor Problems,* ed. John R. Commons (New York, 1905), pp. 246–47; see also John C. Kennedy, *Wages and Family Budgets in the Chicago Stock Yards District* (Chicago, 1914), pp. 5, 8.

23. Immigration Commission, *Reports,* vol. 8, pt. 2, pp. 591–92; for Cambria see pp. 360–63 and Byington, *Homestead,* pp. 13, 214.

24. By the late nineteenth century the northern New England mill towns formed a common labor market, and it seems unlikely that similar studies of the Lowell, Lawrence, or Nashua corporations would show major variations. See Donald B. Cole, *Immigrant City* (Chapel Hill, 1963), pp. 226–27; George F. Kenngott, *The Record of a City* (New York, 1912); and Immigration Commission, *Reports,* vol. 10, pt. 3, pp. 226–28. For the carpet industry see Arthur H. Cole and Harold F. Williamson, *The American Carpet Manufacture* (Cambridge, Mass., 1941), pp. 164–66.

25. The Amoskeag statistics do not distinguish between first- and second-generation foreign workers. Presumably the immigrants' children were included with the parents. However, since there was a constant influx of foreign-born workers, this ambiguity probably has little effect on the totals. See Daniel Craemer and Charles W. Coulter, *Labor and the Shut-Down of the Amoskeag Textile Mills,* WPA National Research Project, Report L-5 (Philadelphia, 1939), pp. 166–69.

26. "Happenings," 1912, Amoskeag Papers (Baker Library, Harvard Business School, Cambridge, Mass.), VH-S.

27. Allan Nevins, *Ford,* vol. 1, *The Times, the Man, the Company* (New York, 1954), p. 537.

28. U.S. Bureau of Labor, *Conditions of Employment,* 3:212.

29. U.S. Congress, Senate, *Woman and Child,* 17:23.

30. Sumner H. Slichter, *The Turnover of Factory Labor* (New York, 1919), p. 16.

31. Ibid., p. 33.

32. Ibid., p. 44; Paul H. Douglas, *American Apprenticeship and Industrial Education* (New York, 1921), pp. 101–5.

33. Contemporary estimates of unemployment were haphazard at best. See Stanley Lebergott, *Manpower in Economic Growth* (New York, 1964), pp. 184–90, and Lebergott, "Labor Force and Employment Trends," in *Indicators of Social Change,* ed. Eleanor Sheldon and Wilbert E. Moore (New York, 1968).

34. Lebergott, "Labor Force," p. 123; Lebergott, *Manpower,* pp. 187, 522. Charles Hoffman, *The Depression of the Nineties* (Westport, Conn., 1970), 104–9.

35. See Daniel Nelson, *Unemployment Insurance: The American Experience, 1915–1935* (Madison, 1969), chaps. 2–3.

36. Horace L. Arnold, "Modern Machine-Shop Economics," *Engineering Magazine* 9 (April 1896): 64–65; Commissioner of Labor, *Twelfth Annual Report,* 1897 (Washington, 1898), pp. 70–72.

37. U.S. Bureau of Labor, *Conditions of Employment* 3:97, 263; John A. Fitch, *The Steel Workers* (New York, 1910), pp. 183–84.

38. The contracts were complicated, legalistic documents that included detailed specifications of wages and employment during the life of the agreement. See sample contracts in Pacific Mills Papers (Merrimack Valley Textile Museum, North Andover, Massachusetts), no. 148; see also Daniel Craemer, "Recruiting Contract Laborers for the Amoskeag Mills," *Journal of Economic History* (May 1941): 42–56.

39. New England Cotton Manufacturers Association, *Proceedings, Fifth Annual Meeting,* 1870, p. 20. For a specific case see G. W. Lovering, Agent Lyman Mills, Holyoke, to J. W. Cumnock, Agent, Dwight Manufacturing, March 28, 1880, Dwight Manufacturing Company Papers (Baker Library, Harvard Business School, Cambridge, Mass.), ML-A.

40. See Erickson, *Industry and Immigrants,* chap. 5; for recruitment from Canada see the correspondence of I. M. Boynton to Agent, Dwight Manufacturing Company, 1872) in the Dwight Manufacturing Company Papers, ML-A. Workers were occasionally borrowed from other firms, Harold C. Livesay, "The Lobdell Car Wheel Company, 1830–1867," *Business History Review* 42 (1968): 184; see also, e.g., Immigration Commission, *Reports,* vol. 18, pt. 21, p. 25.

41. Nevins, *Ford,* 1:517.

42. Harrison, *Public Employment Offices,* pp. 69–70; U.S. Congress, Senate, Commission on Industrial Relations, *Final Report,* 1:1247–48; 3:2882, 2890, 2909; 4:3416.

43. For good examples see Harold F. Williamson, *Winchester, The Gun That Won the West* (Washington, 1952), p. 135; U.S. Bureau of Labor, *Conditions of Employment,* 3:143–46. Labor unrest was also a factor in the mechanization of

the factory. "When mule spinners at one Fall River mill in the 1890's demanded higher pay, they were easily replaced. 'On Saturday afternoon after they had gone home,' the superintendent chuckled, 'we started right in and smashed up a room full of mules with sledge hammers. . . . On Monday morning they were astonished to find that there was no work for them. The room is full of ring frames run by girls.'" Berthoff, *British Immigrants*, p. 36.

44. Arnold, "Machine-Shop," p. 62.

45. U.S. Congress, Senate, *Woman and Child*, 3:114, 157–67, 632–33; Ohio, State Inspector of Shops and Factories, *Fifth Annual Report*, 1888, p. 113.

46. Dwight Papers, HC-4.

47. See Douglas Flamming, *Creating the Modern South: Millhands and Managers in Dalton, Georgia, 1884–1984* (Chapel Hill, 1992), pp. 30–31.

48. August Kohn, *Cotton Mills of South Carolina* (Charleston, S.C., 1907), p. 62; David L. Carlton, *Mill and Town in South Carolina, 1880–1920* (Baton Rouge, 1982), pp. 113–15; Jacquelyn Dowd Hall, et al. *Like a Family: The Making of a Southern Cotton Mill World* (Chapel Hill, 1987), pp. 110–11; Cathy L. McHugh, *Mill Family: The Labor System in the Southern Textile Industry, 1880–1915* (New York, 1988), p. 8.

49. U.S. Congress, Senate, *Woman and Child*, 1:120.

50. Kohn, *Cotton Mills*, p. 61; Robert S. Smith, *Mill on the Dan* (Durham, N.C., 1960), pp. 104–5; Blicksilver, *Cotton Manufacturing*, p. 32.

51. Kohn, *Cotton Mills*, pp. 200–203; U.S. Congress, Senate, *Woman and Child*, 1:125; Carlton, *Mill and Town*, pp. 113–14.

52. Holland Thompson, *From the Cotton Field to the Cotton Mill* (New York, 1906), p. 166.

53. The following discussion is based on a comparative study of company towns operated by manufacturing firms largely in northern New England (textiles), New Jersey and Pennsylvania (glass, iron, and steel), the Carolinas (textiles), and Alabama (iron and steel). The sources for this study included government documents (especially the Immigration Commission reports), city histories, industry studies, and works on company towns. Only quotations or paraphrases of statements in these works are documented.

54. See Joseph Walker, *Hopewell Village* (Philadelphia, 1966), pp. 365–72.

55. "Housing by Employers in the United States," *BLS Bulletin* 263 (1920): 141.

56. Henry Roland, "Six Examples of Successful Shop Management, II". *Engineering Magazine* 12 (November 1896): 278.

57. Smith, *Mill on the Dan*, p. 107.

58. Charles B. Going, "Village Communities of the Factory, Machine Works, and Mine," *Engineering Magazine* 21 (April 1901): 70.

59. Isaac J. Quillen, "Industrial City: A History of Gary, Indiana, to 1929," (Ph.D. Diss., Yale University, 1942), pp. 143–44.

60. Pennsylvania, Secretary of Internal Affairs, *Annual Report*, vol. 15, 1887, pp. 12–13E; U.S. Congress, Senate, *Woman and Child*, 14:157; Byington, *Homestead*, p. 48; Hareven, *Family Time*, chap. 3.

61. See New Jersey, Bureau of Statistics of Labor and Industry, *Twenty-third*

Annual Report, 1900, p. 255. Also see Hall et al., *Like a Family,* pp. 116–27, and Edward H. Beardsley, *A History of Neglect; Health Care for Blacks and Mill Workers in the Twentieth Century South* (Knoxville, 1987), chap. 2.

62. Pennsylvania, Secretary of Internal Affairs, *Annual Report,* vol. 15, 1887, p. 24E.

63. U.S. Congress, Senate, *Woman and Child,* 1589; also Thompson, *Cotton Fields,* p. 165; Blicksilver, *Cotton Manufacturing,* p. 39; Harry C. Silcox, *A Place to Live and Work; The Henry Disston Saw Works and the Tacony Community of Philadelphia* (University Park, 1994), pp. 20–21.

64. Henry Roland, "Six Examples of Successful Shop Management," *Engineering Magazine* 12 (October 1896): 80; Victor S. Clark, *History of Manufactures in the United States,* vol. 2 (New York, 1949), p. 398; U.S. Congress, Senate, *Woman and Child,* 1:537–38; Silcox, *A Place to Live and Work,* p. 78.

65. U.S. Congress, Senate, *Woman and Child,* 3:632–33; on the extent of the company stores and payment in kind in the North see E. Levasseur, *The American Workman* (Baltimore, 1900), p. 118.

66. Immigration Commission, *Reports,* vol. 9, pt. 2, p. 190.

67. New Jersey, Department of Statistics of Labor and Industry, *Twenty-second Annual Report,* 1899, p. 142.

68. In this respect the company town apparently differed from the "small industrial town" with multiple employers and a more complex economic and social life. See Herbert G. Gutman, "The Workers' Search for Power," in *The Gilded Age,* ed. H. Wayne Morgan (Syracuse, 1970), pp. 31–53, and Herbert G. Gutman, "Class, Status, and Community Power in Nineteenth Century American Industrial Cities—Paterson, New Jersey: A Case Study," in *The Age of Industrialism in America,* ed. Frederick Cople Jaher (New York, 1968), pp. 263–83.

69. Melton Alonza McLaurin, *Paternalism and Protest* (Westport, Conn., 1971) discusses the obstacles to union organization, chaps. 2–6. See also Brody, *Steelworkers,* chap. 6.

70. "Manuscript History of the Amoskeag Manufacturing Company and the Amoskeag Company" (Baker Library, Harvard Business School, Cambridge, Mass.), sec. 3, pp. 19–20; Craemer and Coulter, *Shut-Down,* p. 172; Hareven, *Family Time and Industrial Time,* pp. 40–61.

71. There are numerous examples of this situation in the Immigration Commission reports on individual company towns. See also Brody, *Steelworkers,* chaps. 4–5.

72. U.S., Senate, *Woman and Child,* 17:25.

73. Flamming, *Creating the Modern South,* p. 123. Also see the perceptive article by Gertrude Beeks, "Welfare Work in Southern Cotton Mills," National Civic Federation *Review* 2 (July–August 1906): 15 esp.

74. Immigration Commission, *Reports,* vol. 9, pt. 2, p. 194.

75. Ibid., vol. 8, pt. 2, p. 385.

76. Ibid., p. 694.

77. U.S. Congress, House of Representatives, *Hearings . . . U.S. Steel,* 3:3380. U.S. Steel reported: "No industry in this country has, so far, solved satisfactorily the problem of housing unskilled foreign laborers, whose families have

not yet followed them to this country. These men . . . have been accustomed to ways of living which we must try to change, and yet which are much cheaper than those ways in which we wish to have them live." Quillen, "Gary," p. 128.

78. Frederick W. Taylor, "Testimony," *Scientific Management* (New York, 1947), p. 35.

79. A few large firms, like Ford and Packard, established training courses to provide skilled and semiskilled workers.

80. "Boot and Shoe Industry in Massachusetts," *BLS Bulletin* 180 (1915): 43–47; Frederick J. Allen, *The Shoe Industry* (Boston, 1916), pp. 266–67.

81. Jessie Davis, "My Vacation in a Woolen Mill," *Survey* 40 (August 10, 1918): 539–40; Licht, *Getting Work,* chap. 4.

82. The *American Machinist* polled 116 machinery manufacturers in 1896 and found to the editors' surprise that eighty-five, or 73 percent, took apprentices. *American Machinist* 19 (December 24, 1896): 1204–36; see also E. H. Parks, "The Question of Apprentices," *Cassier's Magazine* 23 (November 1902): 199–201, and Harless D. Wagoner, *The U.S. Machine Tool Industry from 1900 to 1950* (Cambridge, Mass., 1966), pp. 86–88.

83. Douglas, *American Apprenticeship,* pp. 74–78, 80–83. But see also Addison B. Burk, "Apprenticeship as It Was and Is," *Papers of the Philadelphia Social Science Association* (Philadelphia, 1882).

84. O. M. Becker, "A Modern Adaptation of the Apprenticeship System," *Engineering Magazine* 32 (November 1906): 173–74.

85. Because of the physical strength required to do the work, he was usually an "improver" or "holder on" rather than a mere handyman. Walter E. Weyl and A. M. Sakolski, "Conditions of Entrance to the Principal Trades," *BLS Bulletin* 67 (November 1906): 770.

86. Ibid., p. 776.

87. See Douglas, *American Apprenticeship,* pp. 117–19.

88. *American Machinist* 2 (October 25, 1879): 8; *Machinery* 23 (February 1917): 455–57; L. D. Burlingame, "An Example of the Modern Development," *Engineering Magazine* 26 (January 1904): 512–16. Brown & Sharpe and Pratt & Whitney later introduced shop instructors.

89. Douglas, *American Apprenticeship,* pp. 212–213. Of the firms listed above only Allis-Chalmers had no definite education plan. Philetus W. Gates, "The Apprenticeship System of the Allis-Chalmers Company," *Engineering Magazine* 27 (April 1904): 26.

90. *Railway Age Gazette* 50 (June 2, 1911): 1257–58.

91. S. M. Vauclain, "The System of Apprenticeship at the Baldwin Locomotive Works," *Engineering Magazine* 27 (June 1904): 322–23.

92. See Commissioner of Labor, *Twenty-fifth Report,* 1910, pp. 146–47, 150–51; *American Machinist* 36 (January 25, 1912): 143; Clarence O. Price, "How an Industry Trains Its Men," *Engineering Magazine* 52 (October 1916): 24.

93. Magnus W. Alexander, "A Plan to Provide for a Supply of Skilled Workmen," *ASME Transactions* 28 (1906): 479. Many manufacturers disagreed with Alexander's view, arguing that contact with the workmen was highly desirable, and his plan was not widely imitated in the prewar period. See *ASME Transac-*

tions 23 (1903): 464, 470; 29 (1907): 1126. See also Calvert, *Mechanical Engineer*, pp. 74–75.

94. W. B. Russell, "Industrial Education," *ASME Transactions* 29 (1907): 1123–24.

95. Douglas, *American Apprenticeship,* pp. 213–14; Charles A. Bennett, *History of Manual and Industrial Education 1870 to 1917* (Peoria, Ill., 1937), p. 536; Berenice M. Fisher, *Industrial Education: American Ideals and Institutions* (Madison, 1967), p. 111.

96. See Douglas, *American Apprenticeship,* pp. 176–93; Bennett, *Manual and Industrial Education,* pp. 528–34.

97. See U.S. Commissioner of Labor, *Seventeenth Report,* 1902; *Twenty-third Report,* 1908.

98. Pennsylvania, Secretary of Internal Affairs, *Annual Report,* vol. 16, 1888, p. 4E.

99. U.S. Industrial Commission, *Report on Immigration and on Education,* vol. 15 (Washington, 1901), p. 74.

100. Pennsylvania, Secretary of Internal Affairs, *Annual Report,* vol. 16, 1888, p. 2E; Licht, *Getting Work,* chaps. 3, 4.

101. Frederick W. Coburn, *History of Lowell and Its People* (New York, 1920), 2:415–16; Thomas W. Leavitt, "Textile Manufacturers and the Expansion of Technical Education in Massachusetts, 1869–1904," *Essex Institute Historical Collections* (July 1972), pp. 249–51.

102. See U.S. Commissioner of Labor, *Seventeenth Report,* 1902, pp. 148, 153.

CHAPTER 6. THE RISE OF WELFARE WORK

1. "What Is Welfare Work," National Civic Federation *Monthly Review* 1 (August 1904): 5.

2. The following account considers welfare work in manufacturing plants. Welfare programs were also introduced in many department stores and mining communities.

3. Quoted in Marion C. Cahill, *Shorter Hours* (New Hours, 1932), p. 228; also see Josephine Goldmark, *Fatigue and Efficiency* (New York, 1912), pp. 131–32, 168.

4. Stuart D. Brandes, *American Welfare Capitalism, 1880–1940* (Chicago, 1976), chap. 4. The Massachusetts Bureau of Statistics of Labor found more Massachusetts towns with reading rooms than with relief societies. Massachusetts Bureau of Statistics of Labor, *Twentieth Annual Report,* 1899, pp. 237–71.

5. Massachusetts Bureau of Statistics of Labor, *Thirteenth Annual Report,* 1882, p. 269.

6. Gertrude Beeks to Stanley McCormick, November 3, 1802; McCormick Papers (State Historical Society of Wisconsin, Madison), ser. 3B, box 27. Robert C. Alberts, *The Good Provider: H. J. Heinz and His 57 Varieties* (Boston, 1973), pp. 135–48.

7. Henry Roland, "Six Examples of Successful Shop Management," *Engineering Magazine* 12 (October 1896): 81.

8. New Jersey, Bureau of Statistics of Labor, *Fourth Annual Report,* 1881, p. 131.

9. Budgett Meakin, *Model Factories and Villages* (London, 1905), p. 401.

10. U.S. Industrial Commission, *Report on the Relations and Conditions of Capital and Labor,* vol. 14 (Washington, 1901), pp. 728–29; also Massachusetts Bureau of Statistics of Labor, *Twelfth Annual Report,* 1881, p. 473.

11. Information on these firms is derived from many sources. For Peacedale see William R. Bagnall, *The Textile Industries of the United States,* vol. 2 (Cambridge, Mass., 1893), pp. 301–3; Nicholas P. Gilman, *Profit Sharing between Employer and Employee* (Boston, 1889), pp. 296–300; National Civic Federation, *Profit Sharing* (New York, 1921), pp. 334–35; G. W. W. Hanger, "Housing of the Working People in the United States," *BLS Bulletin* 54 (1904): 1221, 1223. For the Cheney Mills the best sources are Gertrude Beeks to Stanley McCormick, November 3, 1902, McCormick Papers, ser. 3B, box 27, and Roland, "Six Examples," pp. 276–85. For Willimantic see Massachusetts Bureau of Statistics of Labor, *Twelfth Annual Report,* pp. 459, 472, and Gertrude Beeks to Stanley McCormick, November 3, 1902, McCormick Papers, ser. 3B, box 27. For Ludlow see Hanger, "Housing of the Working People," pp. 211–13, and Meakin, *Model Factories,* pp. 401, 404.

12. Massachusetts Bureau of Statistics of Labor, *Twelfth Annual Report,* p. 472; Gertrude Beeks to Stanley McCormick, November 3, 1902, McCormick Papers, ser. 3B, box 27.

13. Massachusetts Bureau of Statistics of Labor, *Sixteenth Annual Report,* p. 472; Gertrude Beeks to Stanley McCormick, November 3, 1902, McCormick Papers, ser. 3B, box 27.

14. See Stanley Buder, *Pullman* (New York, 1967); Almont Lindsey, *The Pullman Strike* (Chicago, 1942); and R. T. Ely, "Pullman, A Social Study," *Harpers Weekly* 70 (February 1885): 452–66.

15. Buder, *Pullman,* pp. 62–63, 71–78, 85, 126–27, 141; Lindsey, *Pullman Strike,* pp. 50–51.

16. Quoted in Buder, *Pullman,* p. 45.

17. *American Machinist* 20 (October 28, 1897): 822; see also Buder, *Pullman,* pp. 139–44.

18. U.S. Congress, Senate, Commission on Industrial Relations, *Final Report and Testimony,* 64th Cong., 1st sess. (Washington, 1916), 10:9547, 9563. Captain H. S. Norton, director of the U.S. Steel housing project at Gary after 1906, recalled his orders from the corporation managers that "Gary was not to be another Pullman, nor Indiana Harbor nor South Chicago . . . but a model town." Quoted in Isaac J. Quillen, "Industrial City, A History of Gary, Indiana, to 1929" (Ph.D. Diss., Yale University, 1942), p. 125.

19. Paul Monroe, "Profit-Sharing in the United States," *American Journal of Sociology* 1 (May 1896): 691; Frank W. Blackmar, "Two Examples of Successful Profit Sharing," *Forum* 19 (March 1895): 62–67.

20. U.S. Industrial Commission, *Report,* 14:358–61; N. O. Nelson, "The Nelson Profit Sharing Plan," *Industrial Management* 53 (September 1917): 909–10.

21. Nicholas P. Gilman, *A Dividend to Labor* (Boston, 1899).

22. Monroe, "Profit Sharing," p. 701; National Industrial Conference Board, *Practical Experience with Profit Sharing in Industrial Establishments* (Boston, 1920), p. 6.

23. Monroe, "Profit Sharing," p. 686. For the failure of the Brewster plan in 1892, which "set back [profit sharing] over ten years," see U.S. Senate, Committee on Education and Labor, *Relations between Labor and Capital*, vol. 1 (Washington, 1885), pp. 1104–9, and Edward Bemis, *Cooperation in the Middle States* (Baltimore, 1888), p. 169; Gilman, *Profit Sharing*, pp. 347–51. For later failures, see Boris Emmet, "Profit Sharing in the United States," *BLS Bulletin* 207 (1916): 166–68.

24. Herbert Feis, *Labor Relations* (New York, 1928), p. 17.

25. I. W. Howerth, "Profit Sharing at Ivorydale," *American Journal of Sociology* 2 (July 1896): 48–52. In 1883 W. C. Procter considered a model town, but George Pullman discouraged him. Buder, *Pullman*, pp. 132–33.

26. Feis, *Labor Relations*, p. 32.

27. NICB, *Practical Experience*, p. 28.

28. See Brandes, *American Welfare Capitalism*; Sanford M. Jacoby, *Employing Bureaucracy; Managers, Unions, and the Transformation of Work in American Industry, 1900–1945* (New York, 1985), chap. 2, 4; Edward Berkowitz and Kim McQuaid, *Creating the Welfare State: The Political Economy of Twentieth-Century Reform* (Lawrence, 1992), chap. 1; H. M. Gitelman, "Welfare Capitalism Reconsidered," *Labor History* 33 (Winter 1992): 1–31.

29. This was a minor distinction, since workers performing similar functions, such as "Mother" Dunn at the H. J. Heinz Company, had operated at least as early as the 1880s and since welfare workers in later years were seldom professionals.

30. See John R. Commons, *Industrial Government* (New York, 1921), ch. 5; Daniel Nelson, "'A Newly Appreciated Art': The Development of Personnel Work at Leeds & Northrup, 1915–1923," *Business History Review* 44 (1970): 524, 533.

31. See S. Crowther, *J. H. Patterson, Pioneer in Industrial Welfare* (Garden City, New York, 1923), pp. 4–5, 168–79; Lena Harvey Tracy, *How My Heart Sang* (New York, 1950), p. 139.

32. Paul Monroe, "Possibilities of the Present Industrial System," *American Journal of Sociology* 3 (May 1898): 733; Crowther, *Patterson*, p. 185.

33. Charles U. Carpenter, "Money-Making Management for Workshop and Factory, V," *Engineering Magazine* 23 (June 1902): 414–15.

34. Monroe, "Possibilities," p. 744.

35. Tracy, *How My Heart Sang*, p. 104.

36. Gertrude Beeks to Stanley McCormick, November 3, 1902, McCormick Papers, ser. 3B, box 27.

37. For details see Daniel Nelson, "The New Factory System and the Unions: The NCR Company Dispute of 1901," *Labor History* 15 (Winter 1974): 89–97; Judith Sealander, *Grand Plans: Business Progressivism and Social Change in Ohio's Miami Valley, 1890–1929* (Lexington, 1988), pp. 18–42; Jacoby, *Employing Bureaucracy*, pp. 61–64.

38. Henry Eilbert, "The Development of Personnel Management in the United States," *Business History Review* 33 (1959): 345–64.

39. Charles U. Carpenter, "The Working of a Labor Department in Industrial Establishments," *Engineering Magazine* 25 (April 1903): 5–6.

40. "Get-Together Club Historical Sketch," *Social Service* 2 (April 1900): 5–9. See also "The Need for a Positive Program," p. 11.

41. See various lists of members and contributors—for example, *Social Service* 2 (February 1900): 20; (September 1900): 1; (December 1900): 2, 3 (February 1901): 2; (November 1901): 180–82.

42. N. P. Gilman, "Social Economics at the Paris Exposition," *Bureau of Labor Bulletin* 34 (1901): 440–89.

43. William H. Tolman, "Social Engineering in Cleveland, Pittsburgh and Dayton," *Social Services* 3 (February 1901): 47; see also "Industrial Betterment in Cleveland, Ohio," pp. 43–44; "Welfare Institutions in Shop Life," *Iron Trade Review* 34 (April 11, 1901): 20.

44. See Charles E. Adams to Ralph W. Easley, April 17, 1901, National Civic Federation Papers (New York Public Library, New York City), box 105; "Welfare Workers Confer," *NCF Monthly Review* 3 (September 1908): 19; William H. Tolman, *Social Engineering* (New York, 1909), p. 146; Brandes, "Welfarism," pp. 68–69.

45. "How the Welfare Department Was Organized," *NCF Monthly Review* 1 (June 1904): 13–14.

46. "The Welfare Department to Widen Its Operations," *NCF Monthly Review* 2 (May 15, 1905): 12–13.

47. "National Civic Federation in 1907," *NCF Monthly Review* 3 (February 1908): 16.

48. William H. Tolman, "The Social Secretary," *Social Service* 2 (November 1900): 1.

49. Charles Henderson, *Citizens in Industry* (New York, 1915), pp. 278–80; also see Eilbert, "Development," p. 317; "What Is Welfare Work," pp. 5–6; Brandes, "Welfarism," pp. 325–27; "Wanted: A Social Secretary," *Social Service* 2 (February 1900): 4.

50. Daniel Nelson and Stuart Campbell, "Taylorism versus Welfare Work in American Industry: H. L. Gantt and the Bancrofts," *Business History Review* 46 (Spring 1972): 6–9; Harvey Bounds, "Bancroft Mills, 1831–1961," Joseph Bancroft & Sons Company Papers (Eleutherian Mills Historical Library, Wilmington, Del.).

51. Elizabeth F. Briscoe to E. E. Pratt, February 12, 1910, Brancroft Papers, add. 876, no. 893; compare with Dorothy Drake, "The Social Secretary," *Social Service* 3 (February 1901): 33–37.

52. Elizabeth F. Briscoe to Gertrude Beeks, August 3, 1907, and to Minnie C. Clark, December 20, 1906, and June 3, 1907, all in Bancroft Papers, acc. 736, no. 893.

53. E. H. Cooper to Mrs. Robert F. Armstrong, August 19, 1920, Bancroft Papers, acc. 736, no. 893.

54. Elizabeth F. Briscoe to Cowell Publishing Company, October 10, 1906, to Lillian D. Wald, December 4, 1907, and to Social Secretary, NCR, April 18 and May 16, 1911, Bancroft Papers, acc. 736, no. 893.

55. Elizabeth F. Briscoe to Mrs. Joseph Zarita, August 25, 1906, Bancroft Papers, acc. 736, no. 893.

56. Elizabeth F. Briscoe to Mrs. James Healy, October 20, 1909, Bancroft Papers, acc. 736, no. 893.

57. Elizabeth F. Briscoe to Joseph Berry, June 30, 1911, and to Mrs. John S. Elliott, October 25, 1906, both in Bancroft Papers, acc. 736, no. 893.

58. See Nelson and Campbell, "Taylorism versus Welfare Work," pp. 10–16.

59. "Wanted: A Social Secretary," p. 4.

60. O. M. Becker, "The Square Deal in Works Management," *Engineering Magazine* 30 (January 1906): 554.

61. Eilbert, "Development," p. 314; Eilbert, "An Analysis of the Changes in Employee Counseling since 1900" (Ph.D. Diss., New York University, 1956), p. 44.

62. W. Jett Lauck and Edgar Sydenstricker, *Conditions of Labor in American Industries* (New York, 1917), pp. 229–30.

63. The confusion was illustrated in an exchange between Gertrude Beeks and the manager of the Brown & Sharpe plant, who had introduced numerous safety and sanitation measures but rejected welfare work. "I laughed at Mr. Viall for his emphatic opposition to welfare work. . . . I laughed for his inconsistency was so amusing." Gertrude Beeks to Stanley McCormick, November 3, 1902, McCormick Papers, ser. 3B, box 27.

64. The major omissions are department stores and mining companies such as Pittsburgh Coal, Cleveland Cliffs, and Calumet and Hecla. Many of the listed firms also introduced scientific management after 1910 (see table 6). This was usually a sign of imaginative management rather than dissatisfaction with welfare work. See Nelson and Campbell, "Taylorism versus Welfare Work."

65. For other comparative studies based on these works see Oscar N. Nestor, "A History of Personnel Administration, 1890 to 1910" (Ph.D. Diss., University of Pennsylvania, 1954), pp. 51–53, 100–105, 111–13.

66. Brandes, "Welfarism," p. 54.

67. See Jacoby, *Employing Bureaucracy,* p. 49–51; Tamara K. Hareven, *Family Time and Industrial Time: The Relationship between the Family and Work in a New England Industrial Community* (New York, 1982), pp. 58–68; Jacquelyn Dowd Hall, et al., *Like a Family: The Making of a Southern Cotton Mill World* (Chapel Hill, 1987), pp. 131–39.

68. See Carroll Wright, "The Factory System of the United States," *Tenth Census of the United States,* 1880, vol. 2, *Manufactures,* (Washington, 1883), for an early defense of the factory system against such allegations.

69. John A. Garraty, *Right Hand Man* (New York, 1960), Ch. 6; David Brody, *Steelworkers in America* (Cambridge, Mass., 1960), esp. chap. 4. U.S. Steel was a good example of a firm that employed large numbers of unskilled immigrants but that introduced a welfare program largely for the skilled workers.

70. *Engineering and Mining Journal* 83 (June 29, 1907): 1233–38; Hanger, "Housing," pp. 1202–5.

71. Hugh Allen, *The House of Goodyear* (Akron, 1936), pp. 165–70; Alfred Lief, *The Firestone Story* (New York, 1951), pp. 81–83.

72. For an illuminating account of the importance of location see Abraham Berglund, George T. Starnes, Frank T. DeVyver, *Labor in the Industrial South* (Charlottesville, 1930), pp. 106–9, 115.

73. For examples see August Kohn, *Cotton Mills of South Carolina* (Charles-

ton, S.C., 1907); Holland Thompson, *From the Cotton Field to the Cotton Mill* (New York, 1906), Nelson and Campbell, "Taylorism versus Welfare Work," pp. 6–9; Harriet L. Herring, *Welfare Work in Mill Villages* (Chapel Hill, 1929).

74. Margaret F. Byington, *Homestead: The Households of a Mill Town* (New York, 1910), pp. 124, 178.

75. Garraty, "Right Hand Man," pp. 109–16; Brody, *Steelworkers,* pp. 167–69; Allen, *Goodyear,* pp. 174–75; Lief, *Firestone,* pp. 78–87; ARMCO, *The First Twenty Years* (Middletown, O., 1922), pp. 241–45.

76. "Employers Welfare Work," *BLS Bulletin* 123 (1913): 19–21; Alexander Taylor, "Machine Shop Practice of General Interest," *American Machinist* 38 (January 30, 1913): 194–200; Ethan Viall, "The Westinghouse Air Brake Shops," *American Machinist* 36 (April 11, 1912): 567–72; Westinghouse Air Brake Company to Gertrude Beeks, August 9, 1901, McCormick Papers, ser. 2C, box 39; Gertrude Beeks to Stanley McCormick, November, 3, 1902, McCormick Papers, ser. 3B, box 27.

77. The NCF Papers, box 111, contains letters from numerous General Electric welfare workers. Also see Chester L. Lucas, "Safety and Welfare Work in an Electrical Plant," *Machinery* 22 (November 1915): 210–14.

78. Arundel Cotter, *United States Steel* (Garden City, 1921), pp. 181–82; Charles A. Gulick, *Labor Policy of the United States Steel Corporation* (New York, 1924), p. 173.

79. "Interview with M. W. Alexander," n.d., General Electric, NCF Papers, box 111.

80. U.S. Industrial Commission, *Report,* 14:657.

81. See, for example, "Interview with Mr. G. E. Emmons, April 28, 1904," NCF Papers, box 111.

82. See Eilbert, "Analysis," pp. 51–59.

83. Clarence J. Hicks, *My Life in Industrial Relations* (New York, 1941), pp. 42–43; see also Louis A. Boettiger, *Employee Welfare Work* (New York, 1923), pp. 122–23.

84. See Robert Ozanne, *A Century of Labor Management Relations at McCormick and International Harvester* (Madison, 1967), chaps. 2, 4, for several examples.

85. A. M. Parks (Sherwin Williams) to McCormick Harvesting Machine Company, May 27, 1909, McCormick Papers, ser. 2C, box 39.

86. Quoted in Raynol C. Boling, "Rendering Labor Safe in Mine and Mill," *Yearbook of the American Iron and Steel Institute, 1912* (New York, 1912), p. 112.

87. Gerald Zahavi, *Workers, Managers, and Welfare Capitalism; The Shoeworkers and Tanners of Endicott Johnson 1890–1950* (Urbana, 1988), chap. 4.

CHAPTER 7. THE NEW FACTORY SYSTEM AND THE WORKER

1. See Richard B. Freeman and James L. Medoff, *What Do Unions Do?* (New York, 1984), chaps. 1, 6.

2. For examples, see U.S. Commissioner of Labor, *Regulation and Restriction of Output, Eleventh Special Report* (Washington, 1904); Stanley B. Math-

ewson, *Restrictions of Output among Unorganized Workers* (New York, 1931); David Montgomery, *The Fall of the House of Labor: the Workplace, the State, and American Labor Activism, 1865–1925* (New York, 1987), chap. 1.

3. See Richard Gillespie, *Manufacturing Knowledge: A History of the Hawthorne Experiments* (New York, 1991); Daniel A. Wren, *White Collar Hobo: the Travels of Whiting Williams* (Ames, 1987), chaps. 4–5.

4. See Alan Dawley, *Class and Community: The Industrial Revolution in Lynn* (Cambridge, 1976); Paul G. Faler, *Mechanics and Manufacturers in the Early Industrial Revolution: Lynn, Massachusetts, 1780–1860* (Albany, 1981); Mary H. Blewett, *Men, Women, and Work: Class, Gender, and Protest in the New England Shoe Industry, 1780–1910* (Urbana, 1988); John T. Cumbler, *Working Class Community in Industrial America: Work, Leisure, and Struggle in Two Industrial Cities, 1880–1930* (Westport, Conn., 1979); Augusta E. Galster, *The Labor Movement in the Shoe Industry* (New York, 1924).

5. The mean number of male and female strikers between 1887 and 1894 divided by male and female employment in manufacturing in 1890 provides striker to total worker ratios of .021 for men and .015 for women.

6. See Benson Soffer, "A Theory of Trade Union Development: The Role of the 'Autonomous' Workman," *Labor History* 1 (Spring 1960), 141–63; Dorothee Schneider, *Trade Unions and Community: The German Working Class in New York City, 1870–1900* (Urbana, 1994), chaps. 3–5; Patricia A. Cooper, *Once a Cigar Maker: Men, Women, and Work Culture in American Cigar Factories, 1900–1920* (Urbana, 1987), chaps. 1–2; Carolyn Daniel McCreesh, *Women in the Campaign to Organize Garment Workers* (New York, 1985), chaps. 1–2; Benjamin Stolberg, *Tailor's Progress* (New York, 1942), chap. 2.

7. Compare the accounts in Philip Scranton, *Proprietary Capitalism: the Textile Manufacture at Philadelphia, 1800–1885* (Philadelphia, 1983), Scranton, *Figured Tapestry: Production, Markets, and Power in Philadelphia Textiles, 1885–1941* (New York, 1989), and the essays in Scranton, ed., *Silk City: Studies on the Paterson Silk Industry, 1860–1940* (Newark, 1985) with the chapters on Fall River in Cumbler, *Working Class Community*. Also see Daniel Walkowitz, *Worker City, Company Town: Iron and Cotton-Worker Protest in Troy and Cohoes, New York, 1855–1884* (Urbana, 1978), chap. 7.

8. Norman Ware, *The Labor Movement in the United States, 1860–1895: A Study in Democracy* (New York, 1929), 69.

9. See Ware and Gerald N. Grob, *Workers and Utopia: A Study of Ideological Conflict in the American Labor Movement* (Evanston, 1961), for general histories. Among recent case studies of local and regional developments, see Richard J. Oestreicher, *Solidarity and Fragmentation: Working People and Class Consciousness in Detroit, 1875–1900* (Urbana, 1986); Melton Alonza McLaurin, *The Knights of Labor in the South* (Westport, Conn., 19); Leon Fink, *Workingmen's Democracy: The Knights of Labor and American Politics* (Urbana, 1982); Susan Levine, "Labor's True Woman: Domesticity and Equal Rights in the Knights of Labor," *Journal of American History* 70 (September 1983): 323–39; Paul Buhle, "The Knights of Labor in Rhode Island," *Radical History Review* 17 (Spring 1978): 48–66; Jama Lazerow, "'The Workingman's Hour': The 1886 Labor Uprising in Boston," *Labor History* 21 (Spring 1980): 200–220; and Faye

Dudden, "Small Town Knights: The Knights of Labor in Homer, New York," *Labor History* 28 (Summer 1987): 307–27.

10. See Fink, *Workingmen's Democracy,* 196–202; Thomas Gavett, *Development of the Labor Movement in Milwaukee* (Madison, 1965), 68–71; Steven J. Ross, *Workers on the Edge; Work, Leisure, and Politics in Industrializing Cincinnati, 1788–1890* (New York, 1985), 294–312.

11. Commons, *History of Labor in the United States, Volume 2* (New York, 1926), 76, 79.

12. Blewett, *Men, Women, and Work,* chap. 6.

13. Cumbler, *Working Class Community,* chaps. 2–5.

14. Doris B. McLaughlin, *Michigan Labor: A Brief History from 1818 to the Present* (Ann Arbor, 1970), 32–49; Jeremy W. Kilar, "Community and Authority Response to the Saginaw Valley Lumber Strike of 1885," *Journal of Forest History* 20 (April 1976): 73–77.

15. See Paul Avrich, *The Haymarket Tragedy* (Princeton, 1984); Robert Ozanne, *A Century of Labor-Management Relations at McCormick and International Harvester* (Madison, 1967), 22–23; Gavett, *Development of the Labor Movement,* 64; Oestreicher, *Solidarity and Fragmentation,* 150–55.

16. Melton Alonza McLaurin, *Paternalism and Protest: Southern Cotton Mills Workers and Organized Labor, 1875–1905* (Westport, Conn., 1971), 77, 92.

17. Elizabeth and Kenneth Fones-Wolf, "The War at Mingo Junction: The Autonomous Workman and the Decline of the Knights of Labor," *Ohio History* 92 (1983): 49.

18. John N. Ingham, *Making Iron and Steel: Independent Mills in Pittsburgh, 1820–1920* (Columbus, 1991), chaps. 4–5; Michael Santos, "Laboring on the Periphery: Managers and Workers at the A. M. Byers Company, 1900–1956," *Business History Review* 61 (Spring 1987), 113–33.

19. Paul Krause, *The Battle for Homestead, 1880–1892; Politics, Culture, and Steel* (Pittsburgh, 1992), 160–350.

20. See, for example, Michael Nuwer, "From Batch to Flow: Production Technology and Work Force Skills in the Steel Industry, 1880–1920," *Technology and Culture* 29 (October 1988): 808–38.

21. See Richard Oestreicher, "A Note on Knights of Labor Membership Statistics," *Labor History* 25 (Winter 1984): 102–108.

22. Richard J. Jensen, *The Winning of the Midwest: Social and Political Conflict, 1888–1896* (Chicago, 1971), 239–51.

23. See Warren R. Van Tine, *The Making of the Labor Bureaucrat: Union Leadership in the United States, 1870–1920* (Amherst, 1973), 66–68.

24. Robert A. Christie, *Empire in Wood: A History of the Carpenters' Union* (Ithaca, 1956), 110–19.

25. Leo Wolman, *Ebb and Flow in Trade Unionism* (New York, 1936), appendix table 1. For the industrial union issue in the AFL, see James O. Morris, *Conflict Within the AFL: A Study of Craft versus Industrial Unionism, 1901–1938* (Ithaca, 1958), chap. 1.

26. Christopher L. Tomlins, "AFL Unions in the 1930's: Their Performance in Historical Perspective," *Journal of American History* 65 (March 1979): 1026–27.

27. Ozanne, *A Century of Labor-Management Relations,* 46–59; David Brody, *The Butcher Workmen; A Study of Unionization* (Cambridge, 1964), 34–61.

28. Marc Jeffrey Stern, *The Pottery Industry of Trenton: A Skilled Trade in Transition, 1850–1929* (New Brunswick, 1994), 115–22; John T. Cumbler, *A Social History of Economic Decline: Business, Politics, and Work in Trenton* (New Brunswick, 1989), 29–31.

29. See Selig Perlman and Philip Taft, *History of Labor in the United States, 1896–1932,* vol. 4 (New York, 1935), 110–16.

30. Daniel Nelson, *American Rubber Workers and Organized Labor, 1900–1941* (Princeton, 1988), 13–15; Brody, *Butcher Workmen,* 48–58; Blewett, *Men, Women, and Work,* chap. 9; Scranton, *Figured Tapestry,* 207–8; McLaurin, *Paternalism and Protest,* 186–87.

31. Alfred D. Chandler, Jr., *The Visible Hand: The Managerial Revolution in American Business* (Cambridge, 1977), chap. 10; Naomi Lamoreaux, *The Great Merger Movement in American Business, 1895–1904* (New York, 1985).

32. Perlman and Taft, *History of Labor,* 129–34; Robert H. Wiebe, *Businessmen and Reform: A Study of the Progressive Movement* (Cambridge, 1962) chaps. 2, 7; Montgomery, *The Fall of the House of Labor,* 269–74.

33. Thomas Klug, "Employers' Strategies in the Detroit Labor Market," in *On the Line: Essays in the History of Auto Work,* ed. Nelson Lichtenstein and Stephen Meyer (Urbana, 1989), 51.

34. Howell John Harris, "Getting It Together: The Metal Manufacturers Association of Philadelphia, c. 1900–1930," in *Masters to Managers; Historical and Comparative Perspectives on American Employers,* ed. Sanford M. Jacoby (New York, 1991), 125.

35. Olivier Zunz, *The Changing Face of Inequality: Urbanization, Industrial Development, and Immigrants in Detroit, 1880–1920* (Chicago, 1982), 310. Also see Raymond R. Fragnoli, "Progressive Coalitions and Municipal Reform: Charter Revision in Detroit, 1912–1918," *Detroit in Perspective* 4 (1980): 119–65.

36. Frederick W. Taylor, *The Principles of Scientific Management* (New York, 1911).

37. Bruno Ramirez, *When Workers Fight: The Politics of Industrial Relations in the Progressive Era, 1898–1916* (Westport, Conn., 1978), 67–68; James Weinstein, *The Corporate Ideal in the Liberal State* (Boston, 1968), chap. 1; James O. Morris, "The Acquisitive Spirit of John Mitchell, UWM President (1899–1908)," *Labor History* 20 (Winter 1979): 5–44.

38. Milton J. Nadworny, *Scientific Management and the Unions, 1900–1932: A Historical Analysis* (Cambridge, 1955), chaps. 4–8.

39. Daniel Nelson, "Scientific Management in Retrospect," in Nelson, *A Mental Revolution; Scientific Management since Taylor* (Columbus, 1992), 12–14.

40. See John Ingham, "A Strike in the Progressive Era: McKees Rocks, 1909," *Pennsylvania History* 90 (July 1966): 355–56; David Brody, *Steelworkers in America: The Nonunion Era* (Cambridge, Mass., 1960), pp. 138–39.

41. Ingham, "A Strike in the Progressive Era," 358–76; Melvyn Dubofsky, *We Shall Be All; A History of the IWW* (Chicago, 1969), 199–209; Philip S.

Foner, *History of the Labor Movement in the United States,* vol. 4, *The Industrial Workers of the World, 1905–1917* (New York, 1965), 282–95.

42. Dubofsky, *We Shall Be All,* 150.

43. AFL organizers often tried to undermine IWW strike leaders, generally with disastrous consequences for both groups. See for examples, see Dubofsky, *We Shall Be All,* 236, 276; Steve Golin, *The Fragile Bridge; Paterson Silk Strike, 1913* (Philadelphia, 1988), 85–88; Anne Huber Tripp, *The IWW and the Paterson Silk Strike of 1913* (Urbana, 1987), 27, 111–17; Robert E. Snyder, "Women, Wobblies, and Workers Rights: The 1912 Textile Strike in Little Falls, New York," in *At the Point of Production; the Local History of the IWW,* ed. Joseph R. Conlin (Westport, Conn., 1981), 39–40; Nelson, *American Rubber Workers,* 33–34.

44. See Dubofsky, *We Shall Be All,* 126–290.

45. For example, see Tripp, *The IWW and the Paterson Silk Strike,* chap. 4, and *American Rubber Workers,* 27–29.

46. In 1900, for example, the typical cotton textile worker used 23 times as much power and 1.5 times as much capital as the typical men's clothing worker. See *Twelfth Census of the United States, 1900,* vol. 7, *Manufactures* (Washington, 1902), table 2, p. cccxvii.

47. *Twelfth Census,* vol. 7, *Manufactures,* table 2, p. cccvii, *Thirteenth Census of the United States, 1909,* vol. 8, *Manufactures,* p. 261.

48. McCreesh, *Women in the Campaign to Organize Garment Workers,* 95–127; Diane Kirkby, "The Wage Earning Woman and the State: The National Women's Trade Union League and Protective Labor Legislation, 1903–1923," *Labor History* 28 (Winter 1987), 54–74.

49. Melvyn Dubofsky, *When Workers Organize: New York City in the Progressive Era* (Amherst, 1968), 58.

50. See Jesse Thomas Carpenter, *Competition and Collective Bargaining in the Needle Trades, 1910–1967* (Ithaca, 1972), 48–54; Stolberg, *Tailor's Progress,* chap. 5.

51. Steve Fraser, *Labor Will Rule: Sidney Hillman and the Rise of American Labor* (New York, 1991), 45–93; Mathew Josephson, *Sidney Hillman, Statesman of American Labor* (Garden City, 1952), 47–98.

52. Gary M. Fink, *The Fulton Bag and Cotton Mills Strike of 1914–1915: Espionage, Labor Conflict, and New South Industrial Relations* (Ithaca, 1993).

CHAPTER 8. THE IMPACT OF PROGRESSIVE GOVERNMENT

1. William F. Willoughby, "The Inspection of Factories and Workshops in the United States," *Bureau of Labor Bulletin* 12 (1897): 552–59. New Jersey initiated factory inspection in 1883 and New York in 1886 to regulate child labor.

2. Ibid., p. 21.

3. Leonard W. Hatch, "The Prevention of Accidents," *American Labor Legislation Review* 1 (June 1911): 105–6.

4. U.S. Industrial Commission, *Report in the Relations and Conditions of Capital and Labor,* vol. 7 (Washington, 1901), pp. 251–52.

5. Quoted in Earl R. Beckner, *A History of Labor Legislation in Illinois* (Chicago, 1929), p. 228.

6. Ibid., p. 239.

7. Elizabeth Brandeis, "Labor Legislation," in J. R. Commons, *History of Labor* (New York, 1935), 3:567–69.

8. They enacted laws in 1915. Ibid., pp. 575–76.

9. Workmen's Compensation Laws of the United States and Foreign Countries," *BLS Bulletin* 203 (1917): 51. See also Edward D. Berkowitz and Kim McQuaid, *Creating the Welfare State: The Political Economy of Twentieth-Century Reform* (Lawrence, 1992), chap. 2. For an excellent survey of the historiography of this and other types of legislation, see Joseph F. Tripp, "Law and Social Control: Historians' Views of Progressive Era Labor Legislation," *Labor History* 28 (Fall 1987): 447–83.

10. In New York and Ohio the state constitutions were amended before the compulsory laws were passed. Brandeis, "Labor Legislation," pp. 578–79; H. R. Mengert, "The Ohio Workmen's Compensation Laws," *Ohio Archeological and Historical Publications* 29 (1920): 16–21; Robert F. Wesser, "Conflict and Compromise: The Workmen's Compensation Movement in New York, 1890's–1913," *Labor History* 11 (Summer 1971): 361–71.

11. Carl Hookstadt, "Comparison of Workmen's Compensation Laws of the United States up to December 31, 1917," *BLS Bulletin* 240 (1918): 6.

12. Ibid., p. 14. For the campaign to secure state insurance programs after 1917 see Robert Asher, "Radicalism and Reform: State Insurance of Workmen's Compensation in Minnesota, 1910–1933," *Labor History* 14 (Winter 1973): 19–41.

13. "Workmen's Compensation Laws," pp. 87–90, 125–26; Hookstadt, "Comparison," p. 7.

14. For arbitration in the Massachusetts boot and shoe industry see *Annual Report of the State Board of Conciliation and Arbitration, 1886–1919*. For the employment office issue see Frances A. Kellor, *Out of Work* (New York, 1915), chaps. 5–6, 8–11; Shelby M. Harrison et al., *Public Employment Offices* (New York, 1924); and Don D. Lescohier, "Working Conditions," in Commons, *History of Labor*, pp. 185–97.

15. U.S. Congress, Senate, *Report on the Condition of Woman and Child Wage-Earners in the United States*, 61st Cong., 2d sess., doc. 645, vol. 6 (Washington, 1910), pp. 219–20. See also Alice Kessler-Harris, *Out to Work: A History of Wage-Earning Women in the United States* (New York, 1982), chap. 7.

16. Massachusetts Bureau of Statistics of Labor, *Fifth Annual Report*, 1874, p. 5; see also John K. Towles, "Factory Legislation in Rhode Island," *American Economic Association Quarterly* 9 (1908): 28–29.

17. G. A. Weber, "Labor Legislation in the United States," *Bureau of Labor Bulletin* 54 (1904): 1444–45; U.S. Congress, Senate, *Woman and Child*, 6:210–22.

18. U.S. Congress, Senate, *Woman and Child*, 1:1551–52, 6:210–11; Brandeis, "Labor Legislation," p. 429. See also David L. Carlton, *Mill and Town in South Carolina, 1880–1920* (Baton Rouge, 1982), pp. 173–212.

19. Brandeis, "Labor Legislation," p. 421.

20. Sarah Scovill Whittelsey, *Massachusetts Labor Legislation* (n.p., n.d.), pp. 12–15, 26–27; 78; Marion C. Cahill, *Shorter Hours* (New York, 1932), pp. 106–10. The ten-hour day was hardly a new or experimental idea. Adult males generally worked under the ten-hour day by the 1870s; labor unions, moreover, were beginning to agitate for the eight-hour day.

21. U.S. Industrial Commission, *Report*, 5:50–52.

22. Josephine Goldmark, *Fatigue and Efficiency* (New York, 1912), p. 271. Between 1909 and 1911 Arizona, California, and Washington had adopted the eight-hour day and forty-eight-hour week for some occupations. The Supreme Court confirmed the constitutionality of the ten-hour day in 1908 and of the eight-hour day in 1915.

23. Arthur S. Field, "The Child Labor Policy of New Jersey," *American Economic Association Quarterly* 11 (1910): 47–48.

24. Beckner, *Illinois Legislation*, pp. 188–89.

25. Field, "Child Labor Policy," p. 93.

26. For specific measures see "Legislation for Women in Industry," *American Labor Legislation Review* 6 (December 1916): 401; Weber, "Labor Laws," pp. 1442–43.

27. "There is simply no material on the reactions of individual workers." Robert Asher, "Workmen's Compensation in the United States, 1880–1935" (Ph.D. Diss., University of Minnesota, 1971), p. 678.

28. The laws that many legislatures passed in the mid-nineteenth century establishing the ten- or eight-hour day in the absence of contracts specifying otherwise were notorious examples of meaningless legislature. The Pepperell Manufacturing Company Papers (Baker Library, Harvard Business School, Cambridge, Mass.) contain examples of such contracts. For the shorter hours movement see David Montgomery, *Beyond Equality* (New York, 1967), chaps. 6–8, and Cahill, *Shorter Hours,* chap. 4. For the argument that regulatory laws were passed for the benefit of managers, see Roy Lubove, *The Struggle for Social Security, 1900–35* (Cambridge, Mass., 1968), pp. 45–65; James Weinstein, "Big Business and the Origins of Workmen's Compensation," *Labor History* 8 (Spring 1967): 156–74; and Weinstein, *The Corporate Ideal in the Liberal State, 1900–18* (Boston, 1968), chap. 2.

29. Beckner, *Illinois Legislation,* p. 505; Irwin Yellowitz, *Labor and the Progressive Movement in New York State, 1897–1916* (Ithaca, 1965), p. 89; Fred R. Fairchild, "The Factory Legislation of the State of New York," *Publication of the American Economic Association* 6 (1905): 28; Wesser, "Conflict and Compromise," pp. 351, 361, 365–71.

30. Goldmark, *Fatigue*, p. 122.

31. Beckner, *Illinois Legislation*, pp. 230–31.

32. The *Yearbook of the American Iron and Steel Institute*, 1910–1920 has numerous articles on accident prevention that emphasize this point.

33. Lubove, *Struggle,* p. 52.

34. Daniel Nelson, *Unemployment Insurance* (Madison, 1969), chaps. 1–5.

35. James Weinstein, *Corporate Ideal*, p. 50. The most complete survey of business attitudes toward workmen's compensation legislation is Asher, "Workmen's Compensation in the United States," chap. 6. Also, see Asher's critique of Weinstein's treatment of the National Civic Federation on p. 226.

36. Asher describes the campaigns in New York, Wisconsin, Ohio, Minnesota, and Massachusetts. See Asher, "Workmen's Compensation in the United States," and Asher, "Business and the Workers' Welfare in the Progressive Era: Workmen's Compensation Reform in Massachusetts, 1880–1911," *Business History Review* 43 (1969): 474; Wesser, "Conflict and Compromise," pp. 351, 354–55, 365, 371.

37. Francis Feehan, "Proposed Workmen's Compensation Law for Pennsylvania," *American Labor Legislation Review* 5 (March 1915): 107.

38. See Fairchild, "Factory Legislation . . . of New York," pp. 40–45; Jeremy P. Felt, *Hostages of Fortune* (Syracuse, 1965), pp. 18–19; Field "Child Labor Policy," p. 74; Beckner, *Illinois Legislation*, p. 160; J. Lynn Barnard, *Factory Legislation in Pennsylvania, Its History and Administration* (Philadelphia, 1907), p. 56.

39. Walter I. Trattner, *Crusade for the Children* (Chicago, 1970), pp. 54–56; Louis L. Athey, "The Consumers' Leagues and Social Reform, 1890–1923" (Ph.D. Diss., University of Delaware, 1965), pp. 119–30.

40. "In the legislative struggles," the historian of the NCLC has written, "it was often difficult to tell which opponents of child labor legislation were self-interested and which were not." Trattner, *Crusade,* pp. 83–83.

41. See Elizabeth H. Davidson, *Child Labor Legislation in the Southern Textile States* (Chapel Hill, 1939).

42. U.S. Congress, Senate, *Woman and Child,* 6:140–41; Holland Thompson, *From the Cotton Field to the Cotton Mill* (New York, 1906), p. 134; Davidson, *Child Labor Legislation,* pp. 114–16.

43. U.S. Congress, Senate, *Woman and Child,* 6:139.

44. Edith Reeves and Caroline Manning, "The Standing of Massachusetts in the Administration of Labor Legislation," in *Labor Laws and Their Enforcement,* ed. Susan Kingsbury (New York, 1911), pp. 230–35; Brandeis, "Labor Legislation," pp. 636–37.

45. Willoughby, "Factory Inspection," p. 563; U.S. Congress, Senate, Commission on Industrial Relations, *Final Report and Testimony,* 64th Cong., 1st sess. (Washington, 1916), 4:899. The southern industrial states established inspection departments much later—Alabama in 1907, South Carolina in 1909, Georgia in 1915, and North Carolina in 1919—and in general did not initiate effective regulation before 1915.

46. John A. Fitch, *The Steel Workers* (New York, 1910), p. 71.

47. Towles, "Factory Legislation in Rhode Island," p. 46.

48. In Illinois Consumers' League members checked school certificates. In Massachusetts they "cooperated closely with government agencies in checking and enforcing labor legislation." Athey, "The Consumers' Leagues," pp. 117, 149.

49. U.S. Industrial Commission, *Report,* 14:562.

50. U.S. Congress, Senate, *Woman and Child,* 6:204; Davidson, *Child Labor Legislation,* p. 237.

51. Goldmark, *Fatigue,* p. 211, 226.

52. Felt, *Hostages,* p. 31. For additional evidence see Moses Stambler, "The Effects of Compulsory Education and Child Labor Laws on High School Attendance in New York City, 1898–1917," *History of Education Quarterly* 8 (1963): 199–204.

53. U.S. Congress, Senate, *Woman and Child*, 19:44; also Yellowitz, *Labor and the Progressive Movement*, pp. 150–51.

54. U.S. Industrial Commission, *Report*, 7:78.

55. U.S. Congress, Senate, *Woman and Child*, 19:27.

56. Ibid., pp. 39–40; see also Alba M. Edwards, "The Labor Legislation of Connecticut," *Publications of the American Economic Association* 7 (1907): 67–72.

57. Towles, "Factory Legislation in Rhode Island," p. 53. In New Hampshire school officials "enforced" the child labor laws.

58. U.S. Congress, Senate, *Woman and Child*, 19:30. For comparisons of expenditures by the Massachusetts factory inspectors with those of other industrial states see Asher, "Workmen's Compensation in the United States," p. 231.

59. New York Factory Investigating Commission, *Preliminary Report*, 1912 (Albany, 1912), 2:557.

60. Field, *Child Labor Policy*, p. 171.

61. Barnard, *Factory Legislation in Pennsylvania*, p. 165.

62. New York Factory Investigating Commission, *Preliminary Report*, 1912, 3:1436.

63. Whittelsey, *Massachusetts Labor Legislation*, p. 28.

64. New Jersey, Inspector of Factories and Workshops, *Eleventh Annual Report*, 1893, p. 7; Connecticut, Inspector of Factories, *Second Annual Report*, 1888, p. 5; Pennsylvania, Department of Factory Inspector, *Sixth Annual Report*, 1885, p. 5.

65. U.S. Congress, Senate, *Woman and Child*, 19:297; Reeves and Manning in Kingsbury, ed., *Labor Laws*, p. 227.

66. New York, Factory Inspector, *First Annual Report*, 1886, p. 13; *Ninth Annual Report*, 1894, p. 33. For the background of the child labor problem at Harmony Mills, see Daniel J. Walkowitz, "Working Class Women in the Gilded Age: Factory, Community and Family Life Among Cohoes, New York, Cotton Workers," *Journal of Social History* 5 (Summer 1972): 464–87.

67. New York, Factory Inspector, *Twelfth Annual Report*, 1897, p. 21.

68. Fairchild, "Factory Legislation . . . of New York," p. 124. But other abuses remained. In 1901 women employees of Harmony Mills complained of a seventy-seven-to-eighty-four-hour week. Felt, *Hostages*, p. 37.

69. Illinois, Factory Inspectors, *Third Annual Report*, 1895, p. 14; *Fourth Annual Report*, 1896, p. 15.

70. U.S. Congress, Senate, *Woman and Child*, 19:143.

71. Ibid., 1:194.

72. Department of Commerce and Labor, Bureau of the Census, *Census of Manufacturers*, 1905, pt. 1, p. lxxv.

73. U.S. Congress, Senate, *Woman and Child*, 1:188. The total number of children gainfully employed apparently grew rapidly until 1890, and then slowly between 1890 and 1910 and declined sharply thereafter. The census figures on manufacturing and mechanical industries suggest a similar trend. In 1910 there were supposedly 260,932 children between the ages of ten and fifteen, including 32,746 between ten and thirteen, in these industries. In 1920 the numbers had fallen to 185, 337 and 9,473. By far the most important employers of children

between ten and thirteen were the textile manufacturers. U.S. Dept. of Commerce, *Fourteenth Census of the U.S.* (1920), vol. 4, (Washington, 1923), pp. 475–80.

74. Arthur H. Cole, *The American Wool Manufacture* (Cambridge, Mass., 1926), 2:104.

75. Melvin T. Copeland, *The Cotton Manufacturing Industry of the United States* (Cambridge, Mass., 1912), p. 43; Jack Blicksilver, *Cotton Manufacturing in the Southeast* (Atlanta, 1959), pp. 30–31.

76. Martin Brown, Jens Christiansen, and Peter Philips, "The Decline of Child Labor in the U.S. Fruit and Vegetable Canning Industry: Law or Economics" *Business History Review* 66 (Winter 1992): 769.

77. National Industrial Conference Board, *Health Service in Industry* (New York, 1921), pp. 3, 30.

78. Arandel Cotter, *United States Steel* (Garden City, 1921), p. 181.

79. Brandeis, "Labor Legislation," p. 651.

80. Gerd Korman, *Industrialization, Immigrants, and Americanizers* (Madison, 1967), p. 125.

81. Pennsylvania, Commissioner of Labor and Industries, *First Annual Report,* 1913–14, 2:13, 305; *Second Annual Report,* 1914, 1:vii; *Third Annual Report,* 1915, 1:vii, ix, 50, 58.

82. Korman, *Industrialization,* p. 131.

CHAPTER 9. WORLD WAR I

1. W. Jett Lauck and Edgar Sydenstricker, *Conditions of Labor in American Industries* (New York, 1917), p. 71.

2. Solomon Fabricant, *Employment in Manufacturing, 1899–1939* (New York, 1942), pp. 211–12.

3. For the leading munitions manufacturers see Benedict Crowell, *America's Munitions, 1917–18* (Washington, 1919).

4. H. H. Pierce to P. S. DuPont, Jan. 22, 1940, Longwood Papers (Hagley Library, Wilmington, Del.), ser. B, group 10.

5. "Proceedings of the Fourth Annual Meeting of the International Association of Industrial Accident Boards and Commission," *BLS Bulletin* 248 (1919): 195; J. Donald Pryor and Frank V. Sackett, "Some Economic Aspects of Fire Protection Problems and Hazards in War Times," *ASME Transactions* 40 (1918): 404; Lucian W. Chaney and Hugh S. Hanna, "The Safety Movement in the Iron and Steel Industry, 1907 to 1919." *BLS Bulletin* 234 (1918): 24–25, 28.

6. William Smith to B. F. Roeller, August 4, 1916, Phoenix Iron Company Papers (Hagley Library, Wilmington, Del.), "Safety First, no. 1" (1916).

7. "Industrial Poisons Used or Produced in the Manufacture of Explosives," *BLS Bulletin* 219 (1917): 6.

8. Zenas L. Potter, "War Boom Towns I—Bridgeport," *Survey* 35 (December 4, 1915): 237.

9. John Ihlder, "How the War Came to Chester," *Survey* 40 (June 1, 1918): 249.

10. John Ihlder, "Hopewell, A City Eighteen Months Old," *Survey* 37 (December 2, 1916): 229.

11. Joseph Marcus, "Supplementary Report on Trip to Nitro, West Virginia," October 7, 1918, War Labor Policies Board Records (National Archives, Washington), RG 1.

12. Zenas L. Potter, "Penns Grove, A Shipping Place for Sudden Death," *Survey* 36 (February 5, 1916): 544.

13. Ernest Fox Nichols, "The Employment Manager," *Annals of the American Academy of Political and Social Science* 65 (May 1916): 2.

14. Quoted in David Brody, *Labor in Crisis: The Steel Strike of 1919* (Philadelphia, 1965), pp. 45, 47.

15. Pennsylvania, Commissioner of Labor and Industries, *Third Annual Report*, 1916, p. 1112.

16. E. G. Keith, "The Financial History of Two Textile Cities: A Study of the Effects of Industrial Growth and Decline Upon the Financial Policies and Practices of Lowell and Fall River" (Ph.D. Diss., Harvard University, 1937), p. 369.

17. Charles B. Barnes, "A Report on the Condition and Management of Public Employment Offices in the United States, Together with Some Account of the Private Employment Agencies of the Country," *BLS Bulletin* 192 (1916): 66.

18. Shelby M. Harrison et al., *Public Employment Offices* (New York, 1924), pp. 131–32.

19. W. A. Grieves and S. R. Rectansu, "Visit to Nitro, West Virginia," September 9, 1918, War Labor Policies Board Papers, RG 1.

20. Harrison, *Public Employment Offices,* pp. 89, 132–33, 455–56; John A. Fitch, "Employment Managers in Conference," *Survey* 40 (May 18, 1918): 190.

21. Edward G. Hartmann, *The Movement to Americanize the Immigrant* (New York, 1967), pp. 88–93.

22. Gerd Korman, *Industrialization, Immigrants and Americanizers* (Madison, 1967), p. 142.

23. Korman, *Industrialization,* p. 144.

24. Allan Nevins, *Ford,* vol. 1, *The Times, the Man, the Company* (New York, 1954), pp. 557–58; Samuel J. Marquis, Memo on Profit Sharing (ca. 1916), Fort Motor Company Archives (Henry Ford Museum, Dearborn, Mich.), 63-1. At the Long Island City, New York, Ford plants, the graduation ceremonies were especially imaginative. The graduates marched from a model ship into a "melting pot," where they changed clothes (as teachers stirred the pot with U.S. flags) and emerged "fully dressed as Americans." "Notes on Interview with Clinton C. DeWitt and William G. Moore" (ca. 1916), National Civic Federation Papers (New York Public Library, New York City), box 111.

25. Hartmann, *Movement,* pp. 129–30.

26. Hugh Allen, *The House of Goodyear* (Akron, 1936), p. 180.

27. "War Time Experience with Women in the Metal Trades," *Machinery* 25 (September 1918): 85.

28. Fred H. Colvin, "Women in Machine Shops," *American Machinist* 47 (September 29, 1917): 510.

29. See Charlton L. Edholm, "Solving New Haven's Man-power Problem," *American Machinist* 49 (October 17, 1918): 721–23; Harry Franklin Porter, "Detroit's Plans for Recruiting Women for Industries," *Engineering Magazine* 53 (August 1917): 655.

30. John W. Upp, "The Woman Worker," *ASME Transactions* 39 (1917): 1132–33; John C. Bower, "Westinghouse Employment Department," *Machinery* 26 (November 1919): 243.

31. Porter, "Detroit's Plans," pp. 657–58.

32. C. B. Lord, "How to Deal Successfully with Women in Industry," *Engineering Magazine* 53 (September 1917): 841–45.

33. C. U. Carpenter, "How We Trained 5000 Women," *Industrial Management* 55 (April 1918): 354.

34. "War Time Experience," *Machinery* 25 (September 1918): 85. Vestibule schools were also established for male workers in a few firms. A similar innovation was the use of shop instructors to train new employees in the shipyards. See Sumner H. Slichter, *The Turnover of Factory Labor* (New York, 1919), p. 335; Roy W. Kelly and Frederick J. Allen, *The Shipbuilding Industry* (Boston, 1918), pp. 10, 250–51. For government policy toward women workers, see Maurine Weiner Greenwald, *Women, War, and Work; The Impact of World War I on Women Workers in the United States* (Westport, 1980), chap. 2.

35. George E. Haynes, "Negroes Move North, II," *Survey* 41 (January 4, 1919): 456; U.S. Department of Labor, *Negro Migration in 1916–17* (Washington, 1919), pp. 147–57. Also Jack Temple Kirby, "The Southern Exodus, 1910–1960: A Primer for Historians," *Journal of Southern History* 49 (November 1983): 585–600; James R. Grossman, *Land of Hope; Chicago, Black Southerners, and the Great Migration* (Chicago, 1989), pp. 74–85; and Joe William Trotter, Jr., *The Great Migration in Historical Perspective: New Dimensions of Race, Class, and Gender* (Bloomington, Indiana, 1991).

36. Sterling D. Spero and Abram L. Harris, *The Black Worker* (New York, 1931), p. 155.

37. Emmett J. Scott, *Negro Migration During the War* (Washington, 1920), p. 36. Frances D. Tyson, A. U.S. Department of Labor investigator, estimated that labor agents accounted for 19 to 20 percent of the migrants. U.S. Department of Labor, *Negro Migration*, p. 120.

38. Pennsylvania, Commissioner of Labor and Industries, *Third Annual Report*, 1916, p. 1093. See U.S. Department of Labor, *Negro Migration*, pp. 121–24, for turnover estimates.

39. Scott, *Negro Migration;* U.S. Department of Labor, *Negro Migration*, pp. 21–30, 53–66, 78–79, 93–111; and the Chicago Commission on Race Relations, *The Negro in Chicago* (Chicago, 1922), pp. 80–87; Florette Henri, *Black Migration: Movement North, 1900–1920* (New York, 1975), chap. 2; Grossman, *Land of Hope,* chap. 1; William Tuttle, Jr., *Race Riot* (New York, 1970), pp. 75–95; and Elliott Rudwick, *Race Riot in East St. Louis, July 2, 1917* (Carbondale, 1964), pp. 168–70.

40. Scott, *Negro Migration*, p. 26.

41. Ibid., p. 39.

42. Ibid., p. 70.

43. Ibid., p. 69.

44. Haynes, "Negroes Move North, I," p. 116.

45. "Negro Welfare Workers in Pittsburgh," *Survey* 40 (August 3, 1918): 513; ARMCO, *The First Twenty Years* (Middletown, Ohio, 1922), chap. 21;

Meyer Bloomfield, "Employment Problems," *Engineering Magazine* 53 (September 1917): 908.

46. Sanford M. Jacoby, *Employing Bureaucracy: Managers, Unions, and the Transformation of Work in American Industry, 1900–1945* (New York, 1985), pp. 137–40.

47. Henry Eilbert, "The Development of Personnel Management in the United States," *Business History Review* 33 (1959): 350–53.

48. Meyer Bloomfield, "The Aim and Work of Employment Managers' Association," *Annals of the American Academy of Political and Social Science* 65 (May 1916): 77.

49. Daniel Nelson and Stuart Campbell, "Taylorism versus Welfare Work in American Industry: H. L. Gantt and the Bancrofts," *Business History Review* 46 (Spring 1972): 1–16.

50. Majority Report of Sub-Committee on Administration, "The Present State of the Art of Industrial Management," *ASME Transactions* 34 (1912): 1137.

51. Samuel S. Marquis, "Testimony before Judge Alschuler, November 23, 1920," Ford Archives, acc. 293, box 1, pp. 36–37.

52. Nevins, *Ford,* pp. 526–27.

53. Ibid., pp. 529–530; C. J. Abell, "Labor Classified on a Skill-Wages Basis," *Iron Age* 93 (January 1914): 48–50.

54. Horace L. Arnold and Fay Leone Faurote, *Ford Methods and the Ford Shops* (New York, 1919), p. 43; see George Bundy, "Work of the Employment Department of the Ford Motor Company," *BLS Bulletin* 196 (1916): 65–71, for the forms and procedures.

55. S. M. Marquis, "Memo on Profit Sharing" (ca. 1916), Ford Archives, 63-A; Daniel M. G. Raff, "Wage Determination Theory and the Five-Dollar Day at Ford," *Journal of Economic History* 48 (June 1988): 387–99; Daniel M. G. Raff, "Ford Welfare Capitalism in Its Economic Context," in *Masters to Managers; Historical and Comparative Perspective on American Enterprise,* ed. Sanford M. Jacoby (New York, 1991), pp. 90–110.

56. Marquis, "Testimony before Judge Alschuler, Nov. 23, 1920," Ford Archives, acc. 293, box 1, 45–46.

57. See Magnus W. Alexander, "Hiring and Firing: Its Economic Waste and How to Avoid It," *Annals of the American Academy of Political and Social Science* 65 (May 1916).

58. Paul H. Douglas, "Plant Administration of Labor," *Journal of Political Economy* 27 (July 1919): 545.

59. Meyer Bloomfield, "The New Profession of Handling Men," *Engineering Magazine* 52 (January 1917): 446.

60. Prewar industrial psychologists had been more interested in fatigue, lighting, and work methods, and the few vocational tests that had been devised were unsatisfactory. See Charles W. Allen to Gorham Manufacturing Company, April 6, 1905, National Civic Federation Papers, box 105. Hugo Munsterberg's book, *Psychology and Industrial Efficiency* (Boston, 1913), included a chapter on "The Best Man." See also Douglas, "Plant Administration," p. 554. For the intellectual milieu in which industrial psychology developed see John Chynoweth Burnham, "Psychiatry, Psychology and the Progressive Movement," *American Quarterly* 12 (1960): 457–65.

61. Edmund C. Lynch, "Walter Dill Scott, Pioneer Industrial Psychologist," *Business History Review* 42 (1968): 155–57, 162.

62. Ibid., pp. 162–67; Loren Baritz, *The Servants of Power* (Middletown, Conn., 1960), pp. 52, 68.

63. Boyd Fisher, "Methods of Reducing Labor Turnover," *BLS Bulletin* 196 (1916): 19; William O. Lichtner, *Time Study and Job Analysis* (New York, 1921).

64. W. D. Stearns, "Placing the Right Man in the Right Job," *Machinery* 26 (September 1919): 30.

65. Douglas, "Plant Administration," p. 553.

66. Meyer Bloomfield, "Employment Manager's Department," *Engineering Magazine* 53 (June 1917): 439. For an early foremen's club, see Harold F. Williamson and Kenneth H. Meyers, II, *Designed for Digging* (Evanston, 1955), p. 70.

67. G. W. Bowie, "Foreman—Such As America Needs," in *Employment Management*, ed. Daniel Bloomfield (New York, 1919), pp. 317–26.

68. Fred H. Rindge, Jr., "From Boss to the Foreman," *Engineering Magazine* 53 (July 1917): 510. See also Bloomfield, "Employment Manager's Department," pp. 439–40; "Relations of Foremen to the Working Force," *Engineering Magazine* 53 (June 1917): 340; Meyer Bloomfield, "The New Foremanship," *Industrial Management* 55 (February 1918): 145.

69. Paul W. Litchfield, *Industrial Voyage* (Garden City, New York, 1954), p. 127.

70. Daniel Nelson, *American Rubber Workers and Organized Labor, 1900–1941* (Princeton, 1988), pp. 56–58, 81.

71. Boyd Fisher, "How to Reduce Labor Turnover," *BLS Bulletin* 227 (1917): 45–47.

72. "Welfare Work for Employees in Industrial Establishments in the United States," *BLS Bulletin* 250 (1919): 119–27 esp.

73. However, see National Industrial Conference Board, *Cost of Health Service in Industry* (New York, 1921), for the influence of the war on industrial health programs.

74. See Harriet L. Herring, *Welfare Work in Mill Villages* (Chapel Hill, 1929), pp. 29, 120–21.

75. "Welfare Work for Employees," pp. 36–37.

76. Roy W. Kelly, "Hiring the Worker, I," *Engineering Magazine* 52 (February 1917): 599.

77. Clarence J. Hicks, *My Life in Industrial Relations* (New York, 1941), p. 111; see also Harlow S. Person, "University Schools of Business and the Training of Employment Executives," *Annals of the American Academy of Political and Social Science* 65 (May 1916): 118–119, and E. C. Gould, "A Modern Industrial Relations Department," in Bloomfield, ed., *Employment Management*, pp. 193–96.

78. Henry Eilbert, "An Analysis of the Changes in Employee Counseling Since 1900" (Ph.D. Diss., New York University, 1956).

79. Robert G. Valentine might have had a comparable influence except for his premature death in 1916. His associates, notably Ordway Tead, became leaders of the personnel management movement. See Milton J. Nadworny, *Scientific Management and the Unions* (Cambridge, Mass., 1955), pp. 75–76, 98–99, for Val-

entine's career. The Carl Barth Papers, drawer 4, include a copy of an "Industrial Audit" that Tead made for the Osborn Mills of Fall River in 1916.

80. Meyer Jacobstein, "Government Course for Training Employment Managers," *BLS Bulletin* 247 (1919): 21.

81. Douglas, "Plant Administration," p. 550.

82. Bloomfield, "Aims and Work," pp. 78–79.

83. L. P. Alford, "Ten Years' Progress in Management," *ASME Transactions* 44 (1922): 1259–60.

84. Douglas, "Plant Administration," p. 551; Jacoby, *Employing Bureaucracy,* pp. 147–49.

85. The following discussion is based largely on Mary B. Gilson, *What's Past is Prologue* (New York, 1940), chap. 6; on a series of articles that appeared in the *BLS Bulletin* 277 (1917), H. L. Gardner, "The Selection Problem of Cheney Brothers, South Manchester, Connecticut," pp. 12–25, Jane C. Williams, "The Reduction of Turnover in the Plimpton Press," pp. 82–91, Henry S. Dennison, "What the Employment Department Should Be in Industry," pp. 77–81, and Jean C. Hoskins, "Service Work of the Eastern Manufacturing Company," pp. 153–57, and on articles in the *Annals of the American Academy of Political and Social Science* 65 (May 1916), Philip J. Reilly, "The Work of the Employment Department of the Dennison Manufacturing Company, Framingham, Massachusetts," pp. 87–93, and Mary B. Gilson, "The Relation of Home Conditions to Industrial Efficiency," 277–88. See also ARMCO, *The First Twenty Years,* pp. 210–228; H. L. Gardner, "Methods Used in an Employment Department," *Industrial Management* 52 (January 1917): 560–62; and R. C. Clothier, "Employment Department of the Curtis Publishing Company," *BLS Bulletin* 202 (1916): 60–62.

86. David J. Goldberg, "Richard A. Feiss, Mary Barnett Gilson, and Scientific Management at Joseph & Feiss, 1909–1925," in *A Mental Revolution: Scientific Management Since Taylor,* ed. Daniel Nelson (Columbus, 1992), pp. 45–47; Gilson, *What's Past Is Prologue,* chap. 6; Nelson and Campbell, "Taylorism versus Welfare Work," pp. 1–16.

87. Keppele Hall, "Discussion," *Bulletin of the Taylor Society* 2 (October 1916): 11.

88. Hoskins, "Service Work," p. 156.

89. Where scientific management had been introduced—at the Plimpton Press, Joseph Feiss, Eastern Manufacturing, and Dennison Manufacturing—rate setting was not left to the foreman either.

90. Roy W. Kelly, "Hiring the Worker," *Engineering Magazine* 52 (March 1917): 839–40. This group included General Electric, Lynn; United Shoe Machinery; Norton Manufacturing; American Rubber Company; Filene's store; and Cheney Brothers and Dennison Manufacturing.

91. See Melvyn Dubofsky, *The State and Labor in Modern America* (Chapel Hill, 1994), chap. 3; David Montgomery, *The Fall of the House of Labor: the Workplace, the State, and American Labor Activism, 1865–1925* (New York, 1987), chap. 8.

92. Carroll E. French, *Shop Committees* (Baltimore, 1923), pp. 9–12.

93. John R. Commons, *Industrial Government* (New York, 1921), chap. 5.

94. H. F. J. Porter, "Discussion," *ASME Transactions* 41 (1919): 193.

95. H. F. J. Porter, "The Higher Law in the Industrial World," *Engineering Magazine* 29 (August 1905): 547.

96. Porter, "Discussion," p. 193.

97. Ibid.

98. But this experiment apparently lasted less than a year. See F. W. Taylor to H. F. J. Porter, November 4, 1907, Frederick W. Taylor Collection (Stevens Institute of Technology, Hoboken, N.J.), file 63C.

99. H. F. J. Porter, "Shop Management," *Engineering News* 60 (September 10, 1908): 289.

100. H. F. J. Porter, "Obtaining the Cooperation of Men," *American Machinist* 33 (October 13, 1910): 670.

101. Howard M. Gitelman, *Legacy of the Ludlow Massacre: A Chapter in American Industrial Relations* (Philadelphia, 1988); Ben Selekman, *Employee Representation in the Steel Mills* (New York, 1924).

102. Quoted in Selekman, *Employee Representation,* p. 256.

103. Ibid., p. 133.

104. Allen, *Goodyear,* p. 181. Compare this with the Leeds & Northrup situation, Daniel Nelson, "'A Newly Appreciated Art': The Development of Personnel Work at Leeds & Northrup," *Business History Review* 44 (1970): 522–24.

105. Robert Whaples, "Winning the Eight-Hour Day, 1909–1919," *Journal of Economic History* 50 (June 1990): 393–406.

106. U.S. Department of Commerce, Bureau of the Census, *Historical Statistics of the United States, Colonial Times to 1957* (Washington, 1960), ser. D 770–73, p. 99.

107. Brody, *Labor in Crisis,* p. 72.

108. See Brody, *Labor in Crisis,* pp. 57–58; Dubofsky, *State and Labor,* pp. 74–79; Robert L. Friedheim, *The Seattle General Strike* (Seattle, 1964), p. 59.

109. See David Brody, *The Butcher Workmen* (Cambridge, Mass., 1964), pp. 77–105; Allan H. Spear, *Black Chicago* (Chicago, 1967), pp. 159–63; William Tuttle, Jr., "Labor Conflict and Racial Violence: The Black Worker in Chicago, 1894–1919," *Labor History* 10 (Summer 1969): 408–32; Grossman, *Land of Hope,* pp. 209–13.

110. "History of the Shipbuilding Labor Adjustment Board, 1917 to 1919," *BLS Bulletin* 282 (1921): 63; French, "Shop Committees," pp. 22–24.

111. See John A. Fitch, "The War Labor Board," *Survey* 43 (May 3, 1919): 192–95, for a succinct summary. French, "Shop Committees," pp. 22–24.

112. Valerie Jean Conner, The National War Labor Board, *Stability Social Justice, and the Voluntary State in World War I* (Chapel Hill, 1983), chaps. 7–8; Montgomery, *Fall of the House of Labor,* pp. 443–49; Joseph A. McMartin, "Using 'the Gun Act': Federal Regulation and the Politics of the Strike Threat during World War I," *Labor History* 33 (Fall 1992): 527–28.

113. Leo Wolman, *The Growth of American Trade Unions, 1880–1923* (New York, 1924), p. 113.

114. David Goldberg, *A Tale of Three Cities: Labor Organization and Protest in Paterson, Passaic, and Lawrence, 1916–1921* (New Brunswick, 1989), pp. 116–204.

115. Willard G. Aborn and William L. Shafter, "Representative Shop Committees," *Industrial Management* 58 (July 1919): 30.

116. Guy P. Miller, "Discussion," *ASME Transactions* 41 (1919): 197–98.

117. National Industrial Conference Board, *Experience with Works Councils* (New York, 1922), p. 34.

118. NICB, *Collective Bargaining Through Employee Representation* (New York, 1933), p. 19.

119. NICB, *Works Councils,* pp. 51–58; see also 5, 78–81.

120. NICB, Works Councils, pp. 66–67. For a related case study, see Gerald Zahavi, *Workers, Managers, and Welfare Capitalism: The Shoeworkers and Tanners of Endicott Johnson, 1890–1950* (Urbana, 1988), chap. 2.

121. NICB, Works Councils, p. 99.

Bibliographical Note

Since the twentieth-century factory system was ultimately the product of decisions by thousands of executives, supervisors, and workers, I have emphasized the role of specific firms and individuals whenever possible. Most of my data have thus been culled from company archives, trade and professional journals, government reports, and company and industry histories.

The Baker Library (Harvard Graduate School of Business Administration, Cambridge) business collections were by far the most important group of unpublished records that I consulted. The Amoskeag and Dwight Company Papers, in particular, were helpful. The mammoth Ford Motor Company (Henry Ford Museum, Dearborn) and the McCormick (State Historical Society of Wisconsin, Madison) archives and the smaller Studebaker-Packard (Syracuse University Library, Syracuse), Phoenix Iron Company (Hagley Library, Wilmington), Joseph Bancroft & Sons Company (Hagley Library, Wilmington), Samuel Vauclain (Historical Society of Pennsylvania, Philadelphia) and War Labor Policies Board (National Archives) collections were also useful. The papers of Frederick W. Taylor (Stevens Institute of Technology, Hoboken) and his disciples Carl Barth (Baker Library), Frank B. Gilbreth (Purdue University Library, Lafayette), Harrington Emerson (New York Public Library, New York City), and Morris L. Cooke (Franklin D. Roosevelt Library, Hyde Park) are indispensable for an understanding of scientific management. The National Civic Federation—Welfare Department Papers (New York Public Library, New York City) are almost as valuable for the development of welfare work.

Of the numerous journals that reported the activities of manufacturers, I found the *Engineering Magazine, American Machinist, Cassier's Magazine, Engineering News, Machinery, Scientific American, Iron Trade Review, Iron Age, Bulletin of the (Taylor) Society to Promote the Science of Management, Social Service, Industrial Engineering and Engineering Digest, Transactions of the American Society of Mechanical Engineers, Proceedings of the New England Cotton Textile Manufacturers Association,* and *Yearbook of the American Iron and Steel Institute* most helpful. The *American Labor Legislation Review* and *The Survey* were important for legislative developments and the impact of World War I. I also read the monthly publications of the Molders, Machinists, Iron and Steel Workers, and Boot and Shoe Workers for the years 1880–1920 (when appropriate), with considerably less success. The labor journals devoted most of their space to union—as opposed to industrial—affairs.

An extraordinary number of state and federal government publications pertain to the new factory system. The most significant are six major federal studies: the Senate hearings on *Capital and Labor* of the early 1880s, the Industrial Commission reports of the 1900–1902 period, the Senate reports on *Woman and Child Wage-Earners*, 1909–1910, the Bureau of Labor study of *Conditions of Employment in the Iron and Steel Industry* of 1911–1913, the Immigration Commission *Reports* of 1911, and the Commission on Industrial Relations studies of 1913–1915. In addition the Bulletins of the Bureau of Labor Statistics and reports of the U.S. Commissioner of Labor and the state departments of labor statistics and factory inspection contain a wealth of material.

Finally, there are hundreds of relevant company and industry histories and other secondary works. Among the most valuable groups are the Harvard Studies in Business History and the volumes of the Pittsburgh Survey. The *Business History Review*, the *Journal of Economic History*, and *Labor History* also contain many useful articles.

Index